PRAISE FOR THIS BOOK

This has got to be the most comprehensive guide for job-seekers on the market! Gabriela has done a marvelous job covering all bases by taking the job-seeker step by step from "Where do I even start?", to confidently interviewing and landing the job. If you're looking for a job and you're an introvert or otherwise, get this book!

> *Bento C. Leal III, Author of Amazon best-seller "4 Essential Keys to Effective Communication in Love, Life, Work—Anywhere!"*

With this book, Gabriela leaves no stone unturned as she explores the specifics of the introvert psychology, invites the reader to a new depth of self-knowledge, and lays the foundation for the job search project from the mindset to the mundane (but extremely important). As an introvert reader of this excellent volume, I felt my confidence growing with each page as I better understood my strengths, and how to manage my limitations.

> *Tad Frizzell, Owner, Renara Music www.renaramusic.com*

Finally, a career book that's designed specifically for introverts! Presents very well the challenges us introverts face and how to overcome them. I loved the simple and yet easy step-by-step approach in finding a career that's aligned to your authentic self. If you're an introvert and you're stuck in your career or struggling to get the job you want—this is a must have book for your book collection!

> *Petros Eshetu, Author of "I Came! I Saw! I Jumped ! How I Found My Dream Job and You Can Too"*

This book is a treasure trove of information and inspiration for the introverted job seeker. Being an introvert and in the job market myself, I found that this book really resonates with my own inherent struggles in this process. The book is definitely high value and a must read for anyone in the job market, let alone introverts. Five stars!

Juanita R Jones, Project Management Professional

Becoming over specialized in your field and changing careers at 40 don't go well together... that's what I thought until I read this book. It invites you to an inner journey of self-discovery, of finding out your own strengths, and reevaluating and reclaiming the best version of yourself. Relying on her own journey in changing careers and her extensive experience in coaching hundreds of people in their own career search, Gabriela guides you step by step throughout her book, opening a door to unlimited possibilities and your dream job.

Melania Lumezanu, B.A, Psych., M.ADS, Behaviour Consultant/Therapist

Apart from its professional comprehensiveness, what stood out for me while reading this book was a sense of being thoroughly nurtured and propped along. I felt I am not alone and someone really cares about me and my process, taking me by the hand from beginning to end. I heartily recommend this book for any introvert tackling job search.

Uta Gabbay, Author/ Spiritual Psychotherapist, www.hechal.org

This practical and inspirational book is full of great advice, tools and real-life examples, all presented in an interactive style, which I really like. It takes my job searching thoughts and processes to a new level! It also presents many ways in which one can tap into the hidden job market, which is something I really wanted to learn more about. The concepts of The Wheel of Life and The Wheel of Job Search were new and very meaningful concepts to me. This book makes me feel strong and empowered in my search for the next step in my career!

Nina Engstrand, Entrepreneur/ Author, www.theinvitationtochange.com

The book you need if you want to go from desperate and intimidated to having a structured, empowered attitude towards reaching your goals. Gabriela's real life experience is evident in this well laid out guide from "shy" to focusing on strengths and positives. As a Life Skills Coach, I definitely recommend this book to my clients who want to make an empowering career change. Also highly recommended for coaches who wants to refine their skills at helping their clients!

Louise VN Liebenberg, www.i-nfinitepotential.com

Taken to heart, it will open your eyes to how you can create new opportunities by changing your own approach, and aligning it with the strengths of what it means to be introverted. It is written with care, experience and research and stands out with pearls of details to help you to where you decide to go!

Thea Nygaard

A breakthrough book for struggling introverts! I've never thought that my introvert qualities could be considered strengths (especially during a job interview). And I didn't realize either how much my mindset can affect my performance. Well written book with a great balance between theory and practice.

E. Theodore Aranda

INTROVERTS: LEVERAGE YOUR STRENGTHS FOR AN EFFECTIVE JOB SEARCH

GABRIELA CASINEANU

Thoughts Designer

Writing: Gabriela Casineanu

Images: Presenter Media and Gabriela Casineanu

Editing: Stacey Kopp

Follow the author on:

Facebook: GC.ThoughtsDesigner

Twitter: thoughtdesigner

Instagram: thoughtsdesigner

Website/Blog: GabrielaCasineanu.com

Library and Archives Canada Cataloguing in Publication

Casineanu, Gabriela, 1961   , author

Introverts: Leverage Your Strengths for an Effective Job Search, 1st ed.

ISBN: 978-0-9959677-0-0 (softcover)

CONTENTS

DISCLAIMER

The book *Introverts: Leverage Your Strengths for an Effective Job Search* is meant to help introverted people who feel challenged to find jobs and advance their careers in a world that appreciates more extroverted behavior. It could also serve as a reference for professionals (career coaches, employment counselors, recruiters) who would like to better understand and serve their introverted clients. Parents of introverted students ready to enter the workforce will find valuable information and resources as well.

This book does not replace employment counseling, professional coaching, or therapy. The information and resources in this book are provided for informational and educational purposes.

There are several examples and case studies presented in this book, but the real names were replaced with fictitious ones to preserve confidentiality.

Whenever a gender-specific term was used, it should be understood as referring to both genders, unless explicitly stated. This is done solely for the purpose of making the text easier to read, and no offense or sexism is intended.

Neither the author or the publisher can be held responsible for the use of the information provided within this book.

I would like to dedicate this book to the following people:

- *my daughter, Irina, my best cheerleader*
- *my son, Andrei, whose opinion often challenged mine, forcing me to reflect twice before making important decisions*
- *my parents, Maria and Ioan, who made me feel supported and encouraged (even when they didn't agree with my life turns)*
- *my muse, for the inspiration for writing this book and helping me to put the content of highly experiential workshops in a written format.*

Thank you!

FOREWORD

Rich, Intelligent, Enlightening, Engaging, Captivating and Valuable for (not only) the introverted job seeker!

What makes this book stand out is its unique fusion of concepts, techniques, exercises and real life examples. Its conversational style will keep you hooked from the first paragraph to the last.

Under Gabriela's professional advice, an introvert herself, you will embark on a journey that will take you - step by step - through the fundamental aspects that make an effective job search. I guarantee you too, will end up learning valuable skills to enhance your life!

My belief is that if all my introverted clients read this book, our collaborations may prove even more fruitful!

Mihaela Ignat

Founder & Executive Director of Global Talent Placement Inc.

INTRODUCTION

Why a Book about Introverts' Strengths and Job Search?

• Through my experience helping thousands of unemployed people find jobs and advance their careers, I noticed that introverts are struggling to find their way in a world that appreciates the extroverted behavior more, hence the need for a book addressed specifically to introverts.

• Susan Cain did a great job in her book *Quiet*, of helping us understand introverts' strengths. It also includes research studies showing the difference between the introvert and extrovert traits, which are mainly inborn. Mainly, their brain pathways are different, which translates into a difference of behavior and where they get the energy from (for extroverts by interacting with others, while introverts can regenerate only in a quiet space). I counted over 160 differences between extroverts and introverts in Susan's book, which helps us understand all the great qualities that introverts have and need to tap into to be more effective in their job search.

• There are so many books about job search on the market, but their advice is general. With so many differences between introverts and extroverts, a book showing introverts how to tap into their strengths during the job search process was long overdue.

What Is This Book about?

• Presents the whole job search process from a more holistic perspective, shedding light on some useful areas that are usually overlooked in the traditional job search approach and how this perspective can help introverts

• Invites readers to put their current job search into the perspective of their long-term objective, telling why this approach works and how it helps the current job hunting process

• Empowers the readers to shift from a reactive to a more proactive approach to job search by tapping into their strengths

• Breaks down the whole job hunting process into easy to digest tasks, providing proven concepts, techniques, and twenty-one strategies that are well-suited to the introvert's personality

• Presents several case studies that illustrate how and why the principles and strategies presented are useful for introverts

• Shows introverts how to take charge of the whole process, by considering that they own the job search project, and how to manage it in an effective way that maximizes their chances of getting the job they want.

Who Wrote This Book?

An introvert myself, I thrived by designing my career path the way I want. My purpose for writing this book is to help other introverts do the same.

My background spans through various fields, and I worked in both private and non-profit sectors. I successfully navigated several career transitions over the years: engineering, quality assurance, IT programming, program coordination, professional coaching, employment counseling, business, and art.

During the last seven years I helped thousands of job seekers (mainly introverts) through individual coaching, simulation interviews, and job search related workshops that I designed and facilitated: How Your Mindset Affects Job Search Results, Attitudes for Effective Communication, Moving Your Career Forward, Effective Job Search Strategies, Job Search Tools (targeted resume, cover letter), Using Social Media for Job Search, Tips for a Successful Interview, and Understanding the Workplace Culture. I also organized three bilingual job fairs, putting me in touch with employers and recruiters, which helped me understand their perspective.

This book was written based on my experience and knowledge accumulated over the years and the feedback received from my introverted clients who successfully applied the concepts and strategies presented in this book.

Why Is It Important to Read This Book?

• Drawing on the experience and knowledge from several fields, this book helps introverts look at job search with a whole new, empowering perspective. No more feeling at the mercy of an employer or another, the readers discovers how using their strengths can actually give them an equal balance of power.

• Don't know how to talk about yourself in a job interview? No problem! The book shows you how to shift to a new perspective that shows not tells, which is actually even more effective.

• Don't know how to tap into the hidden job market, which offers more opportunities than you can imagine? Read further, there are many ways to do this presented throughout the book.

• Not interested in networking events to increase your visibility and build credibility? Inside, you'll find other useful job search strategies more suited to the introvert's personality or adapted to meet their needs.

• Don't know exactly what you want? Two chapters will help you figure that out, or at least enough to get you started and going until you identify this in more detail.

• Fear that you don't have enough energy to carry on the stressful job search? You'll find some ideas on how to manage your energy and stay motivated throughout the entire process.

• There is even a chapter on what to do after you find the job, to help you prepare for the next step of your career and make the transition even more smoothly.

Do You Have Any Proof that Your Ideas Work?

Here's what some readers and clients said about the job search approach that I laid out in this book:

I had a revelation while reading your book! I spent so much energy in jobs where I was not at my best that I started to believe I'm not a good employee. While, in fact, I was simply focusing on the wrong type of jobs. It was like wearing gloves that were not the right size! I finally understood what I want, and I can't tell you how much it opened my eyes! ~ Sales Professional

This is an excellent, excellent topic, and you are very experienced with it. The book is easy to read and follow, straightforward, and does not make drama for people looking for a job. The tools and the exercises inspired by your job search workshops are very useful! ~ Coach and Recruiter

I participated at two of your workshops, those on Mindset and LinkedIn. The first one helped me understand what was missing. LinkedIn became an incredible tool: in less than three weeks of job search, I got the job! ~ Marketing Professional

Before meeting you, I had six months of unsuccessful job search. I was quite unhappy and didn't know what to do. I start applying your advice and guidance, and it paid off in a very short term, in unexpected ways. ~ Financial Analyst

I started my job search by trying all the strategies you taught me. Then I narrowed down to what worked best in my situation. Within a month, I got the desired position with the type of company I was looking for. ~ Online Marketing Expert

Why Do I Need to Read This Book Now?

Whether you're looking to integrate the job market for the first time or you already have work experience under your belt, this book will help you take charge and accelerate your job search based on your strength. Isn't this what you want?

It also gives proven strategies to build the career you want, by avoiding unnecessary detours and managing your resources more effectively.

All you have to do is keep reading. Each chapter will give you new insights and important strategies to keep you from falling back to a reactive job search mode.

Take control of your job hunting process to make employers more willing to hire you while you enjoy walking the path toward the career of your dreams.

What's the Book Structure?

The chapters of the book build on each other, taking you on a journey. By reading them in a sequential order, you'll get information and insights that will help in conducting a more effective job search.

• Part One ("Preparation") presents a more holistic approach to the job search, which is often overlooked. Through exercises and concepts you might not be familiar with, this section helps you lay the foundation and identify what you're missing, to be more in control of your job hunting process.

• Part Two ("Job Search for Introverts") is full of tips and strategies for each phase of the job search process, to help you be more effective by using your introvert strengths. It also contains a lot of examples and case studies about job seekers who were successful by using the information presented in this book.

• Part Three ("What's Next") helps you look at the acquired position as a stepping stone meant to take you further on creating the career path you want. It also helps you to integrate more smoothly into the new work environment and provides tips for managing your energy in a way that helps with both performing work tasks and focusing on your plan B (creating the conditions for your next career step).

This book is based on the experience gained from successfully navigating several career transitions and helping over 1,200 job seekers during the last seven years (from newly graduated students to experienced professionals from various fields, and even managers).

I encourage you to actually do the exercises and implement the strategies presented in this book, since just reading it won't provide enough traction to bring the expected results.

Have a notebook and pen ready to capture all your insights, answers and notes in one place for further reference (you'll need them in chapter 14).

With this being said, let's get started! :-)

Part One

PREPARATION

Chapter One

WHERE THIS BOOK IDEA CAME FROM

*Every adversity, every failure, every heartache carries with it
the seed of an equal or greater benefit.*
~ Napoleon Hill

It was the beginning of summer 2016. I was very tired and barely talking due to the daily workshops I was asked to deliver for job seekers and the individual coaching sessions with clients. For an introvert like me, that was a lot to handle daily! I didn't have enough breaks to recharge my batteries, and fatigue was accumulating. My body was screaming for help. Two months passed by and my voice didn't make any improvements while my health deteriorated even more.

Worried that I might have bigger problems with my voice, I asked myself one day, "What will I do with the rest of my life if I can't talk anymore?"

To my surprise, a new thought popped suddenly into my mind: "Write an introvert's guide to job search!"

I was in WOW! I had never thought about this, but I immediately recognized its value: I have a lot of experience helping people find jobs and advance their careers. I've also successfully navigated several career changes myself, and with over ten years of coaching experience I bring a more empowering perspective to job hunting. It totally made sense to put all this information in a book so I can impact more people without forcing my voice so much.

Why a job search guide for . . . introverts?

I already knew that answer. Several years before, I was giving a workshop to students from Ryerson University. It was a group of over forty students, sitting in a circle so I could guide them through some experiential exercises (to help them understand how their mindset affects their career). At one point I asked how many of them were shy, and took a look around. Almost half of the participants raised their hands. I mentioned that I'm an introvert, and I too was shy in the past, but I worked on myself and was able to overcome my shyness.

After the workshop, a student approached me saying, "I can't thank you enough! When you asked us to raise our hands, I realized for the first time I'm not the only shy person in the world! And when you mentioned that you were too and were able to overcome your shyness, I understood that I can too!"

That moment made me understand that introverts and shy people can isolate themselves so much in their own bubble, they don't realize there are other similar people they can relate to. I still get goose bumps each time I recount this story.

That experience put me on the path of helping introverts through my coaching practice and talking more about the difference between extroversion and introversion in my workshops.

As an introvert myself, I easily connect with other introverts at a deeper level. I love to help them turn every situation into a self-discovery and learning opportunity, to come up with their own solutions.

From my experience helping job seekers during the past seven years, I noticed that introverts seem to be more challenged in a professional world that appreciates extroverted behavior more. So I happily embraced that sudden idea of writing this book.

Please don't underestimate the power of asking yourself powerful questions!

I included a special chapter on this topic, so you can learn to use this powerful "tool" to make your job search more effective.

Let's dive in! :-)

Chapter Two

WHEEL OF JOB SEARCH

Stay committed to your decisions, but stay flexible in your approach.
~ Tony Robbins

As an introvert who has successfully navigated many career transitions, I'm about to share with you my secrets and the insights I accumulated over the years about effective job hunting. During the last seven years, I helped more than 1,200 people through job search workshops, one-on-one coaching and simulation interviews. Most of them were introverts.

You have probably noticed there is not much information specific to introverts about how to look for a job. There are a lot of books, workshops, and webinars talking about job search strategies in general, but not really addressing our specific challenges as introverts. Let's talk about networking, for example. They ask us to go out to meet new people. While it might be a powerful strategy, how many introverts have you noticed using it successfully? Not many, if any, because introverts don't like to be in places where they can meet a lot of new people. They prefer to be in quiet spaces or engaging in one-on-one conversations on meaningful topics, or with a small group of friends. Just the thought of reaching out to someone we don't know creates a strong resistance. Some introverts even have social anxiety! Yet networking could become a great strategy for introverts if we tweak it a little bit, to make it also work for us.

There are also various other strategies to use when looking for a new position. Not all of them are effective, and even less of them are well fitted to an introvert's personality. And that's exactly what this book is about: presenting some powerful job search strategies while adjusting them in a way that introverts not only feel more at ease using them, but also can get better results.

If I already piqued your curiosity, I'll start by inviting you to look at your professional life as . . . a journey (not a destination)! What do I mean by that? Let me explain using my own background.

I started my career path as an engineer in electronics and telecommunications. It wasn't my first choice at the end of high school, but I didn't have the courage to step up for myself and apply to the school of architecture (which I thought was a good choice for combining both the logical and creative sides of my brain). I ended up working almost eighteen years in a huge telecom company while continuing to look for the type of job I would enjoy most. I changed departments every three to five years, took IT courses, and even got an MBA to see if that was a direction I could be interested in. Well, I ended up knowing much more about how the different departments of a company work together. And I become even less happy with where I was, since that MBA gave me many ideas about what could be improved in the company I was working for . . . without having the power of a position that would allow me to implement those changes. Really frustrating!

Then I asked myself if now, knowing more, I would really love to have that powerful position, and the answer was simply no!

So I continued my search to find out about what was meaningful to me. About that time, I immigrated to Canada (2003), and things started to change. I became this lady that designs her professional path the way she wants, step by step. While the first two positions were based on my skills and previous experience, I soon discovered coaching — a profession I didn't know existed before moving to Canada. It was love at first sight! :-)

Coaching training followed, and starting my own business while still having a full-time engineering position (that required many hours of overtime). Exhausted, after six months I switched to another full-time position which required program design and coordination for a new mentoring program for professionals. This position allowed me to use my newly acquired coaching skills, and my creativity! After a while, realizing that something was missing, I added workshops (design and facilitation) to that program, to bring a fresh coaching perspective to job search, helping those professionals become even more successful. Without even noticing, I ended up getting my toes into another field: training and adult learning. Curious, I took a course in curriculum development only to realize how much my experiential and interactive approach was aligned with what they taught! :-)

See, this way of continuing to unfold your professional path based on what you really want builds the motivation and willingness to approach the job search in a more efficient way, leading to better results and much more satisfaction! It's a process, an interesting journey that unfolds in time without needing to know from the beginning where it will take you. And that's my wish for you too, instead of allowing life to push you from one direction to another, aimlessly.

Even if you stay in the same field, taking a more proactive approach toward your job search could be very beneficial and opens doors without the hustle of a traditional job search. Stick with me, and you'll understand better what I mean.

In this chapter, I'll introduce you to a powerful coaching concept that I found very useful for job search, especially for introverts.

Before getting there, let's talk about five things introverts don't like:

1. Selling Themselves

As an introvert myself, and from what I noticed working with other introverts, we don't like selling — especially "selling" ourselves. We don't like to talk about ourselves, period! It's not only that we dislike it, but it's also that we would rather enjoy proving our skills and knowledge through the work we do than talking about them.

2. Networking Events

Nope, we don't like networking events. They drain our energy, and we don't feel comfortable being there. As an introvert, it's hard to find someone with whom to have a meaningful conversation at such events, and that's what we normally appreciate and look forward to. Yet taking the time to have a meaningful conversation is not even the purpose of a networking event, where participants are looking to only make new connections that will, eventually, be explored later.

3. Talking (Especially Small Talk)

As we enjoy the power of our mind so much, thinking comes more natural to us. Doing something, instead of talking about it, is much more interesting for us too.

Even if we have a meaningful conversation with someone, we get tired after a while. Writing comes more easily to us (because we can stop it whenever we want!).

Small talk? No way! That's something we definitely avoid! There's not much meaning in small talk, so we'd rather avoid it.

4. Attention/Limelight

Feeling that all the eyes are on us is intimidating. Unlike extroverts, who tend to excel in such situations, introverts would rather be the quiet ones who change the world.

I remember how I felt in a meeting when suddenly the director turned toward me while I was about to say something. I did proceed saying it, because I considered the point very important and no one else had mentioned it, but my voice started trembling and shaking. Does that happen to you too?

Introverted public speakers are more of an exception. Asked them how much practice is required to get out of their comfort zone and how much time they need to recharge their batteries quietly later. You'll usually see them choosing topics they're really passionate about, which give them enough energy and courage to stand up in front of a crowd (workshop participants, in my case).

5. Supervision/Authority

Allowing us to do the work, without feeling supervised, suits us better. Feeling pressured to do something by someone who has power or is considered an authority is intimidating as well. We like to do things on our own, and we even perform better this way.

So if you take into consideration the above five aspects about introverts, do you have a better understanding why we (introverts) don't perform well when it comes to finding a new job through the traditional methods?

Traditionally when job hunting, you have to present yourself in a way that projects the best image of you! And since introverts don't like to sell, it's hard for us to "sell" ourselves.

Also, since we don't like networking events, how can we go out to meet new people, to increase our visibility? Yet, nobody will come to knock on your door if they don't even know you exist! So you have to increase your visibility. Networking events might be a way to do it, but as introverts we have to find our own way. I'll talk about this a bit later.

We don't like talking about ourselves, and we don't like small talk either. Guess what? In an interview, that's what you have to do. You have to talk, you have to go through that small talk at the beginning (another uncomfortable place for us). Starting an interview feeling uncomfortable is not the best way to go through an interview, and it doesn't project a good image of you either (especially if other candidates do this very well).

In an interview, we have the whole attention of the interviewer or the panel of interviewers, so we have to figure out a way to deal with that too. Since we don't like authority (and many of us consider the company representatives authority figures), we might feel more stress than we can normally handle. This will affect our performance in the interview and of course the interview results.

Still wondering why as an introvert you have a hard time when it comes to the job search?

Now let's talk about that concept that I borrowed from the area of life coaching, to help you during the job search. The reason I'm showing you this tool is because it brings up a more holistic approach. I'll explain it in the context of your life first. Then you'll get to see how this holistic approach applies to the job search.

Wheel of Life

Let's begin by taking a snapshot of where your life is right now at this moment. Go grab a pen and paper; I'll wait.

Ready?

This exercise is called the **Wheel of Life**. Please **do** this exercise in parallel with my guidance (not just read about it) so you will understand the concept. Later, we'll apply it in the context of a more effective job search.

As a bonus, you'll get a better idea where your life is right now. No one else can score these areas better than you, because they don't know what exactly is going on in your life. So start by drawing a circle with these eight areas, like in the image below:

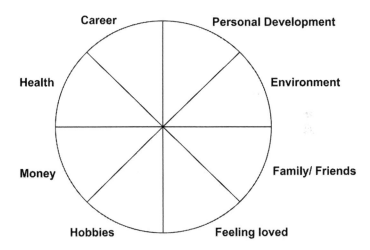

In a moment I'll ask you to mark your satisfaction level for each of these areas, but let me first present what I mean by each of them:

Career: This is about your career right now, how satisfied are you about it at this moment.

I did this exercise with all the people who enrolled in the mentoring program, and I was quite surprised when someone put a zero (not at all) this area, although he had a PhD in physics and already had great work experience. Obviously, to an outsider, his career didn't look like a zero, but that's how satisfied he was with his career at that moment. So you just have to record your own satisfaction level, because that's what is important in this exercise!

Another thing to consider is this: Having or not having a job is not who you really are! I had a client, a neurologist with twenty years' experience, who recently moved to this country. "I'm a zero. I don't have a job," he told me. "Just because you don't have a job now, doesn't mean you're a zero! You're the same person as before, same personality, same knowledge and experience. No one took that away from you! You're just in between jobs!," I answered. His face brightened up.

Health: How satisfied are you about your health level? What do you do to improve your health and have a healthy lifestyle?

Money: This area is not only about how much money you have, but it's also about how much you bring in and how well you manage your spending and investing.

Hobbies: While some people don't consider hobbies too important, but spending some time on hobbies and other fun and recreational activities could actually infuse more energy and enthusiasm into the other aspects of your life (including job search).

Personal Development: This area is about how much time and effort you're putting into expanding your comfort zone, learning new skills, understanding the world around you from a different perspective, and evolving physically, emotionally, and spiritually.

Environment: Think about how satisfied you are regarding the environment you live in at work, at home, in the city, or in the country. Give an average of how you usually feel, when you mark this area in the wheel.

Family/Friends: How much do you feel supported by your family and friends? Also, are you reaching out to them when you need help?

Feeling loved: How much do you feel loved by others? How much do you love yourself? So many people associate love with having a romantic partner, but feeling loved could also come from loving yourself. If you don't, this will negatively impact your life, and even the image you project in an interview. If you look like someone who's not at ease with who you really are, this might come across as a lack of confidence or self-esteem, or maybe as not trusting your experience and skills. If you let employers guess what that means, you might be in for a (negative) surprise. They might get the wrong image of who you really are and how you can help the company. It is important to evaluate this aspect of your life as well.

These are eight different aspects of our life. Now please take the time to score each area from 0 (not at all) to 10 (I'm very happy with it) according to your satisfaction level — at this moment — of each specific aspect mentioned above. Write down in your Wheel of Life the first number that comes to mind regarding each area. Don't think too much, don't analyze why or what it should be — just jot them down! Yes, you can have the same number in different areas.

Take a moment to mark these areas, then come back. I'll show you what to do with these numbers.

Ready to continue? I hope you already have your numbers. If not, please go back to your Wheel of Life and write them down in each area.

The exercise will have much more meaning to you when you come up with your own numbers based on how satisfied you are at this moment.

Now I'd like you to draw some lines. Here's an example: Let's say I came up with these numbers: 8, 5, 7, 4, 6, 9, 3, and 2. The next step is to draw curve lines in each area, corresponding to the numbers chosen. A 0 is the center of the circle, and 10 will be on the circumference. A curve line for 8 would be closer to the edge of the circle than a 2 (which will be closer to the center). Take the time to draw the circular lines corresponding to your numbers, then the lines that unite them when you go from one area to another. Create your own image, as I did in this example:

Ready to continue this exercise?

Now I want you to think about your life as a car, and what you draw represents a wheel of your car. How is your life journey if your car has a wheel like this?

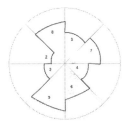

You might understand now why you feel frustrated sometimes, why you're not happy regarding certain areas of your life.

This is a snapshot of where you are right now. It doesn't mean it was similar in the past or it will be the same in the future. It's just where you are today!

When you look at your own picture, there are areas you'd like to improve, right? Pick those areas, and for each of them ask yourself these questions: "How can I improve my satisfaction level in this area? What actions can I take to improve it?"

Write down your answers so you have a reference to work with, if you'd like to make some improvements in those areas.

BTW, lower numbers in any of these areas do have a negative impact on your job search too: they might drain your energy, they might make you feel bad (about yourself and where you are in your life), they might affect your ability to achieve more. So do take a moment to plan some actions (and take them) to raise your satisfaction level so they don't affect your job search so much!

Also, I would like to draw your attention to something else. These areas are so **inter**dependent, they affect each other! For example: if your Health area didn't get a high score and you go to an interview, you will not present yourself in the best way you can, because you don't feel good. So this could affect your Career area. Or, if during your job hunting, you don't give some attention to your hobbies or participate in fun activities, your energy level might drop and the stress will increase. Not the best way to go to an interview, right? You won't even be positive enough to write a good cover letter! Spend some time on your hobbies, especially when you feel stressed out or have low energy. The time spent on hobbies could be your investment in getting more energy and enthusiasm to carry on your job search in a more positive way. Doing only things you think you *have* to do (preparing and sending resumes, for example) won't help you much. Should I mention how your Money area affects the other aspects of your life?

I can go on and on, but I guess you've got the point: all aspects of your life are important, and those with lower marks need more of your attention now. If that means taking a temporary job to put food on the table, why not do it? Decreasing the stress level (caused by lack of money) could improve your mood and increase your chances of getting a better job soon.

I hope by now you have your action list regarding the more general aspects of your life. Spread those actions in your agenda to remind you of the importance of taking them. You'll be surprised by their positive effect on your job search.

Wheel of Job Search

Now let's move on to see how we can apply this holistic approach in the context of job searching. For that, I designed a Wheel of Job Search and tested it successfully with many introverts. If you don't believe me, maybe you'll take into consideration what these clients said:

"I just want to tell you: in less than three weeks of job search I got a job . . . and it was not even advertised internally or externally!"

"I will never forget how your guidance and your words (Walk Your Talk) helped me find this new job!"

"Gabriela clearly spoke from experience. I attended some of her career guidance sessions, and they were very insightful. I highly recommend her sessions."

For the Wheel of Job Search, I'll use a concept similar to the Wheel of Life. That's why I wanted you to test that wheel first, so you understand how this holistic approach works.

Again, I invite you to draw a circle with eight areas. This time there will be different categories, reflecting different aspects of the job search:

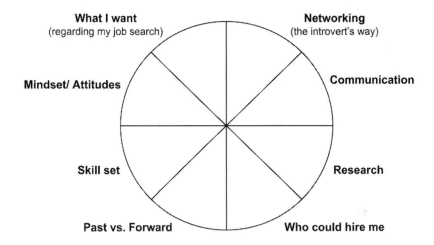

At one point, I will ask you to create your own Strategy Mix by choosing several job search strategies presented in this book that apply to your situation. You may have noticed, I didn't even include "My Job Search Strategies Mix" as a separate area in this wheel, because the effective job strategies for introverts (and how to create a personalized Strategy Mix that suits your needs) will be covered in a separate chapter. In fact, what strategies you'll use in your Strategy Mix will be influenced by what you'll identify first in the areas of your Wheel of Job Search (WoJS).

While I'll elaborate more on each of these area in the following chapters, let me briefly explain them now so you can understand what each of them means in this context. Then we'll do the Wheel of Job Search exercise.

What I want: How clear are you about your short-term and long-term goals? You can even choose a middle-term goal if you want. It's important to know where you're heading because your goal could positively affect your immediate results and how you get there. When you take into consideration your long-term objective in your immediate short-term goal, your job search will be more effective. You'll understand why when you read the chapter about effective strategies for introverts.

Mindset/Attitudes: What do you think about your current job search? Do you believe you will be successful? That there is a job out there waiting for you, even if you have no clue, for now, how you'll find it? Do you believe there is a company that will accept you for who you are, with your skills, your experience, and how you can help them?

Or are you thinking, "There are not enough jobs", "I don't know how to find the job I want", "Nothing works", "I don't even know if the company will hire me because . . ."?

These are different approaches (mindsets) regarding job search. One could help you find what you want, the other one might block you. The mindset and attitudes you have during your job search are very, very important! That's why I put it as a separate area, so you pay attention to it too during your job search. You'll get a better idea how to get a more successful mindset in the chapter dedicated specifically to this topic.

Skill set: By skill set, I mean the set of skills you have, specific to performing a certain job. For example: using a document editor like MS Word (for an administrative assistant) or performing statistical analysis (for marketing research). Your skill set are the skills you bring in your "toolbox" from your past work experiences and even from volunteering.

This area is about the skills you already have and used in the past, and also about the skills required for the new position you're looking for. It might not be exactly the same set of skills. Do you have what it takes? I'll explain more about the different type of skills (soft, hard, and transferable skills) in the "Skill Set" chapter.

Past vs. Forward: I wanted to include this area because way too often I saw people thinking that their past equals their future. It could, but only if you want and allow it! If you have a background in a certain field and you totally love it, it makes sense to continue in the same direction if you want. But if you don't, it makes no sense to continue in the same direction forever if you don't like what you do (or did), just because you have those skills and experience!

This area is about how much you rely on what you bring from your professional background (work experience, skills) while you're moving forward. You might want the same position but in a different company. Then you can bring your skills and experience from the past, but you'll also need to learn about the new company's recruitment process, organizational culture, projects, and values to increase your chances to land a position in the other company. This is even more important when you want to shift directions, even slightly. That's how you can bridge your past with your future: starting with your next step. You'll get more about this in the corresponding chapter.

Who could hire me: Do you know what companies might have a need for what you have to offer?

I see so many people limiting their job search to websites that list a lot of job offers, and just applying to those that might look interesting. I call this a *reactive approach*. Do you know that companies like assertive people? I'll let you guess why. :-) How assertive do you prove you are by using the reactive approach?

Introverts are assertive, and when they're interested in a topic they can go deep. Why not leverage this attitude using a *proactive approach*: think first, do your research, then reach out to those companies that might need your expertise (whether you find a job posting or not). Many managers know what human resources they need, even if they didn't have the time to create and advertise that position. What do you think, do you show your assertiveness more this way? The proactive approach will also help you be more focused than you would be by just applying randomly to positions found on the Internet. Plus, your motivation will be higher, increasing the chances you'll pass a job interview. Should I mention that you'll make the competition less relevant, or even non-existent!

Research: Since introverts love spending time by themselves, researching comes much easier to us than networking. I'm talking about researching information aligned with the proactive approach: making a list of companies you're interested in, finding ways to approach them, connecting with some of their employees to learn about their organizational culture, etc. I'll show you how you can do this the introvert's way. This approach could also increase your visibility in the job market you're interested in, more so than a resume sent as a response to a job listing. It's a different type of research you could do in contrast to extroverts (who are more comfortable using networking when it comes to the job search).

Communication: We all communicate in one way or another. How effective is your communication during the job search? Do you think you really communicate the right message? Do you present yourself in the best way? Is your communication so effective that others understand who you really are and what you can bring to the table? In the context of the job search, communication is much more than just sending a resume and a cover letter. It's also about how you get that resume into the employer's hand. It's one thing to send it via the Internet, responding to a job offer that's already out there (seen by all your competitors too), and another to tap into the hidden market. Also, you don't have to have a huge network of friends willing to help if you're focused and effective in your communication.

Networking (the introvert's way): Networking means talking to people and developing relationships with them. It allows you to develop new contacts and grow your personal network. I know, as introverts we're not very interested in networking. But what if I tell you there's a way to tap into networking's power, and even enjoying it, as an introvert looking for a job? I'll show you how in the chapter "Networking — The Introvert's Way," but for now just notice how much you're using networking in your current job search.

Now do you have a better idea what I mean by the eight areas mentioned in the Wheel of Job Search?

Now grab the piece of paper where you've drawn your Wheel of Job Search, and put a note from 0 to 10 according to how well you're doing in each of these areas in your current job search. Here are a few questions to help you:

1. Do you have in mind a very clear, detailed short-term goal? A long-term goal as well?
2. Do you know all the skills you can bring to the table? I'm talking about soft skills, hard skills, and transferable skills. Do you know what skills are required by the position for which you are looking?
3. Do you have a successful mindset to help you get to where you want? What's your level of confidence, self-esteem, and motivation? (Note the average.)
4. Do you know to bridge the gap between the past and the next step in your professional life?
5. Do you have a list of companies you would like to reach out to, to work with?
6. How is your research? How happy are you with the information you've gathered up to now?
7. Do you believe you communicate well enough to get your message across in the right way?
8. Do you constantly increase your visibility to allow more opportunities to come your way?

Take a moment to mark those eight areas from 0 to 10, if you haven't done so yet. Just write the first number that comes to mind when thinking about a specific area. Don't look for the perfect number, don't analyze. You can come back to measure your progress later on in your job search.

Like you did in the previous exercise, take the time to draw those lines according to the numbers of your current Wheel of Life, and get the image that corresponds to where you are today regarding your job search.

Done? It should look something like this, but adjusted to your numbers:

This is a picture of where you are now in your job search. What do you notice about your Wheel of Job Search? What areas need more of your attention?

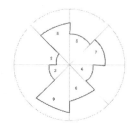

See how much you can get from a picture like this? It's like a snapshot of where you are right now and how else you can approach your job search to make it more effective.

Now I invite you to think about what actions you can take to improve those areas that don't score too high. You'll get more ideas from the following chapters, but for now start with what actions you can think of.

I highly encourage you to find your own way to accelerate your job search, based on what you need most and what grabs your attention from this Wheel of Job Search.

While there are many strategies described in workshops and books, including this one, you'll be most effective when you create a personalized approach to your job search, focused on what you really need and what's missing. There are not two people the same, even if they target the same type of position. Launching yourself blindly into job search will only give you more headaches and will consume more resources (time, energy) than when you start from the beginning with a customized approach.

Use the Wheel of Job Search to understand where you are and your strengths and weaknesses regarding the job hunt. Then create your strategy based on the actions you've identified and what's covered in the following chapters. This way you'll ensure you put your best foot forward and show up as who you really are.

What do you think: How much could a resume represent who you really are — 5 percent, 20 percent, 50 percent? A resume cannot project the whole image of who you are as a human being: your personality, your motivation, your goals. And these are important decision factors for employers. They don't just want another employee; they want someone who's motivated, whose goals are somehow aligned with the company's mission, with a personality that matches their organizational values and culture.

As an introvert, you can leverage your strengths during the job search to find what you want without draining your energy in the process.

As I mentioned with the Wheel of Life, the Wheel of Job Search areas are also **inter**dependent. For example, if you think you're not good enough or there's not enough demand for your skills on the market, will you really have the energy to go out and find the position you want?

If you want to be happy, at least for a while, with your new position, doesn't it make sense to spend some time to define more in detail what you really want —before even starting the job search? I want this type of position, in this type of company, in this sector/industry, with this kind of work environment, and so on.

If you're like the participants in my workshops, thinking that you're limiting your options by narrowing down your wish, I challenge you to think again! I'll explain in the chapter "What I Want" why defining your goals in more details is a better approach than starting with a much broader goal — especially if you're an introvert!

When I worked in an employment center, I used to give a series of job search workshops three times a week. The series included: *Effective Job Search Strategies*,

Tools for Job Search (resume, cover letter, etc.), *Using Social Media for Job Search* (LinkedIn, Twitter, etc.), *Effective Attitudes for Communication*, and *Tips for a Successful Interview*. Many job seekers enrolled at the beginning in only one of these workshops (usually about resumes or strategies), thinking that's all they needed to know when looking for a job. Before the workshop ended, they were ready to enroll in the rest of the series because they understood how each of the other workshops brings in important and different aspects regarding the job search.

Should I mention one of the participants, an introverted marketing & IT specialist, who didn't want to come to the workshop about LinkedIn? Well, she finally did (after I asked her if she really walks her talk by not using such a great resource)! By combining different strategies learned, including using LinkedIn proactively, she was able to get the job of her dreams at a company that matches her values (eco-friendly).

The workshops *Effective Attitudes for Communication* and *How Your Thoughts Affect Your Job Search Results* I introduced first in the mentoring program for professionals, then delivered them many times, in professional organizations as well. Many clients were thinking that having a good resume was enough to land their dream job. Through those workshops they were surprised to discover what else they needed to improve to be more successful. To give you another example: When an introverted participant discovered that lacking assertiveness was her biggest weakness, she used the other strategies learned and landed her ideal job in three weeks (a position that was not even advertised, it was created for her).

I hope I have your attention by now, because I have so much to share with you in the next chapters. See you there! :-)

Chapter Three

PAST VS. FORWARD

The past cannot be changed. The future is yet in your power.
~ Unknown

Thanks for taking the time to read this chapter. I consider it very important to your job search, and here's why:

The past does not equal the future, unless you allow it!

I'm talking about your professional past experience compared to what could be in the future on your career path.

Think about it for a moment: If you simply love what you did in the past and want to continue on the same path, that's great! Your job search will be quite streamlined, and I'll show you how to adapt some strategies to better leverage your introverted strengths to accelerate the process.

But if you found yourself quite frustrated about the skills required or how far you are from living your own values, does it make sense to continue on exactly the same path? Maybe adjusting your direction a little bit, or even moving toward a more drastic career change, will bring you more satisfaction. We're human beings, and each of us has a lot of strengths and talents. We can do a certain job quite well, but the question is, does it bring us satisfaction? That's another story, right? :-)

To better explain what I mean, here's a graphic I created when Jan asked me how to help her friend, who lives well with her salary but has accumulated a lot of frustration. I designed this graphic based on my experience, see if it makes sense to you too:

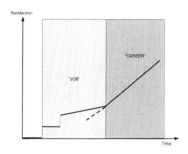

When I moved to Toronto, I started looking for a job and got one two months later. Since I needed to pay the bills and understand how things work here, I focused on finding a starting position as a bilingual customer service representative. To my surprise, I got one with a financial company, without even having a financial background! That's where my satisfaction got the first shift. Two months after, I switched to a better position (corresponding to my background) and almost doubled my salary. My satisfaction level increased again, but still not enough, because I wanted a career change. When I figured out what I wanted, I started on the dotted line in the graphic above, paying for courses with my current salary, preparing myself for the bigger shift: a career change. I made the "CAREER" line an oblique line since it continues evolving, but each stage is quite satisfactory, providing energy and motivation for the next one.

In the graphic, I made the "JOB" line this way because it's an area where we get some satisfaction from getting a salary that pays the bill, but we accumulate frustration from not doing what we love. This is the phase Jan's friend was in. If she figures out what she wants and take steps in that direction, she'll get into the "Career" phase (the oblique line).

What do you think? Where are you on your career path compared to this graphic?

The graphic might have variations, like being without a job for a while, either in the "JOB" or "CAREER" sections. But I want you to understand the difference between moving automatically from one phase to another during your job search (looking for the same position as before, just because you have the experience), and reflecting a little bit on what you really want long term before starting your job search. This way, you can align your short-term goal with the long-term objective, instead of repeating the same pattern from the past (that brought you frustration) or taking a detour in a direction that doesn't support your long-term objective.

For seven years, while I managed a mentoring program for professional newcomers and worked in an employment center, I was exposed to job seekers from various backgrounds. When someone came to me for help with their job search or career path, one of my first questions was, "In an ideal world, what would you really love to do professionally?"

I asked it many times, and now I invite you to reflect on the same question: If you had all the skills you needed, what would you really love to do?

When you come up with something, think about as many details as you can.

If you can't think of anything right now, give yourself a deadline to figure that out. At least what skills you'd like to use and what kind of environment you'd like to be in an ideal world. Don't think about a certain profession. BTW, this was the process I used to figure out what I wanted for my career change from engineering to coaching, then writing. :-)

This question about the ideal world will help you understand what could be a long-term objective for you (let's say, five years from now), which will become very useful in planning the short-term goals for the current job search. We'll dig more into it in the following chapters.

There is another reason I'm inviting you to do this self-reflection first: unlike extroverts (who are driven by external rewards), introverts can motivate themselves. And putting things in perspective (how a short-term goal could help your long-term objective), could help you stay motivated during the job hunting process and present yourself even better at the job interview. Would you like that? :-)

When I asked the question about the ideal world (what they'd love to do), I usually got one of these two answers:

1. Hmm, I've never thought about this before!
2. You know, I have "this" background and experience, and I'm looking for the same type of job.

1. My reaction to "I've never thought about this":

"Well, maybe now is the best time to think (or start thinking) about it! The fact you're looking for a job right now means you're ready for your next step in your career. Would you like it to be toward your long-term objective? Or heading back or aside from what you really want?

"Because if you align your short-term goal with your long-term objective, your path to get there will be much shorter. If not, you might find yourself quite often in a similar 'place' as today, because your frustration will accumulate and affect your job performance."

Then I share my experience, exemplified in the graphic above, and start asking questions to help them figure it out. You'll get such questions in the next chapter. This makes it easier to identify what a possible short-term goal will be, then design a customized strategy mix to reach it faster.

2. When people start giving me the other answer (looking for the same type of job), I interrupt them with a smile:

"That's not what I asked! :-) I understand you have a certain background, but is this really what you love? Do you want to continue in the same direction, or do you envision yourself somewhere else five-ten years from now?"

For those who really love the path they're already on, we'll start planning the job search in the same direction.

But for those who have a different long-term objective, we'll take a totally different approach: create a short-term goal that takes them a step forward toward their long-term objective, which requires some adjustments in the way they present themselves to employers.

Let me give you an example. When Andy, an agricultural engineer, moved to Toronto, we had this conversation:

Me: "In an ideal world, what would you really like to do . . . professionally?"

Andy: "I'm an agricultural engineer with many years of experience in this field . . ."

Me: "That's not what I asked. :-) I'm talking about the future. What would you really love to do five to ten years from now? Do you still want to be in Toronto? Your knowledge applies to large agricultural areas, and there's not much agriculture in Toronto or the surrounding areas."

Andy: "Yes. My English is not too good right now, but I love Toronto! Although I love nature, I'm very creative, and I'd like to incorporate this too in my professional path."

It turns out there is a profession that blends both well: Landscaping. He wasn't aware of it before, but after a little research, he realized he'd like to take that path. In the short term, he took a few jobs while improving his English. Then he returned to school and focused on his long-term objective: getting a master's in landscaping and working in this field.

What do you think? Did this approach help Andy better manage his time and resources than if he first looked for an agricultural engineering position in Toronto or the surrounding areas? Defining his long-term objective first, helped him identify his short-term goals and organize his next steps toward a more fulfilling career path.

I could only imagine his frustration piling up while trying to find a job as an agricultural engineer in Toronto with his level of English, or switching to a path completely different than what he really wants!

Remember? The past doesn't equal the future, unless you allow it!

Want another example?

Chris had an engineering background when he approached me. He was looking for an IT position, no matter the company. When he shared with me his dream of having his own company, I asked, "Wouldn't it make more sense to look for a position in a similar company now, to better understand the industry, the competition, the market, and what is required to have your own company in that field?"

Whatever your short-term goals and long-term objective are right now, please bear with me through the next chapters. The next one, for example, will give you several ways to identify your objectives more clearly.

Don't jump directly to the chapter about job search strategies for introverts. I promise you'll get much more if you go through each chapter at a time, as they build on each other.

In the next chapter, you'll get the chance to further explore what you really want, short-term and long-term.

Chapter Four

WHAT I WANT

I became what I wanted to be.
~ G. Gordon Liddy

Talking about short-term goals and long-term objective, let's dive deeper in this chapter.

"But why, Gabriela? I know what I want short term: to find a job! Just show me the effective job search strategies for introverts so I can get the job sooner!" you might say.

Why?

Let's address this first: Why is it important and useful to know in more detail what your short-term goals AND long-term objective are?

• As you might know, staying motivated during the job hunt is quite a challenge when days go by, there is no news from potential employers, and rejections are piling up. It isn't easy to keep your motivation high in such conditions, right? Knowing your long-term objective and having a short-term goal aligned with it takes you further on that path, keeping you motivated along the way. It keeps your hope alive, especially when you don't see positive results yet. And if you don't get discouraged, you'll find a way to reach your objective, since there are many ways to get there.

• Another benefit of staying motivated is this: Employers love to hire motivated people! Put yourself in their shoes. Would you hire a discouraged candidate or a motivated candidate? The latter could give you that extra point leading to a positive decision. Let's face it: since introverts are inward focused, most of them have a hard time projecting enthusiasm, especially under stress, and we're not good at faking it either. Keeping in mind how your short-term goal serves your long-term objective increases your inner motivation, which could be picked up by interviewers (they are skilled in reading non-verbal cues).

• Knowing your long-term objective also acts like a compass when you want to achieve your short-term goal. How? The details related to your long-term objective could guide you in defining what type of position you can look for short term, which will take you further on that path. Looking for a specific position, in a specific type of company, in a certain industry will provide more insights and direction for your actions, which will build on each other toward positive results. I saw so many introverts rushing into sending their resumes without proper reflection before they started the job search. This approach not only leads to time and energy consumed in vain, but also to the frustration of not getting results sooner.

• "Hey, Gabriela, if I become more specific doesn't that decrease my chances of getting a job?" It might seem counterintuitive, but knowing in more detail what you want will in fact accelerate your job search process. Introverts are good at self-reflection and brainstorming ideas by themselves. Having a more specific goal in mind helps you narrow down a specific direction, giving you ideas about where to look for useful information and how you can achieve your goal (instead of dissipating your energy in too many directions). Also, job hunting doesn't have to be a lonely process. Other people could provide guidance, information, and industry insights, but only if you know what specific position you're looking for. And if you get curious about what kind of information you can gather from others, you'll get that extra boost of energy to approach them.

• Introverts are also perseverant when they know what they want and are self-motivated. Going in too many directions (looking for several types of jobs at the same time) diminishes your focus, and more energy is spent. This is just one more reason to figure out in more detail what you want. By staying focused, your actions build on each other, giving you an idea of what the next proper step is and taking you closer to the expected results.

• Look at your current job search from the perspective of your career. If you want to climb a mountain (your long-term objective), wouldn't it be better to keep that in mind to help you choose the right path along the way, instead of trying many paths (job options) and risking getting lost in the woods?

I hope you're with me by now, curious to find out more about your long-term objective and the specific short-term goal for your job hunting.

The What and the How

With any objective you have in mind, there is a WHAT (what you want) and a HOW (how to get there). This chapter will give you some ideas about how to find your "WHAT," while the following chapters will focus on the "HOW." By the way, did you know that successful people focus first on identifying WHAT they want, then figuring out HOW to get there? They don't know the whole path from the beginning; they figure it out step by step.

If you're one of those who wants to know all the steps from the beginning, or even before you get started, expect to be disappointed! As in life, new information, situations, and opportunities will be revealed to you during the job hunting process. Trust that you'll get what you want, be ready to "dance" with what shows up on your journey, learn from your experience, adjust, and be open to the opportunities coming your way.

I still remember Frank's call: "Gabriela, you won't believe what happened! I sent my resume to someone, and he called me right away. He asked if he could forward my resume to a friend who needs someone with my background. Of course I gave him permission! Wow, these strategies work! He also asked me if I know someone who's looking for a basement apartment. I told him I don't know anyone."

Guess what my reaction was! After congratulating him for having the courage to use the new strategies and sharing his enthusiasm, I also mentioned that a vaguer answer could give him some extra points. Keep in mind that any communication is two-way, and you need to put yourself in the other's "shoes." That person wanted to help Frank, but also had a need. In this case, Frank could say (after taking a breath to formulate a proper answer): "I don't have anyone in mind right now, but I'll keep my eyes open and let you know if I find someone." After that, he could reach out to his connections (like the other one wanted to do), and ask if anyone is looking for a basement apartment. We'll talk more about how to answer unexpected questions in the chapter about job interviews.

Consider Your Job Search Process a Project

Before moving forward, I encourage you to consider your job hunt as your project. Find something meaningful about it, besides the fact that you'll get a new job. You're about to search for a position that could take you further on your path and closer to your dream (long-term objective). Isn't that meaningful enough?

If you consider the job search process a meaningful project, you'll get an extra bonus since introverts' energy is boundless when they are focusing on projects they love. What can you bring to this project to make it more exciting?

Several things make me excited about a project: if I initiated it and it has the potential to positively impact others when I use my strengths (curiosity, brainstorming ideas, creative problem solving, writing, Internet research), and it could lead to personal and professional growth. For me, a job search process definitely fits my definition of a meaningful project.

"Oh, it's easy for you," you might say, "but I'm in a totally different field!" Well, no matter what field you are in, you can positively impact your team, the company, and its clients by working at your best. Don't underestimate your power!

Your turn now: take a few seconds to jot down in your notebook what you love about working on your own job search project. Would it push you to leverage your strengths so you can better understand who you are? Will it help you figure out how to find what you want? What else?

As I mentioned earlier, the extra energy that comes from considering your job search a meaningful project will boost your motivation and positively affect your job search! Did I mention that employers also love motivated people? They don't necessarily need to know where your motivation comes from. :-)

If you need permission to consider yourself the project manager of your job search project, you have mine! :-) How does that feel?

In the following chapters, you'll find the different elements to consider for your job search project, while in chapter 14 you'll gather them all together and find ways to make your project more efficient by maximizing your resources.

If you noticed, I give you the power back! You can influence your project's results by how you conduct your job search. The employers have the power to decide who's hired, while your power lies in what employers you contact, how you approach them, and how well you project the real image of how you can help them achieve their goals (while you achieve yours!). If an employer is not interested in hiring an insightful and perseverant candidate with a strategic mind and creative problem solving (all introvert traits), they do it at their own peril. All you can do is say is "NEXT!" and set your eyes on another company, and another, until you find an employer who understands your real value. We'll talk more about this in chapter 9 ("Effective Job Search Strategies for Introverts").

Long-Term Objective and Short-Term Goal

I'll give you some questions to ponder in this section, to help you figure out your long-term objective and short-term goal(s). Please choose a deadline for answering these questions. You can always add new ideas to your answers later, but it is best to jot down what comes to your mind in the next one to two days (for example), so you can move forward with your job search. BTW, your first answers usually come via your intuition. Jot them down. If you sit too much thinking about your answers, you'll get into analysis mode and might get distracted by your saboteur (that little voice in your head saying things like,

"You don't deserve that", "You don't have what it's needed", "You're not good enough", "What will your friends will say if . . . ?"). This saboteur has its role, but in this phase you can ignore its messages. We'll talk about the saboteur's positive role when you need to take action (in section 2 of this book).

Now let's move on, to figure out what you'd like to achieve with your job search project. We'll dive a little deeper to help you define your long-term objective (something that's meaningful to you) and what could be a good short-term goal to accomplish during this job search project. You're in charge!

Take a look at the following flowchart I designed for you, to understand why I emphasized the importance of first defining your long-term objective, then decide your goal for this job search (short-term goal):

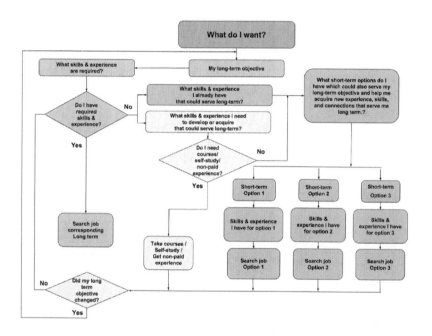

As you can notice in this flowchart, if you start with your long term in mind you'll have a better idea what skills, experience, and mindset are required to get there. If you already have all these, you're good to go! :-) All that's left is to create a good strategy to take you there, and take action.

If you don't have all the skills, experience, and mindset you need, you can identify what you already have and what's missing. With what you already have, you can think of up to three options for short-term positions you can look for during the current job search. Each option has to take into consideration not only what you already have (based on your background), but also what could be useful to take you further on your path toward the long-term objective: what skills you can focus on, what type of company will have a work environment and culture to help you develop the new skills and get the experience, connections, and information that will propel you further.

Introverts thrive in a work environment that caters to their needs, where they are more open to building meaningful connections with their colleagues (who'll understand their strengths), thus opening up a new world of opportunities. This could be the silver lining that will keep your head up when things don't go so well in the current position.

Since introverts don't like to socialize, they have a reduced network of people. Building great relationships in the new workplace could be one of the ways to increase their network, which pays off when they decide to take the next step in their career.

In parallel with identifying your short-term options, you can also identify what else you need (the yellow track) to keep in mind for further personal and professional development inside or outside the workplace.

"Hmm, that's too much to think about. I just want a new job", you might say. I totally understand and have been in your shoes. Yet, I strongly believe that you'll do yourself a favor if you start thinking this way:

• You'll spend less time during this job search because your increased motivation and energy coming from this process will make your job search more effective.

• You'll get to your long-term objective faster, avoiding detours that eat up a lot of resources (time, energy).

• You'll rely more on your own strengths. Thinking thoroughly comes so naturally to introverts; why not benefit from this strength?

Pay attention to one pitfall though: most introverts are also perfectionists. If you're one of them, give yourself a deadline for deciding what your long-term objective and short-term goal options are. Then start focusing on your goals, because you'll get more ideas while you're immersed in the job search process (more about this later).

"Okay, Gabriela. Do you have any suggestions on how to define my long-term objectives and short-term goals?" So glad you asked. I was going in that direction now! Let's take it one at a time.

How Do I Define My Long-Term Objective?

Remember the question I asked you in the previous chapter: "In an ideal world, what would you really love to do professionally?" This answer could help you define your long-term objective.

If you already **have an answer**, great! Write it down in the notebook, with as many details as you have. You could still read the following section ("If You Don't Have an Answer Yet"), and maybe it'll inspire you to find more details about your long-term objective. This will be helpful later, when you identify your short-term goals.

If you **don't have an answer yet**, get your pen and notebook ready, and let's get started.

Now I'll take you through a series of exercises and questions that, hopefully, will give some insights about your long-term objective. You don't have to think of this in terms of "What profession is right for me?" In today's world, when things change so fast, the lines between different professions are not so clearly defined anymore.

A general director told me how much his legal background helps him make great decisions in complex situations (analyzing and synthesizing lots of information is one the skills learned in law school). A specialist in Google Analytics is very excited to work for an eco-friendly company because it matches one of her values.

My coaching background helps bring a different perspective to job search through this book, while my electronics engineering background comes in handy for using computers, learning new software quickly, doing online research, and combining concepts from different fields.

There are many people successfully combining two or more professions or blending skills and experiences from the past while making career changes based on their values.

The key is, since you have some time now, identifying what excites you! When you get a new job, you'll be too busy for a while to figure that out, which could push your long-term objective out even further. I'll help you define it, not in terms of a specific profession or position but in terms of what would be a satisfying long-term objective for you. You would like to get the most of this "in-between jobs" time, wouldn't you?

After you go through these exercises and questions, I'll let you know how to put them together to identify your long-term objective. From there, you'll identify some specific short-term goals to get your job search going in a more effective way.

Ready?

In chapter 2, you were presented with two wheels (one for life, the other for job search), as a way to look at your job search from a more holistic perspective. They gave you an idea where you are today.

What I didn't tell you at that point is this: There's a second part to each of those exercises, which will help you identify your long-term objective and short-term goals.

This book focuses on the job search, so we'll look only at the Career section from your Wheel of Life for this exercise. However this second part of the Wheel of Life exercise can be done with any of the aspects of your wheel needing your attention, though I'll trust you to do the exercise on the other areas if you like.

So for the Career section, check the number you associated with this section in your Wheel of Life.

If it was less than 10, ask yourself this question: What would my career look at a ten? Feel free to let your mind imagine what you'd really love to do when your career gets to that point.

If it's already a 10, great! You can ask yourself, "How would my career look at a 14?"

In either case, let your mind take you wherever you'd love to be professionally five to ten years from now. How does your dream career look if you have all the resources and conditions you need? That will be your long-term objective.

Don't let the "Oh, that will be great, but . . ." derail you from this dreaming process. Jot down your ideas, whatever comes to mind at this point. Pay attention to as many details as you can.

Although introverts are quite good at dreaming, there are some (like me) who have a hard time seeing images in their mind. This is because we're not all the same: some people are visual (easily get pictures and images in their mind), others are kinesthetic (can feel their emotions and the sensations in their body, feel their body's impulse to move, but cannot associate pictures), yet others are auditory (they first perceive information through sounds).

Which ever one of these you are, notice whatever comes to mind when you let yourself think about your dream career or your long-term objective.

Below you'll find some additional questions to help you identify your long-term objective. Create a list with the answers, and later we'll look at this list to help you identify your short-term goals (for this specific job search).

"Oh, there are too many questions!" you might say when you see them bellow. But I know you can do it! Self-reflection suits introverts very well, and with a little help from these questions, you might be surprised by what you'll discover about yourself!

I used these questions too when I identified the career change I wanted for myself. I also used it for helping clients who were stuck in "I don't know". There are some examples presented with these questions, to help you better understand how they work.

Please ponder these questions and capture your thoughts in writing, getting as many details as you can. Grab your notebook and write the title "Long-Term List," then start writing your answers.

- What type of work would you love to do and is meaningful to you? Would you like to work with things, with people, both?

I was still working in the technical field when I went through this process, yet I put on my list that I'd like to help people. Then I asked myself: "What kind of people do I want to help (age group, characteristics)? What challenges do they have? In what way do I want to help them?

- What industry/field are you interested in?
- What are the things you naturally navigate toward (for volunteering, hobbies, etc.)? These are the things you do because they resonate with something important to you.
- Would you like to do this as a career, a hobby, or a combination of both?
- What role would you like to play in that context? Would you like to be the person who thinks strategically? The one who make things happen? The problem solver? The front-line worker? The support person in a field you're interested in? A mix of some of these?
- Which environment would you like to be part of? Write down the company size and culture you'd be interested in, what kind of work environment you prefer, how the atmosphere is at work, your work schedule, and whether it will be independent work, with a team, or combination of both. How are your colleagues and the boss (if you have any)?

Studies show that introverts are more affected by negative experiences and a high level of stimulation (like being in highly interactive areas or surrounded by people while hearing music and having to talk/work at the same time). They notice many details from their environment and absorb everything at a deeper level. They can become overstimulated in such conditions, which drains their energy and affects their productivity. If you did not feel at ease in companies with open office plans (cubicles), in meetings, at lunch time parties, and on team building retreats, that's why.

Those are not proper environments for introverts. They can do well in such environments, but only for a while. If they don't take care of themselves, carving out enough restorative time to relax and recharge their batteries, the stress can accumulate leading to frustration, anxiety, and even burnout. That's why it is good to think upfront about what kind of work environment you'd be interested in. It helps when you do your research, when you ask questions during the interview (to know more about the company), and even to think of alternatives to take care of yourself if you want to accept a certain offer that's less than your ideal.

As an introvert, without having enough restorative niches integrated into your schedule, you can lose interest even in the work you love to do. Has this happened to you? I have surely experienced that: Although I love to interact with people during my workshops, at one point I was asked to facilitate daily workshops and speak with clients the rest of the working day. This soon came to be too much: I became tired, exhausted, stressed out, and some anxiety crept in. I ended up with burnout and stayed away from people for eight months. I gradually recovered, but it did affect my life, and I hope other introverts can avoid such painful experiences.

- What are your values? What is very important to you, both personally and professionally, which you'd like more of or cannot live without?

Below are a few examples of values, to understand what I mean. Search the Internet if you want more examples.

Freedom/ Independence	Moral fulfillment	Intellectual	Variety
Creativity/ Inovation	Assist people	Appreciation	Routine
Expertise	High Standards	Variety	Challenging
Cooperation/ Harmony	Work with things	Democracy	Leisure/ Balance
Security	Learning	Competition	Beauty
Having tight deadlines	Respect/ Status	Fun	Nature/ Outdoors
Belonging	Accomplishment	Interaction with people	Leadership
Commitment	Honesty/ Integrity	Deep relationships	Persuade others

- What activities, which allow you to use your strengths and talents, do you like?

Studies show that extroverts like movement, stimulation, and collaborative work. Introverts have a natural inclination toward concentration, insight, thinking deeply, solving complex problems, strategizing, persistence (especially for something meaningful), creativity (not only art related), and working on independent projects. What's true about you?

- You can also learn more about yourself from what you dislike or what makes you jealous.

Draw a table on your page. On the left side jot down what you don't like. Then go through the list one by one and write on the right side the opposite of each negative term (what you define as the opposite). Go back to the left and strike-through the negative term that led to it. Continue until you get to the bottom of your list. Highlight what you came up with, and we'll use it in a bit. Below is an example how this works, from my list:

Don't like or jealous	Want
office job from 9 to 5	creative work, flexible schedule, I don't work in office all the time
working in a space without a windows	my office has a large window,
ugly environment	I surround myself with art I love
jealous on people who are successful using Internet	use Internet more to grow my business

- In an ideal world where you have all the conditions, skills, and resources you need, what do you really love to do professionally? Again, jot down as many details as you get.

- Another way to approach this quest is to remember the answer you gave when you were a child and people asked you, "What do you want to be when you grow up?" This is not about the specific answer you gave back them. It's more about the meaning, the values lying underneath that answer.

I still remember the answer I gave with emphasis back then, looking straight into the adult's eyes: "I want to be a ballerina!" Well, I love dancing (started dancing in front of the TV at age four), but I don't think becoming a ballerina would really suit me. What I really want and value is activity/movement, non-verbal expression, creativity, being seen without interacting with people, yet touching people's lives in a positive way. I'm happy that almost all of these are part of my life now. It was a journey to get here, and my life is still unfolding. Although dancing was not on my professional path, I still use it daily to lighten up. You should see me dancing to the *Trolls* movie music during the breaks I take from writing this book! Did you see this movie? Lovely, uplifting, with songs so energizing that I can't just sit when I hear them!

So, what values do you uncover by exploring your childhood answer?

- Another way to find out more about yourself is to take personality tests like the Myers-Briggs Type Indicator (MBTI) or Strengths Finder 2.0. They will give information about your preferences and strengths, and books like *Do What You Are* by Paul D. Tieger could even suggest potential career paths corresponding to your MBTI. However, these books and tests only provide general ideas corresponding to your type. You still need to customize them according to your specific preferences (see my questions above).

I personally stumbled upon the MBTI after I asked myself questions to find my long-term objective, like those I gave you in this section, and created a list with everything I want. My MBTI type (INFP) and the Do What You Are book only validated my assumptions. The Strengths Finder test gave some additional information about my strengths and how I can use them more for a fulfilling career. For example, while I knew I am a Maximizer (focused on strengths as a way to stimulate personal and group excellence) and Ideator (fascinated by ideas, able to find connections between seemingly disparate phenomena), it was quite interesting to find out that I am also a Futuristic (inspired by the future and what could be, inspiring others with my visions of the future). All these made sense looking in retrospect at my life, yet I wasn't aware before. The most surprising were the strengths on top: Connectedness (having faith in the links between all things), a belief I noticed showing up in several situations without realizing how it helped me overcome with easiness several life challenges. Now you have a better idea why I'm so passionate about writing this book!

Your strengths might be different from mine, but all strengths are good as long as we use them. This will bring more joy than ignoring them or, even worse, putting them down for whatever reason. Comparing yourself to other people doesn't help either. The most important thing is to become the best version of you you can be! And you can get there by focusing on objectives that are important to you, no matter what others are saying. This way, you'll be more willing and have more energy to acquire the required skills and grab those opportunities that get you there.

Okay, if you did your homework answering the above questions, maybe also adding your personality test results, you've created quite a comprehensive list about how you are and what you really want. Keep the list open because new ideas will pop up in time and you'll want to add them too. Let's move on with what you've already identified; you can incorporate the new ideas later. Quick question: How many elements of your list are already part of your professional life right now?

For me, this question was quite revealing when I went through this process. It helped me understand why I was so unsatisfied by a career that others might consider great (engineering). It also showed me a meaningful direction to look forward to.

The list you created serves the same purpose: to help you define your long-term objective. Even if you don't pinpoint a specific profession or career at this time, this list contains many elements that could lead to a satisfying career for you. It also acts like a filter in defining your short-term goals, leaving out the options that don't correspond at all or correspond too little with what you really want.

Please don't get scared about the lengths of your list! It's not yet organized and is certainly too big to chew all at once!

While the long-term objective might seem hard to identify from such a big list, I suggest three ways of dealing with it below. You can use the one you want or try them all to see if you get the same results.

1st Method

Notice if there are any repeating or similar items on your list. If there are, group them together by categories, and name each category. You can even be a little creative, using metaphoric names. The purpose of grouping them in categories is to shorten the list, more clearly see the big picture, and have it as a more accessible reference in the future. You can come back to this list often, when you feel frustrated or stressed, to understand what's missing and what adjustments need to be made to incorporate more of these items as part of your professional life. You might even be surprised by how many of these items you'd like to have in your personal life as well. Take the time to go through your list and create as many categories as you need, using this template:

category 1: item 1, item 2, item 3, item 4, item 5 . . .

category 2: item 1, item 2, item 3, item 4, item 5 . . .

category 3: item 1, item 2, item 3, item 4, item 5 . . .

category 4: item 1, item 2, item 3, item 4, item 5 . . .

I have a "natural environment" category on my list, which includes: natural light in my workplace, beauty (art on walls), plants, pleasant sounds (if any), harmony when interacting with others, flexibility, and individual work. To me, they all seem to be in the same category, my energy flowing naturally in such conditions. Like other people, I can function in less-than-ideal conditions, but it leads to frustration and stress. So I need to limit my time spent in non-ideal conditions and find ways to be in my "natural environment" more often.

Do you have your wants and likes put into categories? Do so now if you haven't. After you group them, take a look at your list and notice what comes to mind. Do you get a better idea of what your long-term objective could be?

Or at least what elements, once implemented, will represent meaningful work and for you?

As I mentioned earlier, introverts are moved by doing meaningful work. Having enough energy to actually do the work is one of their challenges. Having a meaningful objective in mind could give you a direction, which is also a source of energy to help you overcome the challenges along the way (while achieving the short-term goals leading there). We'll talk about the short-term goals in a bit.

2nd Method

If you'd like to use your intuition, you can work with your list in its raw format, unorganized. Start by putting it in front of you, then take four deep breaths to relax. If you want, you can even go into a deeper, meditative state, to more easily access your intuition. At this point, you'll need to become an observer: you'll look at your list but also notice what's going on inside you.

Start by browsing your list from top to bottom (looking briefly at each item without reading it or dwelling on what it represents). Then browse it bottom to top . . . and again top to bottom . . . bottom to top . . .

Repeat this process until you suddenly get an unrelated thought in your mind. Maybe something not captured in your list, or a totally new thought or image. There's a high probability your intuition spoke to you via that thought/image. Stop here and start exploring this thought/image, trying to understand the meaning behind it. That's how you get new insights about what your long-term objective could be.

Using this idea I identified the career change I wanted (engineering to coaching). The word "coach" simply came to mind while browsing my list, and at that point I had no idea what coaching meant. I heard the term briefly three years earlier when I met two coaches within two weeks after immigrating to Canada.

Yep, serendipity could be another clue from the Universe to help you figure out what you want. What happenstances have you stumbled upon throughout your life, which you still remember? Add them to your list, and check if your newly found long-term objective incorporates these aspects as well. If not, would you like to include them?

3rd Method

This method might look like a combination of the former two, but uses your logic more.

Reduce the list to a number of categories (each containing related items). Then look at this list thinking that it's about someone else, not you.

What can you say about this person? What would be a great long-term objective for her/him that corresponds to what's captured on this list?

Jot down your answer in the notebook, and add as many details you can think of.

Okay! What you find out after using any of these methods (or a combination of them) is a reference for your long-term objective!

Congratulations, you did it! How does it feel?

Give yourself a pat on the back, you deserve it! It's not so easy to go through these exercises and answer the above questions. You are part of the very few who actually took the time to go through them!

If you're unhappy with how much (or little) you've uncovered, don't let your perfectionism spoil your work: you don't need to have it all figured out before you move further. It will become clearer in time, rest assured!

Let me give you an example of how this process worked for Anne. She was unemployed for a few months when she came to me. Her head was spinning, not knowing what to focus on for her job search. She was unhappy, felt defeated and insecure, didn't have much money left, and was struggling with an ankle injury that momentarily restrained her mobility. Anne had many strengths and a background as a project manager in the film industry, yet she couldn't find another contract at this time. Since she was no longer interested in that industry, she was pondering changing directions, but didn't know what else she could do.

As I asked Anne questions similar to those mentioned in this chapter, she began to narrow down what she wanted: she was passionate about helping older adults stay more positive. She had some experience in training, and the project management background could come in handy when putting together programs and activities to help older adults. You should've seen her face lighting up at the idea of making this project her long-term objective. She started to put her project management skills in practice right away: What could be her short-term goal for this job search, which aligned with this project? What resources did the project need? Where could she look for more information? What organizations could be interested in such a project? How could she build her credibility in this field, gaining more skills and experience required by her long-term objective?

At the end of our discussion, I asked her: "On a scale from 1 to 10, where are you now compared to where you were when we started talking?"

"I'm at a 9 right now, while it was 1–2 at the beginning. I like that I now have a direction to focus my energy toward, and it's so motivating! I'm more aware of my short-term goals as well — that's really great! " she answered.

As you see, given a topic that resonated with who she really is, Anne was able to unglue her thinking process and get some clarity, extra energy, and motivation to put into her job search. Did this example help you better understand how your long-term objective helps in defining a more meaningful short-term goal for your job search? I hope it did.

Now write your long-term objective in the notebook.

"Okay. Now tell me **how to define my short-term goal(s)!**"

Thanks for asking. :-)

Remember the flowchart at the beginning of this chapter? After you identify your long-term objective, or at least some elements of it (your list of ideas), it is time to evaluate what you already have and what else you need to get there:

- Do you need to stay in the same industry or same type of company?
- Do you want to do the same type of tasks? Slightly different? Totally different?
- What skills and experience do you already have that could serve you long term?
- What skills and experience do you need to acquire to serve you long term? Where can you get such new skills and experience? (Tip: Throwing yourself into certain experiences can also help you build the skills you need, not just by taking courses.)

The answers to these types of questions will lead you to define your short-term goals. Think of a short-term goal in terms of:

- What tasks relying on your background would you like to perform in the new position? Which provide opportunities to learn the other ones you want?
- What work environment could serve you well, instead of draining your energy? Throwing yourself in an environment hostile to your introverted nature, without taking measures to counterbalance it with enough restorative breaks, leads to stress and drains your energy (and you won't have any left to pour into following your long-term objective).
- What companies could have similar values as yours so you get some extra energy from this alignment as well?

Let me give you another example:

When Zara moved to Toronto, her network comprised only a handful of people. With a background in finance, she wanted to get a position at the same level in one of the big financial companies present here. When we met on a hiking trip, she was quite discouraged, complaining about companies ignoring her applications, and not knowing what else to do since six months had already passed by with no results. I tried to help her understand the recruitment process in big companies and gave her some tips, but I felt her resisting all of my ideas. A month and a half later, I received a message from her. Very happy, she shared how she got a job by implementing my strategies (to integrate into a small company first, in her field, and walk her way up to the type of company and position she wanted). She followed my tips on how to find small companies who'd appreciate her skills and hire her while giving her the type of experience that would make her a more interesting candidate for a big financial institution. I'll give more details about her story in the chapter "Effective Strategies for Introverts."

Zara already knew what her objective was, yet she didn't realize that in her situation this was a long-term objective rather than a short-term goal (since she needed to find a job quickly to pay her bills). If you have an urgent need affecting your life in general (remember the Wheel of Life?), looking for your ideal job right now might not be the most efficient strategy. When she changed her strategy, she got motivated by how fast people and the companies responded to her requests.

When I wanted to leave my engineering background behind, I applied for a position that would allow me to use my newly acquired coaching skills. And I was accepted! This new position was about designing and implementing a new mentoring program for professional newcomers. My coaching skills came in handy: helping newcomers shift their perspectives to facilitate their integration into the Canadian job market, and coaching mentoring relationships when issues occurred. My immigration and professional background helped me to easily relate to my clients' experiences and challenges, while my engineering mindset was useful in designing and implementing a program that lasted five years (until the government cut the funding). Plus, my ability to see things from someone else's perspective made me stand out from other candidates when asked (during the interview) to write promotional messages for this new program, thus inclining the hiring decision in my favor.

Why would an organization hire someone who has a different background? Or no experience for that specific position? I'll tackle this topic in the chapter "Effective Strategies for Introverts."

Now, your turn! Based on your long-term objective, what could be one to three options for your job search goal that align with it? I encourage you to set up to three options for your short-term goal, defining each of these positions with more detail (not just writing down the title). You'll be surprised by how many job offers you can consider when you think in terms of what tasks are required, instead of the job titles.

Why a maximum of three (but ideally only one)? There are more ways to reach your long-term goals, for sure. But by limiting your job search to only one to three options, you won't dissipate yourself in too many directions and get distracted in the process. Your time and energy are important resources!

And since introverts are more inclined to go deeper in their research rather than broader, this process will naturally fit their normal behavior.

Once you've decided what your project is (your long-term objective), it is wise to define the short-term goal for this specific job search in a way that will help you be more successful.

Now write in the notebook the options for your short-term goal: Option 1, Option 2, and Option 3.

SMARRT Goals

We have one more step: to reframe each of the above short-term options using the SMARRT format. You might be familiar with the SMART format for goals; I just added an extra R for introverts.

S: Specific

Your goal should be specific. That's why I asked you to identify as many details you can think of: in what field you'd like to work, what tasks you'd like to perform in this position, what type of company (small, medium, large), from what sector (private, non-profit, government), what work environment and culture, what you'd like to learn while holding this position.

M: Measurable

Having something to measure against is useful in any project. In this context, think of it in terms of measuring against the items listed for your long-term objective. What number of minimum characteristics will you accept for your short-term goal, based on your current situation?

Another aspect of Measurable is dividing your short-term goal into even smaller goals and measuring their implementation to get a sense of your progress. It's kind of like the saying, "When eating an elephant, take one bite at a time!" An example of a smaller goal could be researching and creating a list of twenty companies you'd like to approach (more about this in chapter "Effective Strategies for Introverts").

A: Agreed Upon

You need to be convinced you want this as your short-term goal. Otherwise you might unconsciously sabotage yourself by not putting enough effort into achieving it. It's not only what we do, but it's also about how we do it that helps us reach what we want. And the "how" depends a lot on what we think about our objective (more about this in the next chapter, about mindset).

R: Realistic

Do you consider this goal realistic, attainable, given your situation? If you consider a realistic goal, it is also important to believe it can be achieved!

Don't get discouraged during the job search process when you don't see results yet. Each action you take has an impact, and these actions have a compounding effect, which might not be so visible and tangible like getting a job interview. You can't see what's happening behind the scenes, outside your zone of reach. All you can do is learn from your experience and adjust your job search process to make that goal attainable.

Remember Zara? Due to her situation (she was desperate to get a job), finding a similar position in a big financial company was not a realistic goal. The bigger the company, the longer the recruitment process might be (especially when applying via Internet job boards). Plus, the more experience the position requires, the more trust you need to build (through your actions and networking) to help your application become more attractive to the hiring manager from a big company.

R: Resonance

This is the extra *R* I added to the SMART formula. We're using it often in a coaching context, and for introverts, in particular, is very important! As I mentioned before, introverts need to focus on goals that resonate with them, because they're motivated by what they find meaningful (not by external rewards). This helps them tap into their inner source of energy, to have enough to carry on the demanding job search process. When you understand why putting your focus on this short-term goal facilitates access to your long-term objective, you'll more effectively carry out the different tasks associated with the job search, and project a better image during a job interview, without bragging.

T: Time-Bound

Any goal should have a deadline. This will force you to be proactive and come up with ideas to make it happen. Setting a time-bound goal will also make you more open to noticing and evaluating the opportunities coming your way once you start the job search. It's useful to set a deadline (like I want this type of position in ten weeks), even if you don't have any clue about how long it might take. Setting a deadline will allow you to evaluate your progress along the way (at different checkpoints), to learn what's working and what not. Also, don't get disappointed if you don't reach your goal by that date. If it happens, just say, "Oops! Wrong date!" set a new due date, and get busy adjusting your strategy according to what you've learned in the process and the situation at that point (it might be different from your starting point). At this point, don't forget to acknowledge how much you've learned since you started the job search process.

Okay! It's time to review your previous definitions for your short-term goal options. If they don't correspond to the SMARRT formula, rewrite them in the appropriate section of your notebook.

Please keep in mind that the following chapters will build on what you've talked about up to here. So you'll need to have your long-term objective and these one to three options for your short-term goal ready to use the following strategies.

In this chapter we focused on the Career section of the Wheel of Life. In the next chapters we'll focus on how to use the Wheel of Job Search in the context of one option chosen for your short-term goal. I'll leave it up to you to apply what you learned to your other options.

Chapter Five

HOW MY MINDSET AFFECTS JOB SEARCH RESULTS

A man is but the product of his thoughts. What he thinks, he becomes.
~ Mahatma Gandhi

When I was working as an engineer, some people considered me lucky because I had a great mind. Then, when I switched careers, I was considered lucky because I had the luxury of choosing and doing what I wanted.

What these people might not have considered was our capacity to choose, be perseverant, and succeed! We all have this capacity, but somewhere in childhood we learned to take many things for granted, and we gradually forgot to tap into our innate wisdom and power.

Having the opportunity to help a lot of people find their next job gave me the opportunity to understand how many of them were shooting themselves in the foot, so to speak! :-) Introverts are not an exception; they have just different ways of doing it!

Focusing only on the outside world (what positions are available, what industry has more opportunities, the skills they require, what others are recommending, etc.) is only one side of what will help us find what we want. There is another part that often gets overlooked: your own beliefs and attitudes! In short, your mindset!

According to the Merriam-Webster dictionary, the mindset is a particular way of thinking: a person's attitude or set of opinions about something.

Have you thought about how much your performance in an interview is affected by the stress level you have at that moment? You could be an expert in your field, but you might not be able to articulate that well and make a great impression if you're stressed. It might affect the way you speak (finding the right words, providing good answers) and how you present yourself (nervous, anxious, worried, impatient, etc.). And since the interviewer doesn't know you, he will make his opinion based on what he sees and assumes (which could be something else than what's really going on).

To explore further, your stress level is directly impacted by the beliefs you have. Here are some examples:

• Are you afraid your competitors are better than you? If you are, that attitude of feeling inferior could be picked up by the employer. And they're looking for someone confident to do the job.

• Do you think there are not enough jobs in your field? Or you're not good enough for that position? Notice how these thoughts could add to the stress you already have!

• Do you believe that talking about yourself is selling, and you don't feel like being "salesy"? Then you will not be comfortable doing something you don't like, and without presenting yourself well, how do you expect the employer to understand who you really are and how great of an employee you could be?

• Do you believe that your background is not good enough to get hired? This attitude won't allow you to prepare and present yourself in a way that makes you stand out from other candidates. In a job market where the demand is bigger than the offer, employers increase their standards as well. How much do you understand their standards?

• Do catch yourself thinking, "I don't know how to find companies or how to approach them," or "The economy is down. There are not very many jobs in my field"? Your beliefs can hinder your ability to find the companies that would be interested in what you have to offer.

• Do you expect others to help you? What did you do to gain their trust?

I can go on and on with examples, but I hope you get the point: exploring your own beliefs and attitudes and replacing them with better ones could help you become more successful!

Most of the content of this chapter is based on my workshop called How Our

Thoughts Affect Our Job Search Results. If you're not convinced yet about how your own mindset affects your job search, here are some testimonials from participants in that workshop:

> *So true! It was an unbelievable revelation for me. This workshop gave me all the confidence I needed to start my job search adventure. I discovered what I needed for this adventure. And here it is! My efforts were fruitful: I found a job in the exact field I always wanted! Thank you, Gabriela, for giving me the hope!* ~ Accountant

> *This workshop facilitates wonderful introspection, to understand how our thoughts could ruin our career evolution. We leave this workshop with a new perspective and a new life approach. It was an excellent opportunity to think about ourselves and how our own thoughts are usually limiting us.* ~ Employment Consultant

> *During this workshop, I realized that sometimes I unconsciously designed my job search strategy in a way that my limitations were hiding many skills I have. Even if we know or heard before that our mindset can affect our results, it's totally different when we experience it (like in this workshop).* ~ IT Specialist

> *I just accepted the position of business banking officer. There are several ideas that helped me, that came from your workshop: dream big, the effect of our own thoughts on what's happening to us, don't passively assist your life . . . be yourself, the change agent! Thank you!* ~ Banking Specialist

Before we move forward to show you how to create a more successful mindset, please write down at least ten barriers that you're facing during in your job search.

We'll revisit them later in this chapter, after you learn a method about how to overcome each of these barriers.

What I mean by barriers are all those challenges you think you're facing right now. Here are some ideas to get you started: Low economy? Not good at presenting your skills? Not enough experience? Too much competition? etc.

Write them in the notebook so we can address them later.

Here's what I suggest now: I'll take you through a series of exercises so you can better understand how mindset works in regard to job search, and how to change it to be more successful.

If you're happy with the results you are already getting and are not interested in learning how to get even better, you're good to go. But if you aren't (and I assume you're not since you're reading this book), please do the following:

• **Take the time to actually do** the following exercises, not just read them. Research shows that we retain much more from doing something than reading about it.

• These are experiential exercises, exposing you to new perspectives. By actually doing the exercises, you will **draw your own conclusions** based on your specific situation. Plus, the experience of doing them will provide deeper understanding than reading the information in a book, for example. It's what we in coaching we call "in the bones" learning, because your body will have a memory of the experience which lasts much longer than the information captured intellectually through reading. This gives you access to a way of knowing and doing that will accelerate your job search.

• Go through the exercises with the **beginner's mind,** and leave your opinions at the "door." You could always get them back at the end, if you don't want to incorporate the new learning from these exercises.

You will get as much as you put into these experiential exercises. They are the same as those I used in the workshop How Our Thoughts Affect Our Job Search Results, and you've seen that people did learn something new about themselves, leading to better results.

It might seem counterintuitive, but even though I have quite an extensive background helping people find jobs, I prefer to not give advice. Each person is different, going through a specific situation, and what might work for one person might not work for someone else. The exercises from this book will help you learn from your own experience, specific to your situation and personality.

After each exercise, I'll share with you why I asked you to go through that exercise and how your learning could positively affect your job search. Grab your notebook and pen. Ready?

Exercise 1
How Your Mindset Impacts Others

a) Situation 1: Imagine you're telling a friend about something you're really passionate about (or you're dreaming of).

- Notice your how much energy you have while you're talking about that.
- Bring your attention to the present moment: How does it feel now, while you have that situation in mind (annoyed, frustrated, excited, etc.)?

b) Situation 2: Now remember a moment when a friend told you about what he or she is passionate about (or dreaming of).

- What did you notice about her/his energy level?
- How did you feel while listening (annoyed, frustrated, excited, totally immersed in the story, etc.)?

c) **Debrief**

Now take a moment and notice:

• What did you learn from this exercise?

• How can you apply this learning to your job search?

When I used this exercise in my workshop, people often reported that they felt energized while telling others about their passion or dream, and they felt the same while listening to others doing the same. They also were captivated by and deeply involved in the discussion, like something was drawing them in.

Here's my point on how you can use this in your job search:

• Employers love to hire people who are passionate about their company's culture, products, and services, about the contribution they could make to help the company grow. They are not too interested in hiring people who just want a job that corresponds to the skills and experience they've accumulated. The motivation, the passion, the energy you show during the interview could make a huge difference and set you apart from the competition! And as you might have noticed from this exercise, that's something that's projected through your attitude more than the wording of your answers.

• Look for something you like or, even better, are passionate about that position and about the company you send your application to, and bring that attitude to the interview!

• Don't really love the position you're applying for? Find something else that motivates you to get that position, besides getting a salary. All candidates want the salary that comes with a specific position, so find something else: Is there something about the company's culture, products, projects, or services that you're interested in? Something about the company's position in the market or the awards they've gotten? About how this position could help you understand how things work, so you can help the company more later on? Or about how this position could serve you long term? Before going to the interview — or even better, before applying — get your mind thinking, do your research, and find something you like or are passionate about this position. Because what you put into your application might be influenced by all of these.

• When the interviewers get what you say and understand your drive and motivation to get that position, they'll understand that you're more prone to provide better results than someone who just wants the job to pay the bills.

Like any of these ideas? Make a note to revisit them when you start applying for a new position.

Let's move on to another exercise.

Exercise 2
Exploring the Effect of Your Thoughts on Your Job Search Results

In this exercise, you will be exposed to four situations. Remember, doing the exercise and taking the time to answer the questions will provide you direct insights on what YOU need in your specific situation.

Take your time, go slowly through all four situations. I understand it takes a few seconds to get in touch with yourself and find your answers. Once you do, write them in the notebook.

We'll debrief the exercise at the end, to understand its value in creating a successful mindset.

a) Situation 1:

No matter where you are in your job search, imagine yourself in this situation:

You are at your desk, in front of the computer. You've sent so many resumes but haven't received any answers yet. You don't know why. You believe your resumes are good, and you have the qualifications required by the positions you've applied for.

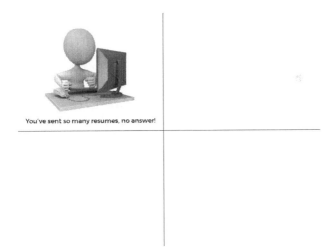

You've sent so many resumes, no answer!

While continuing to imagine yourself in this situation, answer the following questions:

1. How do you feel right now? Notice the sensations in your body. (frustrated? angry? etc.?)
2. While you're feeling that way, score (from 0 to 10) your level of

energy and motivation to continue your job search. Write the scores in your notebook.

3. What actions are you willing you take while feeling this way?

Now look around, choose another spot, and move there while shaking your body as if you leave the situation behind. It's important to do that so you are fully present to the experience of the new situation (2) in this new spot. If you're not willing to move to the new spot, at least face a different direction than you faced imagining situation 1.

b) Situation 2

Imagine that you've already passed the interview successfully and it's your first day at work. Your manager welcomes you and gives you a tour showing you your new office. With your mind's eyes, look around, pay attention to what's around you, what grabs your attention …

You've got the position!
The manager is showing your new office.

While still thinking of this situation, answer these questions:

1. How do you feel now, while having this situation in mind? (frustrated? angry? etc.?)
2. Score (from 0 to 10) your level of energy and motivation to do a great job while feeling this way.
3. What actions are you willing to take while feeling this way?

Now look around, choose another spot, and move there while shaking your body as if you leave situation 2 behind. It's important to do that so you are fully present to experience the new situation (3) in this new spot. If you're not willing to move to the new spot, at least face a new direction different than those for situations 1 and 2.

c) Situation 3

Imagine that it's vacation time! You are in your favorite place, the one that you dreamed of for quite some time. Yep, you're finally here! Take your time and look around and notice the details at that place. How does it feel to be on vacation here?

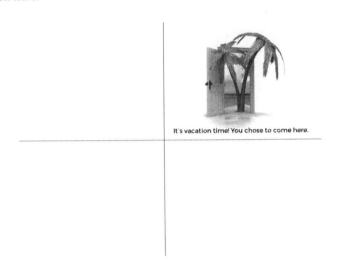

It's vacation time! You chose to come here.

While imagining yourself in that vacation place, answer these questions:

1. How do you feel now while having this situation in mind? (frustrated? angry? etc.?)
2. Score (from 0 to 10) your level of energy and motivation to do a great job or even start looking for a new one.
3. What actions are you willing to take while feeling this way?

Now look around, choose a fourth spot, and move there while shaking your body as if you leave situation 3 behind. It's important to do that so you are fully present to experience the new situation (4) in this new spot. If you're not willing to move to the new spot, at least face a new direction different than those for situations 1, 2 and 3.

d) Situation 4

Imagine that you're back to work: So many tasks are waiting to grab your attention, and your manager and colleagues seem happy that you're back.

You're already back to work.
So many things to do!

While imagining yourself back at work, answer these questions:

- How do you feel now, while having this situation in mind? (frustrated? angry? etc.?)
- Score (from 0 to 10) your level of energy and motivation to start working.
- What actions are you willing to take while feeling this way?

e) Debrief

Shake off the image and experience from situation 4. Look elsewhere and reflect on what you got from the whole exercise.

Here are a few questions to get you started:

- What did you learn from this exercise?

- Did you notice any difference in how you felt in each situation, and what actions were you willing to take each time?
- If you noticed differences from one "place" to another, what caused you feel differently in each situation? (After all, you were physically in the same space, just moving around following my instructions.)
- What else captured your attention regarding this exercise?

Here's why I asked you to go through this exercise:

If you are like the participants who attended my workshop How Your Thoughts Affect Your Job Search Results, you had a different experience with each situation (whether it was a different feeling, energy level, or action you were willing to take).

If you didn't, I wonder if you really followed the instructions and did the exercise, or if you were able to connect with your feelings in the moment (not just paying attention to your thoughts). There are people who are so used to thinking and analyzing, that they have a hard time reconnecting with and noticing the sensations in their body.

If you did notice differences, although you were physically in the same place, the fact that I asked you to imagine a different situation each time had a different impact on you . . . instantly! Did you notice that?

So there is a connection between the image or thought we hold in our mind and the feelings that show up in our body. Those feelings make us have more or less energy, which leads to being more or less motivated to carry on certain actions . . . or prefer other actions. And guess what?! The actions we take and the level of energy and motivation we put into them influence the results we get!

The TFAR Sequence

Have you noticed people doing something without enthusiasm, even with negativity? What was the result of their actions compared to someone enthusiastic and more positive performing the same action? Which one would you like to have on your side?

There is a sequence that many people don't know or simply ignore:

Thoughts > **F**eelings > **A**ctions > **R**esults

Let's call it the **TFAR sequence**.

I have heard many people say: "Tell me what I should do to get the job. What actions should I take?"

As you see in the TFAR sequence, there are two elements that come before actions that these people completely ignore: thoughts and feelings.

If you think that the economy is down or there are no jobs available in your field, how does that feel? How much energy and motivation will you put into your actions to find what you don't believe exists?

If you think the employer has all the power in an interview, won't you be intimidated? In such conditions, will you be able to present yourself in the best way to increase your chances of getting the interview?

At this point I'd like to invite you to go back to your list of what you considered barriers in your job search. Which ones do you still consider 100 percent true? How much energy and motivation do you have thinking they are real barriers?

Before showing you a method that could help you overcome those barriers, let me show you something else.

Exercise 3
Three Levels of Communication

Let's consider three circles as in the image on the right:

• The small one represents the communication you have with yourself.

• The medium circle, communication you have with others.

• The big one, communication you have with the world.

What do you think? On which of these three circles do you have more power to change something?

If you answer, "The small one, communication with myself", you're right. You have much more power to change something when it involves only one person (you), than two or more people. The question is, would you like to? :-)

Some people don't want to change, even though they are not as happy as they'd like to be. As an introvert, if you want to be more successful in your job search, this is an area where you could implement some positive changes if you want a better outcome: get more invitations to interviews, project a better image and gain employer's trust, speed up the job search process, etc.

If you think again about the Thoughts-Feelings-Actions-Results (TFAR) sequence, the first three elements in this sequence depend on you! If you don't like the feelings you have while searching for a new position, you can change your thoughts, leading to more positive emotions. They will bring more energy and motivation to carry on the right actions required to get the expected results. This way you can influence the results by being in the "driver's seat" (adjusting the thoughts as required) instead of being at the mercy of the outside world.

Now go back to your list of barriers you listed earlier in your notebook. Which ones are imaginary barriers, and which ones are real challenges?

Here are two examples, to illustrate what I mean:

• A real challenge is something like this: You're being chased by a bear in the forest, and you're running as fast as you can to escape. If someone around you could witness you actually running away from the bear, that means it's a real challenge.

• An imaginary barrier could be this thought: "The economy is down these days, there are no positions available in my field." Are you sure there is no company that needs your expertise? Maybe you didn't see any positions available on the Internet, but that doesn't mean there are none (maybe you didn't find them). How can you be sure without contacting ALL the companies that could benefit from your expertise? Did you contact them all? Maybe some companies haven't listed their position on the Internet yet. Or they are too small and don't have enough resources to list the position on the websites you're searching on. Maybe there's someone who just moved away and the company needs to hire someone immediately, without going through a formal recruitment process, which takes time. (They didn't even have the chance to create the job description.) As you see, there are many "maybes," which is a sign your barrier could be an imaginary one.

Take a moment and think thoroughly about what you wrote on your list of barriers!

Here's another example, if you have it listed as barrier: "I want to get into this field, but I don't have enough experience. The job openings I see require much more experience." Could this be a real barrier to finding a job? Do you know everything happening in your area or country, to say that no company would be willing to hire you? There might be companies more interested in hiring someone who wants to pursue a career in their field (even with less experience), than someone with more experience who might think of a career change. Not to mention that the latter requires a bigger salary, and if he leaves, the company will need to go through a costly recruitment process to hire a replacement again (the transition will affect their productivity as well). So, your initial thoughts might not represent a real barrier. Your role is to find those companies, but you'll have to change your mindset first. If you go to an interview thinking they won't hire you because _____ (fill in the blank) guess how well you will present yourself during the interview.

That's how I want you to assess the barriers you listed, before proceeding with the next exercise. How many of them did you identify as real barriers? Put a checkmark to each imaginary barrier you identified. We'll get back to them in exercise 5, where I'll show you how to change them into more empowering thoughts, which could actually accelerate your job search.

Since we talked about mindset, let's explore the balance of mindset vs. skill set of successful people through the following exercise.

Exercise 4
Skill Set vs. Mindset

A. Grab your notebook and pen.

B. Think of a person you consider successful. Choose someone you admire, based on your own definition of success.

C. What qualities made this person successful? Write them down. Spend some time with this question, to come up with at least twelve qualities. Don't move to the next point until you're done with this one. If you didn't find enough, think about someone else you consider successful. And continue adding to your list the new qualities you noticed in this person. Choose another one if you need to.

It's important to write what YOU consider to be the qualities that led these people to success. Someone else might notice other qualities or get inspired by other people. The most important thing is to write down what resonates with you, because by doing this exercise you'll come out with something YOU need to know to be more successful in your job search. No book or advice could be more accurate than what you discover by yourself. I'm positive that your discovery could speed up your job search process! Give it a try! It's your choice to believe me or not, but from my experience working with thousands of job seekers, those who were open to discovering and adjusting their mindset to a more successful one were indeed more successful and found jobs sooner. Here are a few examples of qualities that some participants came up with, to get you started:

motivated	risk-taker	curious
self-disciplined	tenacious	continues to improve
confident	open-minded	positive
passionate	good at delegating	visionary

D. Now it's time to review the list of qualities you came up with. Go over the elements of your list, and mark each with an *M* (for mindset), *S* (for skill set), or *M/S* (for both) to note if they are mindset related or part of the skill set of a person. Mindset is a mental inclination, person's attitude or set of opinions. Skill set is a person's range of skills or abilities (something that can be learned).

E. Now step back and look at what you came up with. What do you notice? Are there more *M*s or *S*s on your list?

When I do this exercise in my workshops, we always get more *M*s than *S*s. And that's not surprising at all. Speak to any successful person or read books about successful people, and you'll see that, below the surface, it's always a successful mindset that makes them so driven to get results, to achieve their dreams. Do you now have a better understanding of why I was saying mindset is an important component of a more effective job search?

A skill could always be learned or delegated to someone who does it better and faster than you, but only you can be in charge of your mindset and make it work to your advantage (instead of sabotaging yourself, sometimes unconsciously).

F. How many of the qualities from your list do have? How many of them do you use in your job search? Circle those attitudes (*M*) and skills (*S*) you think you don't use or you're not good enough. What do you think? Could infusing more of these qualities accelerate you in your job search process?

If you ask yourself, "How can I focus on something I don't have or I'm not good at?" you're in good company. :-) Many people have asked the same question. Keep reading, I'll cover that in the next exercise and the other chapters of this book to help you out.

You don't have to become an expert in any of these (if you don't want to), but using those qualities a little more will definitely have a more positive effect on your job search. On the other side, don't go to the other extreme: trying to improve it until it's perfect (it will never be) before taking any further action. Taking baby steps will help you steadily make some progress (which is better than no progress).

Look again at your list of qualities you came up with. Don't discard your results just because you don't understand how some qualities could help your job search. Let's take "good at delegating" for example. How could it help your job search? You don't have to reinvent the wheel and do all the research by yourself. Why not try tapping into what's already out there: company directories, specialty magazines, talking to people who already have good knowledge of what's going on in your chosen field. It's like delegating someone to do part of the tasks you need to do.

G. Revisiting this exercise (Skill Set vs. Mindset), what did you get out of it? What are the attitudes and beliefs you'd like to improve?

Now do you see why you needed to go through this exercise by yourself, instead of just reading a list that I could provide?

If you want to share your insights from any of these exercises, send me a message via my website GabrielaCasineanu.com. I'd like to hear what impact these exercises have on people.

Exercise 5
Create a Successful Mindset (Overcoming an Inner Barrier)

Okay, we have finally arrived at the exercise that will help you understand how you can overcome those imaginary barriers.

First I'll guide you through the exercise, step by step, using one barrier as an example. Then you can take the time to repeat this exercise for each of the barriers you've identified. You don't want to keep bumping into them, do you? :-)

Ready? Grab your notebook and look at your list of barriers now. What did you identify as your bigger challenge or barrier regarding your job search? Pick the one that's the most important for you to overcome. Don't worry about the others, you can get back to them after going through this exercise.

a) Current Perspective

Remember the exercise with different situations? This is a similar exercise. We'll start by replacing Situation 1 with what you consider your bigger barrier or challenge at this moment: replace "Barrier 1" in the image below with the one you chose. This represents your current perspective about which barrier is holding you back the most.

- Consider this perspective like a filter you're looking through, to understand what's going on with your job search. If you look through this filter, what do you notice about your job search? How this barrier is affecting it?
- How does it feel knowing that?
- What's good about this perspective?

You might be tempted to say that nothing is good about this perspective, but please give it a second thought. For example, can you be grateful that you've identified this perspective, because now you can look into how to change it? Or for the fact that you have the power to change something, even if you can't control the existing external circumstances? Etc.?

After exploring this perspective, shake it off and move to another area (or look toward a different direction) for the next step.

b) New Perspective

Here, you'll need to find a new perspective:

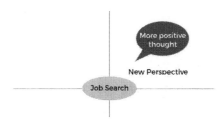

For example: if you don't like selling, maybe the Barrier 1 was, "I don't know how to sell myself, and I don't even want to." Replace this barrier with a more positive perspective: "What are my best qualities related to this position? What examples from my background can I present to highlight those qualities, instead of bragging about myself?"

Your turn: What new perspective do you want to replace "Barrier 1" from the previous step?

If "I don't know" is your immediate answer, you're not the only one. It happened often in my workshops. Did you notice how you feel when you say, "I don't know"? It's hard to come up with something more positive while having that feeling.

To invite a new, more positive thought into your mind, take the thought "I don't know" and put it aside. Then allow your mind to come up with another thought. Don't force it, just wait, you'll get a new thought soon. If the new thought isn't more positive, put that one aside too and wait for the next one. I'm sure you'll get a positive thought soon. We just need practice. Negative thoughts come to mind without effort. The positive ones have to be invited, and we have to quiet our mind to "hear" them. :-)

Here's something else you can do: Say, "I don't know, but I'll find out." :-) If that feels better, start brainstorming ideas for the new perspective now.

Your turn: What new perspective do you want to replace the "Barrier 1" from the previous step? If you've got it, go answer the questions below.

Not yet? Here's another example: a participant's barrier was, "I'm intimidated by HR representatives; they have the power to hire." The new perspective he came up with was, "HR representatives are people too, and they are curious if I'm the right candidate for them. Let's see what I can do about that." That thought made him smile, and he was able to continue the exercise.

Your turn: Find a new, more positive perspective to replace the "Barrier 1" from the step a).

Now proceed to answer the following questions when you have a new, more positive perspective in mind:

- How does it feel thinking this way?
- With this new perspective in mind, what do you notice about your job search?
- What's possible from this perspective?
- Brainstorm ideas of actions you can take to make this new thought more present in your job hunting.

Remember the **TFAR** sequence? You need to take action from this more empowering perspective! Without it, the new thoughts won't lead to better results!

- Pick some of the brainstorming ideas as actions to implement during the following days to help you overcome Barrier 1.
- Choose a reminder for each of these actions (your paper or phone agenda? sticky notes? whatever works for you)
- Take action, one step at a time. It's important!
- Choose to whom you will report the actions you were able to take. It feels good to have someone you can connect with, from time to time, to report your progress. It could be a friend or someone else who's job hunting too. It also keeps you accountable, which is important if you want to make progress. If you don't have anyone with whom to create a "buddy system," put weekly reminders in your agenda to verify what was done during the week and what wasn't.
- Give yourself a pat on the back for whatever you were able to achieve! Not only does it feel great, but it also boosts your motivation and energy to continue.

c) Debrief

That's how you can overcome a challenge or a limiting belief that you consider a barrier to getting the job you want. The important thing is to get unstuck from the place where you were "imprisoned" by your own limiting belief. Once you get out with an action plan and take action, you're free to move forward toward your goal.

"But what about the other barriers I identified earlier?" you might ask.

Get back to what you checked on that list, then apply this exercise to each of them. Yes, go back now, work on them so they don't limit your progress when you get to implement the strategies I'll outline in the next chapter.

Apply these steps:

1. Repeat exercise 5 for each barrier or challenge you checked on your list, those you'd like to work on. Get a list of actions for each barrier.
2. Notice what actions could be done in parallel and which sequentially, so you don't delay your plan too much, taking actions one after another.
3. Put together an action plan with all the actions identified, to help you stay focused during the job search.
4. Create a timeline for your action plan, and add it to your agenda (as a reminder).
5. Verify each day what you'll need to work on, check what was done, and mark what needs to be implemented next or adjusted.
6. Take action! As Leonardo da Vinci said: "I have been impressed with the urgency of doing. Knowing is not enough; we must apply. Being willing is not enough; we must do."
7. Don't worry if it seems like too much and you haven't even start working on the real job search (preparing your applications, contacting companies, etc.). You'll do what you can — even small steps lead to progress. And when it comes to mindset, the positive changes have a cumulative effect over time. Imagine that each action you take to shift your mindset is like a small angle. How much it will open over time?

Congratulations! You've learned a method that helps you overcome any limiting belief, not only those related to the job search — assuming you take action. :-)

And you know what? This exercise, looking at something from two different perspectives, can be applied even for improving those qualities you've identified in successful people that you don't possess strongly enough yet.

Using our exercise again, you just need to put the quality you want to improve into the intersection of the two axes, and look at it from two different perspectives: your current way of thinking about it, and from a more empowering perspective. Then apply the next steps of the method to get your action plan for improving that quality.

Improving your mindset has a short-term and a long-term effect:

- Along with applying effective job search strategies for introverts, it will help you get better results, sooner!
- It will have a positive impact on your life overall (not just your job search results), because the improved qualities and way of thinking will also have a ripple effect on the other aspects of your life.

Creating a more successful mindset takes commitment and patience. The results might not show up overnight. But without proper action they won't show up at all, or not as expected. It's like building a muscle (a mental muscle in this case): you don't expect it to be bigger the day after you exercise, do you? :-)

Chapter Six

SKILL SET INVENTORY

Soft skills get little respect, but will make or break your career.
~ Peggy Klaus

As you've probably guessed, we'll talk more about skills in this chapter.

You'll be asked to assess which of your skills serve your short-term goal and which are required for your long-term objective. Did you identify your goal and objective in chapter 4 ("What I Want")?

If you did, you're great! Continue reading this chapter.

If you didn't, you're still great! :-) But before continuing this chapter, you'll need to go back to chapter 4 to identify your short-term goal options and your long-term objective. You'll need to know your objective and goals from now on, to get the most from the rest of the book.

So let's get started!

Skill set refers to the set of skills you already have, although you might not excel in all of them — which is okay.

By taking an inventory of your skills, you'll realize what skills you already have, which ones you want to focus on more, and what new skills you'd like to learn. Also, it'll make it easier to craft a customized resume for each position you apply. I guess you're already aware that companies are only interested in targeted resumes, not in general resumes presenting all your background.

You'll get more details about resumes in chapter 8: "Preparation (Job Search Tools").

Before moving forward, let's make it clear: the skills required for an effective job search might be different from the skills needed to perform the job (unless you want a job requiring sales skills).

Imagine for a moment you want to buy a certain service: car repair, for example. As a potential client, is your decision influenced by how the technician presents his service and if he satisfactorily answers your questions? Are the skills used in talking with the client different from the skills required to actually perform the task (repairing the car)?

He might be a great technician, but if he doesn't present his services well or he was not referred by someone you trust, your decision will be influenced by your first impression.

It's the same with the job search, although the roles are different: you're the "technician" who needs to present his "services" well (what you can offer, what the company could gain by hiring you), while your "client" is the company's gatekeeper (HR, recruiter, or manager).

Introverts' Job Search Skills

"So what should I do? I'm an introvert, I don't have good sales skills, and I'm not even interested in sales! Plus, I don't like to talk about myself!"

Okay, I get it. As an introvert myself, we're in the same boat. The trick here is how you can reframe the job search process in a way that doesn't seem like a sales process to you. You'll just need to change the perspective to make it easier; you don't have to become a sales expert!

Want an example of selling without being salesy?

I designed and facilitated a series of workshops for several years, with similar content to what I cover in this book. Each workshop was about a different aspect of the job search, but only two workshops attracted new clients: one was about resumes, the other about effective strategies. Most of the people who registered for the workshop on resumes believed that's the only thing they need to land the job: a great resume! The other workshop attracted those frustrated by their job search results, looking for new strategies they didn't try yet.

What approach did I use to "sell" my other workshops? In each of these two workshops, I touched briefly on topics related to the other workshops, highlighting why it is important to consider them too. I also mentioned that I don't have time to cover everything in the current workshop, so they can get more details by attending the other workshops. Well, my strategy worked! Those who came to the workshops on resumes and strategies, registered to at least one other. After attending the new one, they RSVPed to another one, until they completed the whole series!

In one workshop I even mentioned, smiling: "I'm a great seller, right?" They all agreed! Yet, in my mind, this technique had nothing to do with selling! I was so convinced my other workshops would help them become more successful in landing a job, that I was honestly (and confidently) sharing my thoughts! Notice how meaningful the topic is for me? That's why I was successful in getting people enrolled in my other workshops. I told you that we, the introverts, can be successful if we truly believe in what we want.

From a personal perspective, I knew I wouldn't feel good about letting these job hunters go out to struggle again by using only a tiny part of what I had to offer! So my motivation was really high.

You can imagine how happy I am now, putting all my workshops and knowledge about this topic in this book so you have it all at your fingertips!

In the above example, I was the "technician" using some skills to help people come to these workshops, and other skills (facilitation and teaching) to help the clients absorb the content more easily.

If you didn't notice yet, I'm using the same technique in this book to motivate you to keep reading! :-) I truly believe each chapter can help you better understand that job hunting requires a holistic approach, so you'll benefit more from applying these techniques and strategies. If I don't tell you how all these chapters work together, who will? See, I consider this part of my role (to let you know) because keeping this information to myself won't do a service to any of us.

I hope you got the point: It's your responsibility, as a candidate, to talk about the benefits of your "services" for the company you are applying (having in mind what could be a great "service" for them).

There's nothing wrong with selling. Did you ever buy a product or service you love? Selling was part of the process of getting that product or service in your hands!

But if you believe that only extroverts are good at selling, you might need to reconsider your opinion. Extroverts like competition and getting someone else's attention. These are their motivation factors, helping them become good at sales. On the other hand, introverts like collaboration and helping others. There are successful sales professionals who are introverts, and their success is based on the motivation to help others and collaborate for a meaningful purpose. You too can become one of them, if you want to. At least you can become better at talking about your "services", knowing how much you can help the company achieve their goals if you get the job. This also requires speaking with confidence. If you don't believe you can do a great job (given the chance), do you think others will believe?

In the following table, you'll find some skills that many introverts have. In the first column, check the skills you have. On the right column you'll find ideas on how to use these skills during the job search to make it more effective. I'll get back to these ideas in the next chapters, where we'll talk about how you (the "technician") can use these skills combined with certain strategies to be more successful in your job search without feeling like you're selling.

Introverts' Skills and How to Use Them

Focus well in a quiet environment

To be more effective, immerse yourself in a quiet environment, especially when you're doing the self-reflection and experiential exercises, or when you research information.

Desensitization by exposing yourself to smaller, manageable doses

Look at your job search as a process: The more you prepare and practice, the better you become. Also, look at each interview as an opportunity to learn and practice your interview skills, so you become better.

Prefer a passive form of communication (email, online chat/tools)

Use social media (like LinkedIn) to approach new people and learn about them from their profile before asking to meet in person for an information interview. (You'll feel more comfortable talking with someone you're somehow familiar with, and more easily find a topic to start the conversation). Use more emails (instead of the phone) to communicate and share information.

Good at complex, focused problem solving

Let me guess: Isn't a job search a complex, focused problem you need to solve? :-)

Creative, intuitive

Use your intuition to filter the companies and people you'd like to approach, and find creative ways to approach them. The information found via research, and your creativity, will help you identify better ways to approach them.

Imagination/visualization

Often used by sports champions, this is also a great skill to use for your job search. Athletes use this technique by imagining themselves anticipating and practicing the moves until they're confident or they get the feeling of being a winner. There's a psychological explanation of why this method is useful.

Curiosity

While you're curious, you can't be fearful at the same time. Curiosity can help you project a more confident image and decrease your stress during a job interview. It's also useful while doing your research. It could help you figure out what company gets more points when you compare it with the characteristics you identified for your long-term objective and short-term options.

Deep thinker

This is a great skill to use with the self-reflection exercises, to analyze what's working or not in your job search and adjust your strategy.

Work better individually

That's what most of the job search process requires!

Passion for thinking, with attention to details/ subtleties

Picking up on clues during the interview can help you adjust your responses to create a bigger impact. Planning your job search in more detail aids in identifying more precise actions, making it easier to implement and track their progress.

Motivated by meaningful projects

Getting yourself the job you want is a meaningful project, isn't it? In an interview, let your motivation drive your answers in a way that presents the value of your "service" to the potential employer, similar to what I did when I enrolled people in my workshops. Also, this motivation gives you the energy to carry on the job search even when you don't see any results yet.

Need breaks to recharge their batteries after human interaction

When depleted of energy, take a break, or even a day off to recharge. You'll come back more positive and motivated to continue your job search.

Look before you leap

Planning your strategy before diving in will definitively make your job search more effective. Take the time to do the exercises from this book, to better understand where you are and what you need. During a job interview, when asked a surprise question, take the time to understand the reason behind that question so you can formulate a better answer.

Arrange to limit surprises

Preparing answers (to most common interview questions) and questions to ask, and practicing before the interview will decrease the surprises during the job interview. Paying attention to details, screening the job postings well will avoid spending time and energy in interviews for jobs that are not a good match for you (short term and long term). Prepare yourself mentally for the small talk usually used to start an interview (thinking of some answers could give you a great start).

Process info about environment unusually deeply

Train yourself to focus on what's more important: focus on understanding the employer's perspective. Notice his reaction to your answers and adjust accordingly for the next answers. Ignore the noise around you. Don't pay attention to the employer's lack of eye contact if he uses his time to take notes about your answers.

Aware of the consequences of a lapse in your behavior

That's a great skill! In an interview, notice how your answers are and how they are received. Don't spend precious time beating yourself up or dwelling on how bad your answer was. Focus instead on providing better answers to the following questions. The overall performance counts more than a specific answer.

See, that's why I wanted you to pay attention to your introvert strengths! They are also skills that can be effectively used during the job search. You have them for a reason. :-) Did you notice that at least some of them are not similar to the skills required to perform the job you're looking for?

Extroverts' job search skills are different (sometimes quite the opposite), but they also lead to an effective job search. They just use different strategies or apply them differently to get what they want.

Skills Required to Perform the Job

We talked in the previous section about the introverts' skills that could lead to a more effective job search. This section will assist you in identifying the skills required to capably perform the type of job you identified as your short-term goal.

I hope by now you have your long-term objective and the options for your short-term goal. If you don't, please go back to chapter 4 (What I Want). It's very important to define these before moving forward. Otherwise you cannot apply what you'll read from this point on. If you didn't decide yet, now is the best time to do it! :-)

You can always adjust or change your goals and objective later, but you have to start somewhere. Otherwise you lose some precious time, which instead could serve you to move forward.

Still wondering why it is important to take stock of your skills before even thinking of a resume? Here's why:

• Creating a skill set inventory before launching your job search will make your life easier when you have to quickly craft a targeted resume for a certain position. Yep, you have to adjust your resume to each position you apply! So instead of spending time creating the skills section of the resume from scratch, accessing a ready-to-use skills list will simplify and accelerate the process.

• You can leave your list of skills open, to add other skills you remember later. This usually happens when you start looking at job offers similar to what you're looking for, and realize that some of the skills mentioned there are not on your list yet (although you have them and used them before).

• Your skill set inventory should also contain skills you used outside the professional world, while volunteering, for example, or for your own projects. These too could be useful to mention on a resume, if they can make your application more attractive to a potential employer. Someone who's adaptable and proactive, for example, should mention such skills when applying for a position in a fast-growing company.

• A special section of your list should contain the skills you need to acquire for your long-term objective. Thinking of them upfront will help you determine which job postings are more interesting to you. There are many job opportunities out there, you just need to find them. And spending your time and energy applying to those who are not interesting will only delay your job search or make it less satisfactory.

Create a table like this to come up with your list of skills: on the left column add your skills, checking in the other columns what type of skills they are (soft, hard, transferable) and for which objective they are useful (short term, long term). Add as many rows you need.

	Soft skill	Hard skill	Transferable skill	Short term	Long term
skill 1	X			X	
skill 2		X		X	X
...					
long term skill 1	X		X		X
long term skill 2		X			X

If you want to make it even more relevant at this point, you can add a column for the skill level. It doesn't matter much what level a skill is right now, because companies have all kinds of positions — from beginner to advanced — each requiring a different skill level.

If you're not familiar with the terms **soft, hard,** and **transferable skill**, think of a computer: the main unit (the microprocessor) needs software (a program) to tell it how to do calculations or more complicated tasks. The microprocessor itself (the hardware component) will be useless without the software telling it what the steps for a certain operation are (to add numbers, for example).

Soft Skills

When we think about the job search, the **soft skills** are like the software (program) needed to run the microprocessor. They are related to the human attitudes and behaviors that make that person perform well in a specific position.

For example, if your role is part of a team, being able to collaborate with others to achieve the team's objectives is a required soft skill. It's not specific to that position because you can be a good team player in another team (performing other tasks), or even working in another industry.

For a salesperson, perseverance and excellent communication are excellent soft skills to have in order to make great sales. For an IT specialist, the ability to work independently and a keen eye for details are great soft skills to have.

Hard Skills

These are the technical skills required for a specific position, skills allowing you to do this specific job.

For example, if a position requires knowledge and experience operating a certain machine, you cannot get that position if you have no clue what the machine is about. If an IT position requires experience using a certain programming language, you have a very slim chance of getting the position if you don't know that specific language (especially if your competitors do know it).

If you noticed, I didn't say that you have no chance to get that IT position, because if you have transferable skills and the right attitude, you might be able to turn the employer's decision to your advantage.

Transferable skills

These are skills you can use in another industry or position, not necessarily mentioned in the job posting, but showing the potential employer that you could be a good candidate.

Continuing the example with the IT specialist, if he already has knowledge and experience in other programming languages, but not with the one required by the position, he can mention the skills he has, demonstrate that he's a quick learner and loves challenges, and he might be invited to an interview (if the company doesn't have good candidates with the skills mentioned in the job description). You never know what's on the other side, so why not try!

Some of the soft skills could be considered transferable skills, if the employer didn't mention them in the job posting, yet they are useful in performing the job. For example, excellent communication skills used previously for a receptionist position, now applied in a position requiring dealing with client complaints. In the same way, some hard skills could be transferable skills (like knowledge of several programming languages proves the ability to learn new languages).

Now that you have a better idea what soft, hard, and transferable skills are, go back to your notebook and populate your table with the skills you know you have. Check to be sure you didn't miss anything.

Now try to remember and write down all your experiences, paid or unpaid (volunteering, internships, activities with friends/other people, hobbies, etc.):

Experience	When	Skills
Experience 1		
Experience 2		
Experience 3		
...		

This exercise will also help you later when you create your resume, so you don't miss skills and experiences relevant to the position you're applying for. People tend to think only about their professional experiences, leaving aside other types of experiences where they used similar skills to those required for the desired position. This strategy is even more important when you want to shift your direction. I applied for a management position, capturing in my resume the leadership positions I had through volunteering — and I was invited to the job interview!

After listing all your experiences, notice what skills you used in each of them (soft, hard, and transferable skills). Then check with your list of skills (created earlier) to see if you've already listed them all or need to add some more. Repeat this for each experience.

If your mind functions like mine (needs a starting point to get me thinking), here are some example of soft and hard skills:

Soft Skills	Hard Skills
Problem Solving	MS Office Suite (Word, Excel, Power Point)
Adaptability	Computer Programming
Collaboration	Heavy Machinery Operation
Strong Work Ethic	Spanish Fluency (for a position requiring Spanish)
Time Management	Bookkeeping
Critical Thinking	Schedule Management
Self-Confidence	Systems Analysis
Handling Pressure	Automotive Repair
Leadership	Video editing
Creativity	Sales

Want more examples? The following is not an exhaustive list. You can find more examples by searching skills online or looking at job descriptions. Yet, while filling out your list, I encourage you to pay attention to what skills you have already used in your own experiences, and what new skills you'd like to learn (for your long-term objective).

Decide	Counsel	Purchase	Provide medical care
Sort	Teach/train	Cook	Provide animal care
Draw	Manage projects	Edit	Assemble
Write	Estimate	Plan (financial)	Produce crafts
Research	Manage people	Drive	Interview
Facilitate	Paint	Analyze/synthesize	Install
Speak publicly	Coordinate	Decorate	Categorize
Inspect	Create/administrate policies	Draw (technical)	Investigate
See details keenly	Deliver goods	Renovate	Do physical labor
Enter data	Serve customers	Count	Schedule
Operate machines	Develop	Design (industrial)	Design (graphic)
Examine	Photograph	Sew	Negotiate
Sell	Manage data	Do routine work	Grow plants
Use computer	Coach	Clean	Solve problems
Adapt	Collaborate	Overcome challenges	Know multiple languages

Now take the time to compile your own list of skills, preferably directly on your computer. This way, you won't spend time typing them again when you need to craft your resume (copy-paste will do the trick).

Another purpose of taking inventory of your skills is to help you become more aware of how many skills you already have, which will boost your self-esteem (so useful for an effective job search)!

Introverts tend to spend less time with others. They are more often in their head and might not recognize all their strengths. It's helpful to have a good reminder (your skill set inventory), especially when stress makes you forget all those great things about yourself.

Employers do hire candidates with transferable skills or without experience in their specific industry!

I had clients who were surprised to hear that companies hire applicants with transferable skills or without the required experience. Some candidates even get offended when employers hire someone less experienced than them.

To understand why this is happening, you need to put yourself in the employer's shoes:

• The hiring process is costly and time-consuming, and the employers might not be willing to start another recruitment round if they don't find (what they believe to be) the right candidate. The longer the hiring process, the longer they'll need to wait to fill an empty position, affecting the company's productivity, resources, and profit. They keep a constant eye on the risk involved with the recruitment process and will choose the option that minimizes their risk.

• It's well known that the recruitment process does not always guarantee the right candidate will be hired. That's why there is usually a probation period for new employees, whether they have the required skills and experience or not, to see how quickly they adapt to the new position and team.

• The company's culture also plays an important role in the recruitment process. A fast-growing company, for example, might not be willing to hire someone with the right experience for the position but with too many years in a similar position elsewhere. They fear such a candidate might not be adaptable enough to keep pace with their company.

• An employer might lean more toward a candidate who comes across as a motivated person driven by results (even if he is less skilled) instead of one who just wants a job because he has the same background. The former is perceived as someone with higher productivity, the latter as someone who just gets by. Which one would you want on your team? That's why earlier I highlighted the importance of motivation and determination for an effective job search.

• Sometimes organizations don't get candidates with all the skills and experience listed in the job posting, but they are willing to hire someone as soon as possible to move on with their project. If you have the right personality and attitude, similar skills or experience in a different industry, they might be willing to give you a chance. If you have come so far, they assume you have the ability to learn the missing technical skills. But if your soft skills are not appropriate for that position and the company's culture, although you have the right background, you won't get the job. Why? Because it takes time to change someone's personality and attitudes (they also have to be willing to!), and the company might not be willing to wait for that to happen.

• Let's say you're an employer: would you hire an arrogant person for a customer service position, even if the resume mentioned such background? I don't think so. You don't want such treatment for your (potential) clients, do you? You could lose your clients due to this person's behavior, which will affect your profit. And you don't want this person on your team either, to affect the team dynamics. I have to admit: Being an introvert, I used to be so withdrawn in the presence of others that sometimes I was perceived as arrogant (although I'm not, when you get to know me). So pay attention: What we think about ourselves might be different from how others perceive us!

I hope you understand by now why employers pay so much attention to soft skills, sometimes even more than to technical skills and experience: They want employees who are a good fit for their organizational culture and are adaptable. An employee (even a specialist with a lot of experience) who doesn't collaborate well with the rest of the team could negatively impact the team's results. That's why it is important to let employers know about your strengths, especially your soft skills. As an introvert, you might feel tempted not to enter such territory, but in fact, this could be your secret weapon!

As an introvert, you have many strengths employers will benefit from! And in a competitive job market, it's even more important to use your strengths. We'll see in the following chapters the importance of having a good resume and, even more important, how to help employers understand the benefits of hiring you!

Before moving on to the next chapter, take a new look at your skill set inventory. Pay special attention to what skills you checked for your short-term goal, and what for long-term objective. Remember where you put your list, you're gonna need it! :-)

Chapter Seven

WHO COULD HIRE ME

Details matter, it's worth waiting to get it right.
~ Steve Jobs

Let's recap what we've done so far:

• Chapter 2 ("Wheel of Job Search") helped you identify the different elements of a holistic approach that will make your job search more effective. You were also invited to put the current job search in the perspective of your life, thus discovering other life areas that affect your job hunting, and eliminate their negative impact.

• Chapter 3 ("Past vs. Forward") invited you to reflect on how much of your background you want to carry into the future, since you are at a point when you can make a decision: continue on the same path, consider a slight change of direction, or make a career change. Your choice is important and informs how you'll conduct the job search!

• Chapter 4 ("What I Want") helped you identify your long-term objective in more detail and then decide which short-term options you can consider as your short-term goal for this specific job search.

• Chapter 5 ("How My Mindset Affects the Job Search Results") guided you in how to spot your own inner barriers and how to shift your perspective so they don't sabotage your job search.

• Chapter 6 ("Skill Set Inventory") was an invitation to select which of your skills you'd like to focus more on from now on, to make a distinction between the skills required to perform an effective job search and those required by the position you're looking for (short term), and identify the skills you'll need to develop to move forward toward your long-term objective.

Having more clarity about your job search goals (short term and long term), let's dive into what companies could hire you. As you've noticed, this is a different approach from "Let me check the Internet for what positions are available, so I can send my applications." While this latter approach might still work for some people, it is not the most effective strategy for an introvert.

Why? Let's see:

Let me ask you first: What do you think, how much does a resume (or your whole application) represent who you really are and what you can do for an employer?

When I asked this in my workshops, most of the participants admitted they never thought about this. Their answers varied from 5 to 100 percent! Quite a range, right?

The truth is, no piece of paper with words on it could accurately represent who you really are. Those are just words, and from an employer's perspective, they don't how much of the information presented in your application is true, and nothing speaks to them about how well you'll fit into their company's culture. People like to make their own opinion about a candidate. And this is even more important for an introvert not used to talking about himself, his strengths, and his achievements.

So do you want your job search to rely only on what some documents could tell about you? Or do you want to bring more of you into the light, so the employer makes a more informed decision?

In her book *The Introvert Advantage*, Marti Olsen Laney talks about a school director who hired an extrovert to teach the French class, only to find that he hasn't mastered French enough. The school director was an extrovert himself, but if the other candidate (the introvert) would have been able to present himself in a better way, the school director could have at least become more aware of what he was looking for in a candidate, and who would be more appropriate for the job.

For introverts, there are ways to avoid such situations. One of them is to do better research about what companies/organizations could hire you, and find a way to get in front of their decision makers before they even start the recruitment process. This will eliminate or at least decrease the competition, increasing your chances of getting hired.

"How do I find these companies and organizations? How do I figure out who could hire me?" you might ask.

Well, you can use what you've uncovered about yourself up to this point, to give you ideas on how to identify such companies.

Take a look at your answers from chapter 4 ("What I Want"). There were many questions there, and their answers helped you identify the following:

- Sector you're interested in (private, non-profit, government)
- What industry/field
- Size of company (small, medium, large/corporation)
- Work environment you'd prefer
- What organizational culture and values could motivate you
- Type of work you want to do short term (aligned with your long-term objective)
- What expertise and skills you'd like to use short term
- What type of position you'd like: contract, permanent position, temporary, full-time, part-time. What you are willing to accept knowing that you can continue your job search even after you get this position, if you want
- What you don't want at all regarding your next position
- What skills and experience you'd like to gather in this upcoming position, to help you move forward
- What you need to take in consideration about your current situation

When you put these answers together, you'll get a better image of where to focus your energy during your job search, to achieve your short-term goal. Since this direction came from your own answers, being something you'll enjoy, you'll add motivation into your mix to make your job hunting more effective.

Remember the example I gave you earlier about someone who was interested in joining an eco-friendly company? Nancy is an Internet marketing specialist certified in Google Analytics. Working for an eco-friendly company corresponds to one of her most important values, so she was not willing to compromise. She needed a job as soon as possible, so the time was an important element to consider in her strategy. Bigger companies not only have a longer recruitment process, but she also didn't want to spend her time getting into the recruitment hole: too much competition for positions in such companies wasn't to her advantage (fewer chances to stand out).

After doing her homework, Nancy figured out she'd like to work for a medium-sized, fast-growing company with an eco-friendly culture. She started by searching such companies via the Internet, directories of companies, and newspapers, and reaching out to people working in similar companies (approaching them first via LinkedIn, to feel more comfortable). Being at introvert, she felt at ease spending some time researching information about different companies, to use a more targeted approach to job search. Within a month, she got five interviews, rejected two job offers, and got a position in a company that matched her values. She rejected two offers because she felt there wasn't a good fit between her values and the culture of those companies. How she approached those companies, we'll discuss in chapter 14 ("Put It All Together").

Do you believe Nancy was lucky? Her answer: "Behind that luck was a lot of work involved. I made it happen through the actions I took!"

Want another example?

I organized several events with guest speakers who shared their experience with job seekers. Jules was one of them. Although he had HR experience, he didn't look for such a position when he moved to town. He first wanted a position that would allow him to get Canadian experience. Having only a working visa, he thought it might be easier to get a job in a restaurant chain. He walked into one of several such restaurants, asking if they needed help. And got hired! After a while, the HR manager position became available. Knowing that Jules has an HR background, he was asked if he wanted to step into that role. He told us that as an HR manager, he was always aware of the situation of each of his staff members: who would go on maternity leave soon, take a vacation, go back to school, etc. When someone reached him, even for a position that was not yet open or advertised, Jules hired that person if he considered a good fit for the restaurant.

I like two things about this example:

1. How Jules used the short-long term approach to get into the job market, catered to his specific situation. By sending resumes, he had a very slim chance of getting hired, since companies normally prefer candidates with a permanent status (permanent residents or Canadian citizens). By walking in, Jules projected a better image — adding his personality and attitude to the mix (instead of just sending his application).

2. Jules's experience, hiring people without having job openings listed, shows that companies accept being approached by candidates outside the traditional recruitment cycle. I have heard about the same approach from other managers as well.

Isn't this encouraging for an introvert who wants to stand out from the competition?

Yet you still need to do your homework:

• Get back to your answers, to understand what types of companies could be a good fit for you, according to your current situation.

• Start researching and create a list of twenty to thirty companies that correspond with your preferences. Don't list only those companies you already know; there are many other companies that could benefit from your skills and experience. Your chances of getting a job will increase if you also contact the new companies you discover. A well-known company gets more applications, decreasing your chances of standing out from the competition. Less known companies don't get so many applications, and just because they are not as well-known doesn't mean they are not great companies to work for. Start compiling this information into a "list of companies" spreadsheet. It will be very useful when you start implementing the job search strategies from chapter 9.

How do you find companies you'd like to add to your list? Here are some ideas:

- Contact people you already know (via email, if you prefer), and ask if they know companies with the profile you're looking for or people working in such companies.
- Approach other professionals via LinkedIn, people who have a similar type of job as the one you want. Ask for advice and if they know other companies you could approach. How you'll approach these companies is important; we'll talk more about this in later chapters.
- Search LinkedIn profiles of people who have the same or similar position and work in your city (or where you'd like to move): for what companies have they worked and do they work now?
- Go to the local library and speak with a librarian. Mention what you're looking for and ask for help finding directories of companies (printed, online), industry specific magazines, local newspapers, and other information they might find useful for your research. With a library card, you get free online access to resources like companies' directories (which otherwise would require a payment).
- Read industry magazines and newspapers. Keep an eye on news and ads to identify companies that might be a good fit. If you hear about companies that merge with or acquire other companies or have new company projects that could benefit from your skills, add them to your list as well.
- Add to your list the companies you sent applications to before. Maybe the person they hired didn't pass the probation period or they need extra help.
- Professional associations and industry conferences are great places to connect with professionals in the same industry and find out about other companies (check their LinkedIn profile, who they're following, or ask them directly).
- Search online company directories per industry or geographic area. For example, in Canada, search the Yellow Pages, government websites like Industry Canada (click "Just for Businesses" then "Find Canadian Companies"), and Scott's Directories (free access via the library).
- Walk on the streets and see which companies or banners attract your attention. :-) Then research them.

Okay, you already have enough ideas to get started. :-) Now go! Do your own research and create your list of companies so you're ready for the next chapters.

No one else can do this for you, because you know better what you want!

You can continue this research throughout the job search process, and even get some help from others (if you reach out to them). But you'll need to get some companies on your list, to have a starting point when we'll talk about job search strategies for introverts (chapter 9) and how to put all this information together to be more effective (chapter 14).

Part Two

JOB SEARCH FOR INTROVERTS

Chapter Eight

PREPARATION (JOB SEARCH TOOLS)

It's best to have your tools with you.
If you don't, you're apt to find something you didn't expect and get discouraged.
~ Stephen King

Before you even start using any job search strategies that are more effective for introverts, you need to prepare some tools to help you out. You've gotten a glimpse of these strategies in the previous chapters, but there's much more!

In this chapter, we'll cover useful tools to have in your Job Search Toolbox, ten effective steps for creating a targeted resume, what makes a difference in getting a job interview, and the employers perspective on job applications.

Do you remember the example I gave you in a previous chapter, with the technician who needed to present his services to potential clients?

These job search tools are your way of getting the word out, in written format, about your background and potential. Since introverts prefer writing to talking, let's see how you can use this preference in creating more effective job search tools!

What Do You Have in Your Job Search Toolbox?

These are:

- Resume templates
- Cover letter or pain letter templates

- Business card*
- Portfolio*
- Social media profiles* (LinkedIn, Twitter, Facebook…)
- Blog*
- Website*
- References

Those marked with * are optional tools in your toolbox, but they could be very useful to help you stand out from the competition. That's what you want, right?

This chapter is especially for those who don't get job interviews, or get just a few. There could be several reasons why, including the tools or the job strategies used.

If you've already started and are often invited to job interviews, your job search tools are probably good. But you might find some new ideas from this chapter, to help you be even more effective in your job hunting.

I'll start with the optional job tools listed above. Then we'll get into more details about resumes, cover letters, and the employer's perspective.

Do You Have a Business Card?

When I was in charge of a mentoring program, I interviewed the professionals who applied to become a mentor.

That's how I met Glenn, in a coffee shop, close to his workplace. He handed me his business card: no company name on it, just his name, profession, credentials, phone, email address, and his LinkedIn account. He told me, smiling: "While I work for this company at this moment, I want the business card to represent me. I might change companies in the future, and I want people to still be able to stay in touch with me."

I love Glenn's approach, and it was very professional too! You can do the same: create your own business card!

Why Having a Business Card Could Be Useful During Job Hunting

When new people meet, a business card is helpful in starting a discussion. For us introverts, it's not easy to start a discussion. We'd rather listen, right?

When someone hands you his business card, you can make a comment about it (thus inviting the other person to talk first). This way, you're taking the pressure off of you and gaining new information about the other person while listening. After a while, the person will stop talking and ask what you do or what you're looking for. This is your chance to hand out your business card, mentioning that you're open to new opportunities in your field and to any advice. Exchanging business cards also gives you the opportunity to follow up with those you've just met and want to stay in touch (or ask for an information interview).

While you're looking for a job, I suggest creating a business card reflecting where you are heading (not your past). Why? Because you want people you meet to remember what you want. Maybe they can even help with some information, advice, or referrals.

In the example I gave you earlier, Glenn was an accountant and loved what he did, so it made sense to have his profession on his business card. If your short-term goal is to find a similar position to the previous one, go ahead and list on your business card your profession and accreditations.

But if you want something different, you can mention something from your background (skills and/or experience) related to what you're looking for short term. You have full control over what you put on your business card, so create one that represents what you're looking for!

If you don't know what skills and experience to add to your business card, you can simply add an image beside your coordinates (something you love or represents what you want). This way, when someone looks at your card, they might make a comment about your card image — and you can, at that point, add whatever details you want to share with this person.

I remember the first business card I created when I moved to Canada: until I figured out what I wanted (I had several options to focus on), I put an image with a sunrise and my personal details. When someone asked what that picture represented, I answered, "New beginnings", and continued with whatever I wanted that person to know about me and my goal (depending on the situation).

Wondering how to create your business cards?

You can use a computer or an online service like Vistaprint, Staples, or Moo. They even have business card templates, if you don't want to create a new one from scratch, but you cannot buy just a small number of business cards.

I'd suggest creating your own business cards and printing them yourself so you can print just a few at the beginning. After talking with some people you will likely realize that you want to change something on your card, so you can easily do that and print new cards. You can even create several types of business cards, for each short-term option you chose.

To create the business card on your computer, you can download Word templates of ten business cards per page from avery.com. Or simply create a table with ten cells on a blank page. Then add your information inside one cell, and copy-paste on the other nine.

The beauty of using Avery templates in that they have matching business card paper you can buy and print how many business cards you want, to begin with. You'll find the Avery business card paper at any office supply store like Staples, even at Walmart. After printing, just fold the pre-cut paper, and voila, you've got your business cards!

During your job search, your business card could have the following information:

- First and last name
- Something related to your short-term goal (profession/expertise/skills/industry)
- Email
- Phone number
- LinkedIn profile/website (optional)
- Image that represents your style or what you're interested in (optional)

You can use the back of the card for additional information, but do not make your card too crowded. Let it be a starting point for a conversation. You can add more information while you talk.

If you're an experienced professional, you can also present yourself as a consultant looking for new opportunities when you meet someone new. Here's an article about how you can juggle several business cards, depending on who you're talking to, from Forbes.com: "Why You Need Your Own Business Cards."

Portfolio

Not everyone needs a portfolio, but having one is very useful for creative people (graphic designers, artists, copywriters, etc.) to showcase their work and talent, and for those working on projects (marketing & advertising professionals, project managers, IT specialists, etc.).

A portfolio is a way to show your work and what you're capable of, without bragging. Let the portfolio do that "talk" for you. I bet it can do a better job! Employers love to draw their own conclusions based on what they see, instead of relying on what you say in your application or during the job interview.

In a portfolio, printed or online, you can include the most relevant samples of your work and projects. Add awards, numbers that reflect your achievements, and recognition proof, if you have it.

While you can present a printed portfolio in interview or when meeting someone, a link to your online portfolio can reach even more people: it can be mentioned on your resume, LinkedIn profile, email signature, social media profiles and updates, and so on.

And it certainly could include more information than you can capture in your application (without crowding it).

Talking about Social Media!

While I'll elaborate more on this topic in chapter 12 ("Speed Up Your Job Search with Social Media"), I want to emphasize here the benefit of using social media for your job search.

When I was the organizer of a Meetup group for introverts, I noticed that many members were hesitant of using social media. Yet I found it very useful — especially for introverts!

Since we introverts are more at ease behind the curtains and we're not quite comfortable socializing in the real world, social media could be a way to get in touch with the rest of the world. Because, let's face it, we can't do it all by ourselves, hidden in our "ivory tower"! We need information and connections that are out there in order to get a job.

From a job search perspective, social media could open new opportunities for you — if used the right way. I know it can be intimidating and overwhelming, but the beauty of social media is that you can use it as much or as little as you want. And what I like most is this: You can be laser-focused when using it for a job search, to limit the distractions and find the information you need.

With a website like LinkedIn, you can find new job opportunities, companies you might be interested in, people who work in those companies, peers (people working in the same field who might have great advice for you since they're already employed), and even a mentor who can provide guidance and support during your job search!

What I'm saying might sound like too much to you, maybe more like an extroverted approach, but I'll show you how to reap the same benefits while staying true to your introverted nature.

Using Twitter and Facebook could be useful job search tools too, but I don't want to overwhelm you now with too much information.

If I got your attention, in chapter 12, we'll talk about how to use social media from an introvert's perspective to make the strategies from chapter 9 even more effective.

How Can a Blog or Website Help Me?

Glad you're asking! :-)

I used to start one of my workshops by asking: "What does a job seeker need?"

The answers were usually: a great resume and job postings where they can send their application.

Well, in an industry with low competition these might be enough. But do you really think your resume is enough to get an interview in a competitive job market?

Think again. An employer might get many resumes, and the applications that stand out (in one way or another) might get more attention. If you increase your visibility in the industry you're interested in and build credibility and trust over time, employers might be more interested to hear from you than if you let your application get into a pile of a hundred other resumes received.

That's what a blog or website could do for you, when you use them from a professional perspective (to highlight your expertise). You don't necessarily need to make an extra effort to promote your blog or website. When you list their URL on your business card and resume, they can offer additional information about your background and expertise, standing out from other applications (because the employer can check you out even before inviting you to the job interview). This way you can give an extra boost to your application.

That's what Steve did: he created a simple website with four pages (Resume, Projects, About, Contact), to highlight his engineering background and experience in the renewable energy field. He wanted to capture more details about the important projects he worked on, and the resume was not enough. He added his LinkedIn profile on his website (if someone wanted to get in touch with him there), and he listed on his resume both the website and LinkedIn profile. Then he used strategies I'll show you later (chapter 9 and 12) to get the attention of a recruiter from an engineering company, and . . . he got hired!

Garry, a marketing specialist, did the same. He created a website with the projects he was involved in. He made sure to first highlight how the companies were benefiting from those projects he was in charge of, then gave more details about the projects themselves. By adding his website to his resume and

LinkedIn profile, he was able to present more information related to his expertise than he could with a normal resume.

As I said earlier, having a blog or website is optional and takes some extra effort to create or maintain. But, done right, it could have a more positive impact. You can even include testimonials from people you worked with.

Companies love to reduce their risks, so giving them more information (in a less overwhelming format) might help. Plus, doing all this work up front, you're more prepared for job interviews because you can easily take a look at your blog or website to remember what examples could be given in the interview to show your expertise better.

Also, along the lines of what we have already discussed, you can even integrate multiple channels of communication (job application, social media profiles and updates, blog or website) to raise your profile. I didn't mention the video resume because I think most introverts won't be comfortable talking about themselves in a professional manner in front of a camera. But if you are good at this, go ahead, record yourself and post your video resume on YouTube and on your website and add the link to your resume and LinkedIn profile.

It's up to you what you choose to do. I just wanted to give you a few other perspectives than traditional job search tools: resumes and cover letters.

Resumes!!!

Okay, it's finally time to talk about resumes! I already mentioned in a previous chapter that a resume can represent only a small percentage of who you really are. You're much more than what some words on a piece of paper could say about you, right?

In this section, we'll talk about how to craft your resume to increase that percentage, and make it more attractive to employers.

In some job search strategies, you'll need a resume only after you make the first impression, but it still has to be a good resume when you're asked to present it!

Resumes . . . from the Employer's Perspective

When I helped clients with their job search, I noticed a pattern showing up quite often: the background was presented in chronological order, mentioning skills and ALL past work experience — hoping the employer would understand how great the candidate is!

I don't believe this is the right approach in a competitive market, where employers receive a lot of applications for a specific advertised position.

So let's take a look at the employer's perspective:

• The company's representatives are busy, either scanning resumes or performing other tasks required by their position.

• The duration of the recruitment process is established upfront, so they need to hire someone by a certain date no matter how many applications they get.

• They usually get many resumes (sometimes hundreds) for each advertised position, and with the limited time available, they need a way (a scanning process) to select a very small number of candidates to invite to a screening interview or directly to the job interview. The scanning process could be software checking for specific keywords in each resume or someone looking briefly at each application and putting aside only a few of the resumes, those that quickly grabbed their attention by being relevant to the position. You might not know what scanning option the company uses, so you need a resume that can pass more easily through the recruiter's screening gate in any situation.

• Because software can quickly scan hundreds of resumes, if your resume does not have what the software is looking for, your resume is rejected without being seen by human eyes, no matter how great your background is!

• When a person is scanning the resumes, there is not much time to read the details of all the resumes, to understand if the candidate could be a good fit. They will probably start looking from the top of the first page, and if they don't find something related to the position, they will put the resume in the "rejected" pile. That's why it is important to have a resume that grabs the employer's attention from the first page, especially the top one-third of it. The role of the first scan by the employer is to eliminate most of the applications, to have only a few candidates for the interview phase. They don't have time to interview many candidates. So if you put the information relevant to the position further in your resume, they might not even see it during the first scan (increasing the chances of having your resume rejected).

• Only during a second scan will the company representatives read the whole resume. But even now, getting to the next phase depends on how clearly your resume is structured to highlight the qualifications (skills, experience, education) for that specific position.

• To minimize their risk, employers prefer to interview candidates whose work they've previously seen or who are referred by someone they trust. That's why they usually advertise the positions internally first, and if they don't get enough candidates, they open to external candidates. Company employees could refer someone else, but usually they prefer to refer candidates they know could do a good job. Otherwise, their credibility inside their own company will be affected.

• Employers are more interested in candidates who recently used the skills required by the position, because they have a fresh experience about how to use them and it takes less time to become productive (decreasing the company's costs related to new hires).

• Accomplishments listed on resumes show employers that candidates have not only the required skills, but also the capacity to use them to provide outstanding results (helping their company grow!).

I'm not talking about all these to scare you! On the contrary, to help you understand the employer's perspective so you can adjust your resume and job search in a way that will increase your chances of getting job interviews.

Thinking only from your perspective might not help much.

Why? Because if you don't understand the employer's perspective you might be tempted to add more information to your resume than needed, or not organize it properly to catch the employer's attention. In his book *What Color Is Your Parachute?*, Richard N. Bolles shows two pyramids: one about the employer's expectations, and the other about the candidate's perspective. These two pyramids show how opposite the two perspectives are: what is the most important from the employer's point of view (for example, minimizing the risk by hiring someone they already trust), is usually seen as less important from the candidate's perspective (for example, they want the company to "invest" in them first, and they'll prove they're worthy after).

You can grab employers' attention by crafting a targeted resume for a specific position, using one of the three types of resumes. We'll talk about this in a bit.

Use your introvert's strengths when you create a targeted resume:

• Research about the company (culture, projects, products, services,) and the position (new or existing).

• Analyze the information and summarize what's important: what could help in creating a better resume and cover letter? What should you keep in mind if invited to a job interview?

• Use your powerful mind to organize your resume in a way that highlights the information from your background that is relevant to the position you apply, and present it in the best order.

• With your keen eye for detail, take another look over your resume and correct any misspelled words and awkward phrases.

• To summarize, looking from the employer perspective you should keep the following in mind:

• What the employer is looking for in a resume: it contains at least the most important qualifications listed in the job posting (usually they want more, but are willing to accept less), the applicant is interested in their company and in the position he or she is applying for.

• Mentioning your accomplishments will increase the value of your resume and build trust.

• Out of respect for their time, a targeted resume should be no longer than one to two pages (more is not better in this case), targeted to the specific position you apply.

• What resume type could present you in the best light? Using a chronological resume type might not be the ideal if you apply for a different position than your previous one. Rearrange sections if needed, and expand a certain section if it adds more value (or shrink it if it doesn't).

• The resume summarizes at the top what is expanded in the other sections of the resume (if they want to read more). In the Summary of Qualifications, you will include a summary of your skills (soft, hard, and transferable) and experience and education pertinent to the job. Presenting this information at the beginning of the resume gives the employer a brief snapshot of what follows in more detail in the next sections (if they're interested in reading more); otherwise they might not look further.

• If the company has an online application system (allowing only simple text, no file attached), do not format your resume with tables and text boxes that could change the resume content flow when their system extracts the information.

• Use keywords related to the position, if the company uses an online platform to receive resumes (some keywords are captured in the current job posting).

• Copy-paste phrases from the job posting in the resume are not well viewed. If you'd like some inspiration on how to frame your experience in words, look at similar job postings, job descriptions, or LinkedIn profiles of people working in such positions.

• It is not mandatory to start your resume with an objective. A phrase like "I want a position where I can utilize my skills and experience" doesn't say anything important to help the employers make a decision. By including it you would only help them lose some important seconds, which could be more skillfully used to direct their attention to more relevant information (like the Summary of Qualifications). But if your objective is formulated in a way that grabs the employer's attention because you could add extra value, go ahead and use it. An example of such objective could be: "Looking for a marketing specialist position where my PR background could be an asset." This way, if the company is interested in this additional value provided by having a PR background, the resume would be more attractive. If not, at least the person didn't spend time preparing for a job interview with a company that doesn't appreciate his background. Say, "Next!" and continue your job search. :-)

In my workshops I invite participants to do an exercise, asking them to imagine they are in the employer's shoes: they received many resumes for one position, and now they are reviewing them (few seconds each) to decide who they might be interested in. I gave them one of these resumes.

The resume started with a Languages section (spoken/written), followed by Education (sports teacher, sports awards). The Experience section started only at the bottom of the first page (five years' experience as a secretary in a law office). The resume was three pages long, with lots of blank spaces between sections.

After a few seconds I asked participants for what position the candidate applied to with this resume. Some were confused, while others answered, "A sports teacher position".

My next question was, if you received almost two hundred resumes and you have a very limited amount of time to scan them all (a few seconds per resume), would you consider the candidate with this resume for an administrative assistant position?

This time I would get only nos. It's quite logical, isn't it?

When you get many resumes for a position, and most of the first page of the resume talks about something unrelated to the position, you'll want to move on to the next resume.

When you have only a few seconds at disposition for each resume, you'll scan them quickly (starting from the top) to see if they seem to be a good fit for the position. You don't have time to analyze the whole resume to see if this person might have the right skills and experience.

The candidate's resume I used as an example for my workshop did have some administrative experience as a secretary in a lawyer's office, and he could create a more targeted resume if he wanted to increase his chances of getting a job interview for an administrative assistant position. Yet he didn't realize that employers are not interested in ALL of his background.

I have seen many similar resumes. They're like: "Look at what great background I have! I hope you hire me."

Please look at it from the employers' perspective: Would you hire someone with a great background? Or someone who has what it takes for the position you're hiring?

Unless the resume shows a similar background with what the employer is looking for (which is equivalent to a targeted resume), the employers are less interested in other experience and skills you have.

Please don't create a resume that's begging the employer to hire you!

Take your power back: show with your resume what background you have related to the position you want to be considered for, not all your background. And let them know how your values align with their company culture and values.

Doesn't it feel better when you start presenting yourself as someone who can help the company achieve its objectives, instead of begging or hoping to get hired?

Different Types of Resumes

Remember your short-term options defined in chapter 4 ("What I Want") — those positions you are targeting short term, to help you move forward toward your long-term objective?

Now you'll have the chance to choose which type of resume projects a better image of you and your background for each of those specific positions you're targeting (so your applications are more attractive). It all depends on the job description and what you can bring to the table.

As I said earlier, a targeted resume is usually one to two pages, no matter how much experience you have. That's why is called a resume, right? :-) So, a targeted resume might not always be chronological if you want it to project the best image of your background, in which case you will use one of the other two types of resumes (functional or combination), which ever one is more suitable for your purpose.

While I'll elaborate more about the general types of resumes, please keep in mind that different professions, industries, and geographical areas might have a different point of view on resumes. That's why it's important to connect with your peers, people who already have the position you want, and ask for specific details.

I know as an introvert you prefer to do your job search by yourself, but why not delegate some of the work? :-) Your peers could save you hours of research, plus you'll increase your visibility when you approach them. And who knows what other opportunities could open up? I'll talk more about this in chapter 9, when I'll cover effective jobs search strategies for introverts.

If you're looking for a position in a sector where there isn't much competition, you have higher chances of getting hired with a normal resume. But even in this situation, having a targeted resume will help you more, showing the employer that you have the right skills and experience. Plus, you know how to select what's important from what's not — an important skill to have in any position, since employers love goal-oriented and productive employees!

You can find a lot of information and samples of different resume types in books and online. So I won't go into details like what font type to use in your resume, or what letter size.

Yet, with all that information available out there, many of my clients came to me with resumes that were not properly targeted to the desired position. That's why I think it's important to first understand the different types of resumes, then pick the one that serves you best (by projecting a better image) and use it as a template to create your targeted resume.

So I'll start by comparing the different types of resume. Then it will be your turn to:

- Decide which resume type is best for you, according to what parts of your background correspond to the desired short-term position.
- Use that resume type as a template. Then, to make a more effective resume, you'll populate the different sections with information from your background, keeping in mind what is listed in the corresponding sections of the job description. I'll show you which are the corresponding sections.

I found it useful to show people the bigger picture first, before getting into the details. Is this an introverted trait as well? At least that's the approach I use when I learn, and I've met many introverts using the same approach.

Now we'll talk about the resume types from a higher perspective. I have a strong belief that once you understand that eagle view, you'll know how to apply the learning to create better-targeted resumes. If you still need inspiration, check some of the books on resumes available at the library and search samples resumes online.

Type of Resume	When to Use This Resume Type	Reasons for Using this Resume Type
FUNCTIONAL	- Looking for your first job - Making a career change or slight change of direction - Having a gap in your experience (raising a child, for example)	It shows employers your relevant skills and experience in the first part of the resume. By the time they get to the chronological work history, they might already be convinced you have what it takes. This increases your chances of getting an interview.
CHRONOLOGICAL	- Appling for a position similar to your current/previous one - Having progressive work experience in your field	It shows that your most recent experience is similar to what employers are looking for, which is perceived as a shorter time to get productive in the new position (which they prefer).
COMBINATION	- Similar reasons as for a chronological resume, but you want to highlight some aspects of your career (for example, certain projects you worked on that are more pertinent to the new position, and you want to make them stand out)	The employer notices in the first part of the resume the most valuable experience and skills you have for the position.

There are three types of resumes: *functional*, *chronological*, and *combination* (which combines the previous two). We'll talk more about these types of resumes, when to use each type, and why.

The chart above tells you when you can use each of them, to show the employer you can capably perform the tasks they need you to (even your experience is not the most recent or you don't have work experience at all).

As you probably know, the information in each type of resume is organized in sections. To more easily compare the different types of resumes, in the following table I captured the differences between the sections for each resume type, and in what order they usually appear.

1. FUNCTIONAL Resume	2. CHRONOLOGICAL Resume	3. COMBINATION Resume
Personal details	Personal details	Personal details
Summary of Qualifications	Summary of Qualifications	Summary of Qualifications
Professional Experience List of work or volunteering experiences that show you have what it takes to perform the job	N/A (all details are presented in Employment History section)	Professional Accomplishments Accomplishments/important projects directly related to the position
Employment History List each position (in reverse chronological order), company name, city, years/duration	Employment History Positions with details, presented in reverse chronological order	Employment History Positions with details, presented in reverse chronological order
Education	Education	Education
Volunteering (optional)	Volunteering (optional)	Volunteering (optional)
Hobbies (optional)	Hobbies (optional)	Hobbies (optional)

The overall idea is that each type is more useful in some situations and less in others, depending on your background and what you're looking for in your next position (as mentioned in the above table).

For example, if you are applying for a position that is not similar to your previous experience (but you know you have what it takes for the new role), sending your resume in a functional or combined format instead of a chronological one will project a better image of you and how you can help the company. Isn't this what you really want?

Some of the ideas I'll mention for each resume type might be repeated in another resume type (if applicable). I chose to present them this way so that when you choose a certain resume type, you will need to check only what is mentioned for that resume type.

Please keep in mind, these are general guidelines about resumes. There might be specific industry or geographical instructions you need to become familiar with. So please do your own research to find out.

What to Capture in a Functional Resume

Personal details:

- Name, email, phone, address, LinkedIn profile/website (optional)

Summary of Qualifications

- Years of experience relevant to position (No problem if you don't have any experience; that's why you use this resume type.)
- Brief description of your education (if pertinent)
- Soft, hard, and transferable skills you have related to the position
- Computer skills
- Profile: other traits of your personality useful for the position (for example, proactive, assertive, etc.)
- Languages

Professional Experience

- Include examples of work or volunteering experience relevant to the position (even a school project or a summer job could be mentioned here).
- Put the most important experience related to the position first.
- Do not include the experience's duration/years. There's no need to organize the information in reverse chronological order in this section. Here, focus only on what experiences prove you're a good candidate for that specific position
- This is a great place to include achievements. They talk by themselves about how well you can use your skills. Employers like to draw their own conclusions, and good examples speak more about your expertise than a list of skills. You can add numbers and what you were able to achieve in those experiences; for example, increased productivity by 20 percent, improved the process's workflow, received a certificate of appreciation for the quality of the services provided, etc.
- You can group the examples into two or three categories, named by the most important skills for that position. For example, for a receptionist position the categories could be Administration and Customer Service, and under each category, you would list your relevant experience that proves your skills (preferably also using numbers and achievements).

Employment History

- This should be a bulleted list of work experiences in reverse chronological order.
- No need to add the tasks and achievements of each position, since you've already covered the important experiences in the previous section (Professional Experience).
- When you list your employment history, keep in mind that employers are interested in first seeing the type of position you had, then the company, city, and period of time you held that position.

Education

- Give a bulleted list of your training and education, organized to show what's most suited for the position first. List: degree/diploma, specialization, institution, graduation year.
- If the relevant training and education was too long ago, don't mention the years at all.
- If your education is more pertinent to the position than your experience, you can change the order of the sections in the resume: put Education right after the Summary of Qualifications.

Volunteering

- Give a bulleted list of volunteering experiences.
- For each experience mention the title, organization, year/duration, and important tasks (especially those relevant to position).
- Put the most pertinent experience first.
- Don't forget to add any achievements during volunteering. They can display useful skills for the professional environment as well (like leadership, initiative, etc.)

Hobbies

- This is an optional section. If you'd like to have it on your resume, it's enough to mention your hobbies only as a list (without much detail).
- This section might be useful when employers are looking for candidates who have a work-life balance or certain skills not mentioned in the job description. For example, a candidate applying for an engineering position who demonstrates creativity through his hobbies might be more appealing to a dynamic and fast-growing company.

What to Capture in a Chronological Resume

Personal details:

- Name, email, phone, address, LinkedIn profile/website (optional)

Summary of Qualifications

- Years of experience relevant to position
- Brief description of your education (if pertinent)
- Soft, hard, and transferable skills you have related to the position
- Computer skills
- Profile: other traits of your personality useful for the position (for example: proactive, assertive, etc.)
- Languages

Employment History

- Mention your work experiences in reverse chronological order in much more detail than you would in a functional resume.
- For each position, add a brief description of two to three projects (or achievements) that highlight your contribution. It could be one to two phrases for each project or achievement. Employers like to draw their own conclusions, so good examples will be more impressive and will speak more about your skills and expertise than what you could say about yourself.
- You can add numbers and what you achieved while holding that position: for example, increased productivity by 20 percent, improved the process workflow, served one hundred clients per day, received a certificate of appreciation for the quality of the services provided, etc. Anyone can perform tasks, but numbers and achievements show that you performed those tasks well. This way you stand out from other candidates, without feeling that you're bragging or you need to sell yourself.
- Unless you worked for companies known and appreciated by the new employer, HR/the recruiter is more interested in knowing what position you held in the past than the company title. So, for each position, list first the position title, then company, city, and the period of time you held that position.

Education section:

- Give a bulleted list of your training and education, organized to show what's more suited for the position first. List: degree/diploma, specialization, institution, graduation year.
- If the relevant training and education was too long ago, don't mention the years at all.
- If your education is more pertinent to the position than your

experience, you can change the order of sections in your resume: put the Education section right after the Summary of Qualifications (before Employment History).

Volunteering:

- Give a bulleted list of volunteering experiences.
- For each experience mention your title, organization, year/duration, and what you did there (list what is relevant to the position first).
- Put the most pertinent experience first.
- Don't forget to add any achievements during volunteering. They can display useful skills for the professional environment as well (like leadership, initiative, etc.).

Hobbies

- This is an optional section. If you'd like to add it to your resume, it's enough to mention your hobbies as a list (without much detail).
- This section might be useful when the employers are looking for candidates who have a work-life balance or certain skills not mentioned in the job description. For example a candidate applying for an engineering position who demonstrates creativity through his hobbies might be more appealing to a dynamic and fast-growing company.

What to Capture in a Combination Resume

Personal details: Name, email, phone, address, LinkedIn profile/website (optional)

Summary of Qualifications

- Years of experience relevant to the position
- Brief description of your education (if pertinent)
- Soft, hard, and transferable skills you have related to the position
- Computer skills
- Profile: other traits of your personality useful for the position (for example: proactive, assertive, etc.)
- Languages

Professional Experience

- This is a great place to include two to five special projects and achievements illustrating your capability to perform well in the new position — what you want the employer to see first, before looking at the Employment History in reverse chronological order.

- Use full phrases when describing the projects/achievements. They are more powerful and present you in a better light from the beginning. Employers like to draw their own conclusions, and good examples help them better understand your capability and personality. Remember when we talked about soft skills? The employers are versed to read between the lines and understand your soft skills when you talk about your important projects and achievements.
- If you can include numbers or special recognition, it is even better: for example, increased productivity by 20 percent, improved the process workflow, received a certificate of appreciation for the quality of the services provided, etc.

Employment History

- Mention your work experiences in reverse chronological order with much more detail than you would in a functional resume.
- For each position, it's better to talk about your results than mentioning a list of tasks. Anyone can perform tasks, but the numbers and achievements show that you performed those tasks well (which projects a better image).
- Unless you worked for companies known and appreciated by the employer, HR or the recruiter is more interested in knowing what position you held in the past, than the company title. For each position, first list the position title, then the company, city, and period of time you held that position.

Education

- Give a bulleted list of your training and education, organized to show what's more suited for the position first. List: degree/diploma, specialization, institution, graduation year.
- If the relevant training and education was too long ago, don't mention the years at all.
- If your education is more pertinent to the position than your experience, you can change the order of the sections in the resume: put the Education section right after the Summary of Qualifications (before Employment History).

Volunteering

- Give a bulleted list of volunteering experiences.
- For each experience mention your title, organization, year/duration, and what you did there (list what is relevant to the position first).
- Put the most pertinent experience first.

- Don't forget to add any achievements during volunteering. They can display useful skills for the professional environment as well (like leadership, initiative, etc.).

Hobbies

- This is an optional section. If you'd like to have it on your resume, it's enough to mention your hobbies only as a list (without much detail).
- This section might be useful when the employers are looking for candidates who have a work-life balance or certain skills not mentioned in the job description. For example, a candidate applying for an engineering position who demonstrates creativity through his hobbies might be more appealing to a dynamic and fast-growing company.

---

10 Steps for Creating a Good Resume

1. Start with your short-term goal in mind: the position you're looking for.

2. List all skills, experience, and education you already have that is relevant for this position.

3. For each experience, write down three to five examples or accomplishments you're proud of. Make sure you capture your accomplishments are in the SAR format: Situation (the context), Action (what you did) and Results (positive, of course). :-)

4. Decide which resume type will present you in a better light based on what you've listed in step 3. If the most recent experience is relevant to the new position, consider a chronological or combination resume. Use the latter when you have accomplishments or projects you want to highlight. The functional resume will present a better image of you and your background if you're a recent graduate, you want to shift direction, or your pertinent experience is not the most recent.

5. Start populating the different sections of the chosen resume type with the information listed in steps 2 and 3. For inspiration, you can look at similar job postings and LinkedIn profiles of people holding similar positions to the one you're looking for.

6. Search job openings corresponding to your short-term goal. Pick one you're interested in, and start customizing your resume for this position.

7. Read the different sections of the job posting carefully, and adjust your resume according to employers' requirements and the job description.

8. Check for spelling errors. Arrange the information and format your resume to look great.

9. Check if a cover better is required to send with your application. If not, decide if you want to include one or a pain letter when you send your resume.

10. If you decide not to include a cover or pain letter, adjust your resume to be a stand-alone document with all the information you want to show the employer.

Some Suggestions for Resumes

You'll find below a few suggestions based on what I noticed in thousands of resumes I reviewed over the years, and some tips learned from recruiters and mentors.

Global Resume

• At the beginning of your job search, it's better to create a global resume that includes all your skills, experience, and education. This resume is only for you.

• Have it handy when you're looking for jobs, because some job postings might remind you of other skills and experience you forgot to mention in your global resume.

• When crafting a targeted resume for a certain position, import from your global resume only the information pertinent to the new position (instead of creating a new resume from scratch). Customize the information according to the job posting, organize it, and you're done!

Address

• Most employers want to hire local candidates, to avoid relocation costs or delays due to commuting.

Email

• Preferably an email address with your name.

• A Gmail address is considered more professional.

• An email like name@yahoo.fr could indicate you're still in France, while you're already in Canada applying for a job here.

For IT professionals

• An IT recruiter recommends listing all your technical skills briefly in the Summary of Qualifications, grouped by categories (programming languages, OS, computer protocols, etc.), so they become keywords when the resume is scanned. Then mention in the Professional Experience or Employment History what skills were used for each project/work experience.

Do not use tables or text boxes to format your resume

• Unless you send your resume in a PDF format, there might be differences between how a document shows on another computer screen.

• Tables and text boxes could interrupt the normal flow of information. Guide the employer's eye to what you want to be seen first on your resume first, then second, then third.

• If employers use software to scan resumes and extract information in simple text format, tables and text boxes could change the order of the information, making the text less clear and accurate.

Too much white space

• Employers are busy. Too much white space in your resume (between sections, for example) could be viewed as a lack of respect for their time.

Too little white space

• A resume packed with information that is well organized might work well. But if it doesn't have enough white space to grab what the employer wants to see quickly, the resume might be overwhelming and skipped over.

Photo, age, marital status

• In Canada, there is no need to put a photo on the resume, nor age or marital status (so companies don't discriminate candidates based on these criteria). In other countries they are not only acceptable, but sometimes mandatory as well. So please do your own research about what personal information you need to capture in the Personal Details section of your resume.

Age

• Even if you don't put your age (or date of birth) on your resume, employers might get an idea about your age if you list all your professional experience and the graduation years in the Education section.

• If you're an experienced professional and want to hide your age, don't list more than the last ten years of work experience, and remove the years from the Education section (if the education most pertinent to the new position is more than ten years back). Maybe the employers won't notice when they look at the resume. Let them ask when you graduated, if this information is important to them.

CV or resume?

• In the English part of Canada, the terms *CV* and *resume* represent different types of documents.

• A CV is usually used when applying for a management position or in academia, when the candidate explains on several pages all his background to build more credibility (projects, research, publications, books, etc.).

• A resume is a targeted document presenting only the skills, experience, and education required by a job application.

Resume length

• A resume should be no longer than two pages. If you have a lot of relevant experience to the position you're applying, organize your information in a better way (highlighting only what's most relevant) instead of adding more pages.

• If you want to make more information available to the employer, in a way that doesn't negatively impact the employer's first impression (they're busy!), create a website with all your background and add the website URL to your resume. Or list it in your LinkedIn profile, and add the profile link to your resume.

Resume in visual format

• You can create a profile on http://vizualize.me to show your background in a visual format (graphic), and add your profile URL to your resume, in the Personal Details section.

• I personally love this website! I have done several things in parallel (working and volunteering, having a business in parallel with a job), and with their main graphic I am able to present my background in a way that grabs attention for what I've done in parallel. Otherwise, all these experiences will be presented in a sequential order on my resume, and a reader might not realize my ability to manage several projects and situations in parallel. When I applied for positions requiring skills from different domains, I even inserted the main graphic as an image in my resume to grab the viewer's attention quickly.

Cover Letter

Cover letters are important if your application responds to a job posting, and is sent via email, fax, a company's website, or online job boards.

But there are other ways to approach employers that are even more effective, and in those cases you might not even need a cover letter. Sending a pain letter via mail, accompanied by your resume, is one of them. I'll talk more about the pain letter shortly, and in chapter 9 (about effective strategies).

I personally believe a resume is about the past and the cover letter is about the future. Think about it: a resume talks about the past (your background), while a cover letter gives you the chance to think about the future (how this position will take you further on your career path). The motivation you draw from this perspective will help you find the right words to use in your cover letter, to help the employer understand how hiring you will benefit you both: they get help in achieving their goals, while you take this step to advance your career. This proves you're assertive, and employers love assertive candidates! They know that employees with this personality trait perform better, leading to higher productivity and profits. By using this approach you will also tap into your inner motivation and wisdom, and your cover letter will be much more effective.

What to Include in a Cover Letter

On the Internet, you can find templates of cover letters showing you how to put your contact information and employer's coordinates at the top of the cover letter.

In the body of the cover letter you'll have several paragraphs, followed by your signature and a mention of the attached resume.

First Paragraph

If you're responding to an advertised position, start your cover letter by mentioning where you heard about that job posting. Then let them know you're interested in their organization, and explain why.

Employers want to know how the applicants found out about their open positions, to understand what channels are more effective for getting the word out when they need to hire. It's all about decreasing the costs of their recruitment process. By helping them figure that out, you get some good points from the beginning. :-)

If you're sending a spontaneous application, start your cover letter expressing your interest in their company, and mention why you want to work for them.

Second and Third Paragraphs

Here is your chance to make a bridge between your background and something specific to this company and this position, thus showing you could be a great fit for them. No need to repeat what you've already captured in your resume. Find another way to make the point, like presenting specific examples that show a good match with the company's projects and challenges (for example, how you've overcome challenges in similar positions in the past) or what values you have in common. Again, let the examples do the talking for you. Speak confidently about your capacity to help the company achieve its objectives.

Fourth Paragraph

If you plan to follow up on your application, inform the employer when this will happen. Also provide your contact information in case the employer prefers to reach you first. Emphasize your desire to be part of their team.

When you create your cover letter, keep in mind that employers prefer a shorter one since they usually receive many applications.

Pain Letter

The concept of a pain letter was introduced by Liz Ryan, an experienced HR manager, founder, and CEO of Human Workplace, and I totally agree with her approach!

While I'll cover the strategy for using the pain letter (instead of the cover letter) more in depth in the next chapter, check out Liz's article to see an example of a pain letter:

http://www.humanworkplace.com/whats-pain-letter.

What makes a difference?

To make the point, let me share with you another exercise I used in my workshops to help participants understand the employer's perspective. I held this workshop at least twice a month for more than two years, having over nine hundred participants in attendance.

First, I gave participants a job posting and a resume of someone who supposedly applied for that position. Then I asked for their feedback: "If you were the employer with this job opening and you received this resume, would you invite this candidate to the interview?"

Several points stand out about this exercise:

• The answers received were usually divided between "Yes", "No", and "Maybe/Depends", but no general agreement. This shows, in my opinion, that participants and even recruiters could have different opinions about the same resume. That's why sometimes we hear the saying "Job search, like selling, is a numbers game". If this is true, that people have different opinions, it's good to keep saying "NEXT!" after each rejection (and look for another company/position) instead of letting the rejection knock us down! Also, each rejection could be a source of constructive feedback you can use to adjust your resume and job search approach to make them more effective.

• What I showed participants was a functional resume, from the candidate with a different background. The several yeses received mean that even a functional resume could be a way to get an interview if done properly. That's the resume type I used when I switched from an QA engineering position to a mentoring program coordinator, and it worked!

• The argument of those who responded no was that the resume was not convincing enough. Although it mentioned that the candidate had the required skills and experience, there were not enough specific examples provided (when and where the candidate used those skills, and especially what the results were), thus emphasizing the importance of being more specific when giving examples and adding achievements in the resume.

• The "Maybe/Depends" answer was usually follow by: "I'd like to see the other applications before deciding which candidate I'd invite to job interview. If I don't have a better application, I might invite this person". This is another valid point: your application is usually put in the context of other applications if it doesn't stand out from the beginning. All you can do is, do your best, hope for the best, and have a backup strategy to get back on track if this application doesn't end up with a positive result! You can't control the other candidates' applications, but you can control what job search strategies you use! And there are some that are more effective for introverts than replying to online job postings.

• Another point that could not be guessed from reviewing a resume is this: If the person doesn't have the soft skills required for the position (empathy and active listening, for example, for a customer service position), a resume could easily hide this aspect, and the candidate might get the chance for a job interview. But the employer could easily spot the missing soft skills and reject the candidate — even if the resume was crafted very well! Another example: For an engineering position, someone arrogant has less of a chance to pass the interview even if he has a similar background with the successful candidate.

• The moral of the story is this: An employer assesses more than the skills and experience mentioned in the job posting. And a resume, however well crafted, cannot hide everything. Don't underestimate the power of soft skills, since they are very important in the employer's decision! They know that someone can more easily learn the hard skills required to perform the job, but rarely do they want to change their personality and behavior. And even if they want to change, it takes time, and the employer might not be willing to wait for that to happen at their expense.

References

In case you wonder why references are listed in this chapter, it's good to have a list of references in your job search tool box and provide it when an employer asks for your references!

References are important to help you stand out after the job interview, but you don't need to wait for an invitation to a job interview to prepare this list.

There's no need to mention references in your application, unless it is specified in the job posting. I also don't see the need to add the phrase "References upon request" at the end of your resume, unless it is common in your industry or geographical area. The employer will ask for referrals if they want them, even if this phrase is not in your resume.

An employment counselor told me that many of his clients don't know what to include in a referral list. For each person who agrees to provide a reference for you, mention the following in your list:

- Name
- Phone and email address
- What connection you have with this person. For example, "was my manger (or colleague or client) when I worked as (position) at (company)."

The following points might be common sense, but I want to list them because I've met people who didn't apply them:

• Ask the person if he or she wants to provide you a reference (add it to your list).

• Before providing the reference list to an employer, let the persons know when you'll have the job interview (it might take a while since you've asked for permission, and the person might not be available anymore or changed his or her mind)

• Let the person know the type of position you're applying for, so they can think upfront about what to say about you (what examples they can give that are relevant to the position you're applying).

Here are two examples about the first two points:

• I used to tell participants who attended all my job search workshop series that I was willing to provide a reference for them. During the workshops, I could get a sense of their personality, so I could find something to say about them (if they couldn't think of someone else who knew them better).

One day I received a call from a recruiter: "Andy provided your name as a reference. Do you have time to answer a few questions?" That came out of the blue; no one had notified me recently that my name had been used as a referral. My first reaction was, "Sorry, could you please tell me more about this person? I have had a lot of clients recently and I don't remember all their names." The person was kind enough to tell me about Andy's background and what he looks like. And I remembered quickly: he was a participant in my workshop series more than half a year ago! Then I was able to give a positive referral, and he got the position. Phew! I could have easily screwed this up had I not remembered. I can only imagine what the recruiter's impression was when I said, "Sorry, could you please tell me more about this person?" The fact that the candidate didn't tell the me someone would call for a reference could also have had a negative impact on the recruiter's impression of him!

• Another participant, Ana, asked if I could give her a referral. I accepted and start thinking what I could say about someone with a chemical engineering background who applied for a school bus driver position. She was new in town and needed a job as soon as possible. We'd talked a little bit, so I could get to know her:

- "I have no experience as a school bus driver," she told me. Her lack of confidence was so obvious.

- "Do you drive?" I asked.

- "Yes, but only to take my children to kindergarten".

- "So you have driving experience, and you also have experience working with children. The fact they invited someone with your background to this job interview means they might not have more suitable candidates for this position and they're willing to see if you could be a good fit!" I could see the shift in her confidence by the time she left.

Two days later I received the call:

- "I'm the recruiter for the school bus driver position, and Ana listed you as a referral. Do you have a few minutes?"

- "Sure. What would you like to know?"

- "Tell me more about Ana."

- "Ana was a participant in my workshop series about job search. She's a great observer and very smart, although this might not be obvious from the beginning because she doesn't talk much. But when she does, she asks very smart questions!"

- "Yes, I noticed that too. That's what I like about her actually: she's nice and thinks about things thoroughly, which is useful when working with children. I think I'll give her a try!"

And Ana got the position!

Besides being an example that employers do hire candidates who don't quite match the requirements, this example also shows the importance of telling the referrer for what position you applied. Being an introvert myself, I probably wouldn't be able to say something quickly if put on the spot when the recruiter called.

Also, it highlights the importance of telling the truth when you refer someone, since it could be a question mark if the employer noticed something different while interviewing the candidate. So pay attention who you ask to give you a referral.

How to Adjust Your Resume to the Job Posting

We have one last thing to cover before moving on to effective job search strategies for introverts: how to target your application to an advertised position. You usually see these sections on the job posting:

- Company description
- Job description (includes the tasks you'll perform if you're hired)
- Qualifications (what skills, experience, education, and special requirements are needed to apply for the position)

If not all of these sections are present in the job posting, it's your responsibility to research the missing information. An Internet search with the company name as a keyword will help you find out more about the company, its values and culture, projects, products, news, etc. And searching the Internet for similar job postings will help you get an idea about the tasks and qualifications usually required for the position.

Let's now look at the correspondence you'll have to draw between the different sections of the resume, cover letter, and job posting:

Job Posting Section	Resume	Cover Letter
Company description	Will inform your resume style (specific characteristics for the industry, include tables or not, etc.)	- What can you bring to this company? - What's your motivation to join this company?
Job description	In the following sections, give examples showing that you've performed these or similar tasks in the past, with good results: - Professional experience - Employment History - Volunteering	- What can you bring to this position? (Add one to two paragraphs showing additional examples that were not covered in your resume, showing you're a great fit for the position.) - What makes you a good candidate?
Qualifications/ Requirements	What to include in: - Summary of Qualifications: the skills (soft, hard, and transferable), education (briefly), and years of experience you have that correspond to employer's requirements - Professional Experience and Employment History: examples that correspond to those requirements - Education: information about your education pertinent to the position	

In this chapter we've covered useful tools in your Job Search Toolbox, what makes a difference for getting a job interview, and how to adjust the resume to a job posting.

Before moving to the next chapter, take a moment to reflect on what you have taken away from this chapter regarding your specific situation, and write it in your notebook.

Chapter Nine

EFFECTIVE JOB SEARCH STRATEGIES FOR INTROVERTS

It's not that I'm so smart, it's just that I stay with problems longer.
~ Albert Einstein

Persistence is one of the introvert strengths, along with the ability to tackle complex problems. And isn't job search a complex problem that requires persistence?

It's in your power to approach the job search by using your strengths, to make the process more effective.

Einstein was an introvert, and he left a great legacy behind. There are many introverts who became famous and, if you study their biographies, you'll notice that is not the fame they were looking for. The celebrity status came along with focusing on something meaningful to them and getting some allies to help them move forward.

Steve Wozniak (inventor, electronic engineer and programmer) is an introvert, and he teamed up with Steve Jobs to co-found Apple Inc.

Al Gore (politician and environmentalist) is another introvert. He became famous for raising awareness about global warming, but he was helped by someone else to spread his message while using his own perseverance and inner motivation to make an impact.

I'm not saying you have to become famous (unless you want to). All I'm saying is, you can achieve what you want by leveraging your strengths and using effective strategies.

For introverts, it might look like a scary world out there, but you have a powerful engine inside (the combination of your mind, strengths, and talents). Use it to your advantage!

If you read the previous chapters and did your homework, by now you should have the following:

• A better understanding of what's required for an effective job hunt (remember the Wheel of Job Search?)

• Your short-term goal options aligned with your long-term objective (three to five years from now)

• Your global resume and templates for different types of job search tools (resume, cover letter, etc.), plus an understanding of how to target these tools based on your expertise and where you're heading (your goals).

• Removed the limiting beliefs you previously had regarding job search, and replaced them with more empowering ones. I'm curious: did you put reminders in place to help you stick with the newer beliefs until they're fully integrated?

• A list of companies and organizations you'd like to work for, or at least which industry you're interested in and other specific details corresponding to your preferences. Remember Nancy, the Google Analytics specialist who wanted to work for an eco-friendly company and she got the job?

This chapter presents twenty-one job search strategies and how to apply them using your introverted strengths, to make your job hunt more effective.

Since this is already a long chapter, you'll find more examples on how these strategies work in chapter 14 ("Put It All Together").

If you skipped the previous chapters to come directly here, I highly encourage you to go back and read them. This chapter builds on those chapters, taking you a step further to understand how to actually use your introverted strengths to tap into the hidden job market and find positions matching your short-term goal.

Two of the strategies listed here have their own chapters, Networking the Introvert's Way (10) and Speed Up Your Job Search with Social Media (12). They will be briefly mentioned in this chapter to give you a more comprehensive list of strategies.

Later on, chapter 14 ("Put It All Together") will show you:

• How to create your own strategy mix by combining the strategies that work best for your situation.
• How to maximize your time and resources during the job search

process and minimize the risks, to be more efficient during the job search. Managing your time and energy well are important, aren't they (especially for an introvert like you!)?

Using only one strategy or another is not so effective as using a strategy mix. Please don't be like Ron, who attended my workshops and then later told me: "I've sent over three hundred resumes during the last six months, with no results. Now I'll start using the other strategies I learned from you". Using several job strategies in parallel will not only accelerate the process of finding a job, but also keep your head up during this difficult period of time.

What you'll discover in this chapter:

Things do happen behind the scenes!

- 21 points to consider for your job search
- 1 direct job search strategy
- 20 indirect job search strategies (to access the hidden job market)
- 12 employer points of view on candidates (from a job search perspective)

Things Happen Behind the Scenes!

Let me start by sharing with you how I found my first job after I moved to Canada. I talk about this from a job search strategy perspective so you can understand that **things do happen behind the scenes!**

If you release the need to control everything related to your job search and open yourself to opportunities along the way, your job search process will be less stressful and more effective.

My first job in a new city (and country):

A few days after landing, I took the situation in my hands and start looking for information so I could understand how to find a job in this new country. I knew almost nothing about Canadian culture and the job market, but I had both a short-term goal (to find a job as soon as possible, to pay the bills) and a long-term objective (to change careers, although I didn't know in which direction).

Looking at the brochures picked up at the airport, I decided that my first stop would be at the YMCA, a center that has a lot of presentations for newcomers. While waiting for a presentation to start, I grabbed several flyers, and one of them was about a center helping women immigrants. That was my next stop. There I talked with an employment counselor who seemed somehow intimidated by my engineering background. Just talking with her gave me a confidence boost, and the advice received was priceless! While there, I grabbed another brochure about a francophone center. The French language seemed more familiar to me at that point (having the same Latin roots as Romanian, my first language), so I decided to check it out. My first appointment there was with an employment counselor.

Every time I went to these centers, I was dressed like I was going to a job interview, and I could immediately see the positive impact that made on the people I met.

This employment counselor looked at my resume and cover letter, provided additional job search tips, opened a file for my case, and kept my resume. He also was impressed by my background in several fields. Another boost of confidence! Back home, in Romania, someone who changed fields and jobs every three to four years was not viewed so well at that time, while here it seemed to be quite appreciated. What a relief! I get annoyed by staying too long in a certain position, so I was glad to discover a professional culture that better suits my personality.

The employment counselor recommended a three-day job search workshop that started soon, and referred me to another program that could pair me with a Canadian (to help me understand the Canadian culture).

I attended the job search workshop and met new people: the colleagues and the workshop leader (the first professional coach I'd ever met). I also met the manager of that pairing program, and she registered me in her program. Noticing my professional background, she asked me to volunteer to research and create a list of professional organizations from Toronto. I accepted gladly, since I could do the research from home while still looking for jobs.

Almost two weeks after my arrival, prepared with a lot of information regarding the job search process, I was all pumped up to find my first job. I started by contacting recruitment agencies, at least to get my name in their databases.

Those days I was leaving home at 8:00 a.m. in the morning, to find more information, getting back home in the evening quite tired. But I was doing it at my own pace, with breaks when I needed to boost my energy level. Once home, until bed time, I searched the Internet for information related to what I had come across during the day, sent job applications, and made plans for the next day.

BTW, for administrative positions, recruitment agencies usually ask you to pass tests (Word, Excel, PowerPoint), which eat up a few good hours. I couldn't do more than two agencies per day.

Via an online discussion group of Romanians, I met Bobby. He had a similar background and had come to Toronto a couple of months earlier, so we were looking for the same thing: a "door" to get into the job market. We stayed in touch, exchanging information along the way.

The leader of the job search workshop sent us job opportunities from time to time. When I received an email about a ten-day bilingual position at a government booth (for the Winter Agricultural Fair), I jumped on it: I called right away, and the lady asked if I knew other bilingual people (they had ten positions available). I called Bobby to let him know, and I also posted the position in that online discussion group. Funny thing: Bobby was accepted, along with others who saw my message, but I wasn't!

I consoled myself saying that I could use those ten days to continue my job search instead of working ten hours a day for them!

Several days later, while talking with Bobby about his experience, I noticed that his morale was quite down: he kept sending resume without results. So I encouraged him to visit the same francophone center.

Almost two months passed by, and one day, the only day I stayed home (sick with the flu), I received a phone call: "I'm a recruiter, and I would like to invite you to a job interview for a bilingual customer service representative position."

My jaw dropped: How did he find out about me? I'd never applied for any position at his company! And I didn't even think to send an application to a financial company, as I didn't have any financial background!

Of course I accepted the invitation, being ready to start somewhere so I could pay my bills (that was my short-term goal). I had a strong belief that I wouldn't be there for long, and I was also curious to find out how the company found me!

Two days after receiving that call, Bobby told me he had gone to that francophone center and was received by the same employment counselor:

- "How did you find out about our center?"

- "A friend of mine, Gabriela Casineanu, told me".

- "Oh, Gabriela! How is she doing?"

- "She's still looking for a job".

- "She didn't find one yet?"

- "No."

In front of Bobby, the employment counselor took my resume from a folder and faxed it to the company that called me!

Dilemma solved, just in time! Before the job interview started, I was asked to fill out some forms, and one of the questions was: How did you find out about this position?

I did get that job, and stayed there three months. In the meantime I continued my job search and found another position, corresponding to my background, which almost doubled my salary.

21 Points to Consider for Your Job Search

The reason I told you this story has nothing to do with the type of position I was looking for. I just wanted to show you an example that illustrates the following points, something to consider when you're looking for a job:

1) Whatever grabs your attention might have some information for you — check it out!

Remember the flyers I was picking up from different places and how I followed up with actions? They paved my way to finding my first job in Canada. Pay attention to what resonates with you, because it might be of help to you.

2) Don't underestimate the impact of the human factor.

In todays' world, where online communication seems to be predominant and easy to access, people appreciate the direct connection (which I call the "human factor") even more. It helps them get a better understanding of who you are, and they might be more willing to help than if you ask for help via email.

As you noticed from my situation, the human factor had a huge impact on the results of my job search: from the information they openly shared with me to the referrals received because I took the step to meet them in person and even contribute to their cause. As introverts, we are more comfortable in one-on-one conversations than in groups. Why not take advantage of this strength by tapping into the "human factor"?

3) Find out how others see you for a boost of confidence.

Building on the previous point: talking with people during your job search is a way to better understand where you are by allowing them to reflect back to you the image you project (sometimes unconsciously). It's like looking in a mirror, although this mirror shows how others perceive you.

As introverts, we have a tendency to spend more time in our own thoughts, often judging ourselves because we're not where and how we'd like to be. The mirror I'm talking about is like getting a more objective view of how we're perceived by the outside world.

If you get a positive image back, it will boost your confidence, which is great for a successful job search!

If you don't, first check if the feedback is coming from a person who is often negative or pessimistic. If it is, try to find the grain of truth in their opinion and ignore the way they deliver it. Especially during the job search, you don't want your energy being drained by their negativity. If they're not usually negative or pessimists, mirroring back to you an image you don't like can help you understand what you can improve to project a better image of yourself. You can even ask for help in identifying what and how to improve.

4) Trust your intuition.

I learned this point while I was doing a four-month internship in France for my master's degree. While I was there, I decided to check out how my professional background is perceived by the French job market. One of my tasks during that internship was to do a survey: I had to call more than seven hundred companies and get the CEOs or financial managers to answer the survey.

While looking at the list, one company name stood out. I sent only six resumes to companies I was interested in working for, including that company. I got three answers: two companies did not have any openings, and the third one invited me to an interview. It was exactly the company that grabbed my attention when I looked at that list. To my French friends' surprise, that company offered me a permanent position, well paid, and they were willing to pay for my work visa as well.

I suggest you take your intuition into consideration during your job search! In a world with so much information, it could act as your personal compass.

5) Job search is a journey with interesting turns.

As you noticed from my experience, one thing leads to another if you keep filtering the information through the lenses of your short-term goal. And, if you follow through with actions, you'll get to where you want short term (which is part of your long-term strategy).

You don't need to know all the steps from the beginning: take a first step, learn from the experience, adjust if needed, then take another step and so on.

That's why in this chapter I present several job search strategies to choose from, and I invite you to create a strategy mix and be open to adjusting it along the way.

6) Dress to impress during the job search, wherever you go (not only for the interview).

We live in a world that associates being professionally dressed with being competent. You never know who you are going to meet, and you want to make a good impression from the beginning. Otherwise, you might not be given a second chance. Or they might not be willing to refer you to someone else if they don't like the way you present yourself (it's their reputation at stake, after all).

Here's a story to illustrate: After finding the job he wanted, a client came back to share his story with other clients. I was not surprised at all when he shared that he was always dressed professionally during his job search — to a point that someone approached him in a Starbucks to ask if he was a manager. He made a great impression wherever he went, and he found the position he wanted in a financial company.

7) Use curiosity as your ally.

Keep your curiosity alive during the job search. You can't be curious and fearful at the same time. Instead of allowing fear to paralyze you, get curiosity on your side. I'm talking about the fear of not being enough jobs on the market, not being good enough for a certain position, speaking with people you don't know (you know why), being rejected in a job interview, and so on.

When you park these fears and get curious about what's out there, which could help you take a step further, you might be surprised by how much useful information you get (leading you, step by step, toward what you want). I wouldn't get that opportunity for the job interview if I was not curious along the way.

8) Volunteering can help.

If you're one of those people considering volunteering a waste of time during the job search, I encourage you to reconsider your opinion. If you noticed the doors that opened for me, you' understand why. Soon I'll talk more about volunteering as a job search strategy.

9) Increase your visibility.

I strongly believe that your most important task during the job search is to increase your visibility on the job market. Nobody will knock at your door to offer you a job if no one knows you exist!

Sending resumes in response to job offers is not the only way to increase your visibility in a competitive market (and not the best one either). By applying the job search strategies from this chapter and using your introverted strengths, you will become more visible in the job market and increase your chances of getting hired.

10) Combine online and offline job search strategies.

As you've noticed from my example and the previous points, combining these strategies will help you tap into the "human factor" to increase the efficacy of your job search. I'll help you figure out how to do it, while still staying true to your introverted values and strengths.

11) Treat your job search as a full-time job.

If you are working a full-time job, do you work continuously, or take some breaks to replenish your energy? It's the same with your job search.

You need to get organized: allot a certain number of hours per day to your job search, and put structures in place to help you stay organized and focused. Take breaks from the pressure of being in "job search" mode, and disconnect mentally from time to time. It not only helps replenish your energy faster, but it also allows you to notice new opportunities that might be helpful (and overlooked otherwise).

12) Stay in touch with other job seekers.

Remember how staying in touch with Bobby helped me find a job without me doing all the heavy work?

Other people who are going through the same process might be willing to share information about you or with you. Being in that online group, sometimes as observer, other times as an active participant, helped me meet new people and removed the uneasiness when we finally met in person for the first time.

13) The more you help others, the more you get helped.

Am I the only introvert who loves to help others and it comes so naturally? Just because you NEED a job, doesn't mean you cannot GIVE FIRST.

This is the best way to tap into the "human factor" potential during your job search process (and beyond). Humans are propelled to give back, so why not increase your chances by giving first?

A word of caution though: don't expect everyone will give back to you. If helping comes naturally to you, do it with open heart without expecting anything back. It's a form of increasing the generosity pool in the world, and you might be surprised by how the universe pays you back (sometimes in unexpected ways, like in my case). But helping someone else makes us feel good about ourselves — with a positive effect on the job search.

14) It's your job to pick yourself up and move on.

I know you can do it, if you tap into your inner wisdom. Did you noticed how I handled the rejection when I found out that I was not accepted, and others were (although they've heard from me about that position)? I consoled myself by founding a reason why the new situation was actually better for me, and I moved on.

When you feel down, if you prefer to not talk with other people you can be your best ally! I know you can do it, because introverts are so focused within. All you need is to notice the negative thoughts that might creep in, and focus on more positive ones. Remember the exercise about perspectives from the chapter about Mindset?

15) Let the employer decide. Don't cut yourself off.

Your role is to apply for a position you're interested in, even if you don't think you have all the qualifications. Let the employer decide if you are the best candidate for that position, according to what the company needs at the moment.

I accepted an invitation to a job interview with a financial company, without having any financial background, and I got the job. Trust that there are more factors that influence the hiring process than what is captured in the job description, and some might be in your favor. If you're invited to a job interview, even if you don't meet all the requirements, who are you to judge the employer's choice? Prepare for the interview, go there, do you best, and the rest is not your "job." At the very least you may end up with a helpful learning experience.

16) Keep your short-term goal in mind, aligned with your long-term objective

Why was I happy to start with the position with the financial company when I could start sooner with a position in a coffee shop, for example (that would also pay my bills)?

I knew the financial position would give me a strategic start. It was a great opportunity to improve my interpersonal communication skills in both English and French, and improving such skills is always a great long-term investment. Also, having a well-known company listed on my resume would give some extra credibility in the eyes of other employers, which would take me further on my chosen career path.

17) Believe that your job search will be successful, even when you don't see the results yet

If you don't believe in your ability to achieve the desired results, who will? As you noticed in the chapter about mindset, what you believe can affect your results. So start with the result in mind, and build your way into achieving it without letting yourself to get on a downward spiral when you don't see the results yet. In chapter 14 I'll introduce you to a concept that'll help you build a strong belief that you will succeed!

18) Things happen behind the scenes when you increase your visibility.

I guess my example showed clearly enough that this point is true. It happened to me in other situations as well, and to many of my clients who kept taking the right actions.

19) Leave a good impression; people will remember and might even want to help you.

While I'll talk more about this point in the section about information interviews, I invite you to also think about how important it is for the first impression you have on someone else: Would you like to stay in touch with someone who didn't leave you a good first impression?

20) You can reach your goal even if you're only comfortable with one-on-one discussions.

Being an introvert myself, I didn't rely on networking events while searching for that first job. They made me feel uneasy and project a different image than who I really am. I went on to talk with one person at a time, following the leads the discussion opened up. In time, I learned to use my introversion in my advantage so I can make the most of the networking events too. I'll share more about this in the next chapter ("Networking the Introvert's Way").

21) Sometimes it is easier to get where you want with baby steps than waiting for the big step to happen.

This is why I suggested you consider your short-term goal aligned with the long-term objective. Being open to taking a position for a certain period of time (while continuing the job hunt) might be less stressful and even make it easier to get ahead on your path. Because the bigger the step you want to take, the longer it might take, and you could get discouraged in the process (which would make the job search even more difficult).

Now I'm curious! :-)

What's more inspiring and motivating to you: reading the above 21 points in a how-to book? Or hearing a story (like mine) showing how these points intertwine, leading to the desired result?

Which way will you remember them more easily: presented as a list of items, or understanding them through an example?

If you answered yes to the second part of the above questions, then you'll understand why people prefer to understand who you are by seeing and talking with you, instead of reading a piece of paper called a resume.

Remember the "human factor"? Don't underestimate it, because employers and recruiters are people too! And they are more inclined to trust their own impression or someone they already trust.

I know, introverts are not comfortable talking about themselves, but if this could really make a difference, would you be willing to try? At least have one-on-one conversations so people get a better understanding of who you are from the words on the piece of paper called a resume. Depending on their background, expectations, and biases, the image they get from your resume might be different from who you really are and what you can offer.

Later, I'll show you ways to find key people, while being true to your introverted nature, so you can increase your chances of finding what you want.

For the rest of this chapter, you'll be presented with twenty-one job search strategies (including one that combines the strategies you like the most) to maximize your chances. They will accelerate the process of finding your (next) job by more effectively using your time and resources. Stay tuned for the Mind map Strategy. :-)

Some of these strategies might not be new to you, but I hope you'll see them in a different perspective since they are presented with your introverted strengths in mind.

I will divide the 21 job search strategies in two categories: **Direct** (DS) and **Indirect** (IS) strategies.

DS 1) **Direct Job Search Strategy**

I define a *direct job search strategy* as the steps you take to apply for a position when you already have the job posting. Whether you found it online on job boards and company websites or somewhere else, you already have the job posting. It usually contains a few words about the company, a full description of the tasks you will perform if hired (the job description), and what the company is looking for (qualifications or requirements to apply).

From what I've noticed, many job seekers rely only on this strategy. They search online job boards (Eluta, Indeed, Workopolis, etc.) or the LinkedIn Jobs section, and apply directly.

Here's a workflow to increase your chances of getting a job interview with this direct strategy:

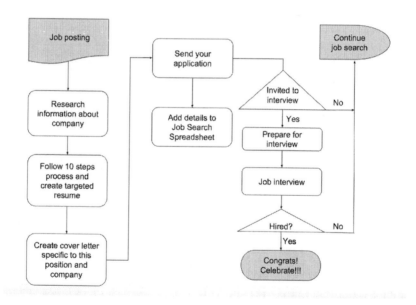

In my opinion, this strategy is not quite effective in a competitive job market, unless you target a very specific niche. And when it comes to introverts, the direct strategy is even less effective.

Many of my introverted clients are more like, "Give me the job first and I'll show you how good I am. Don't make me talk about myself." And, as we've seen in the previous chapters, the employer comes from exactly the opposite perspective (hoping to minimize their risks this way). In the above workflow,

I'm talking about the ten-steps process presented in chapter 8, ("Preparation: Job Search Tools"), on how to create a targeted resume. I explained this process in more detail there, and also gave you tips for creating a more attractive resume, taking in consideration the employer's perspective.

"What's a Job Search Spreadsheet?", you might ask.

It's an Excel file or table where you add information about each job application you've sent. It's a way to help you keep track of all your job applications in one place.

A sudden phone call received from an employer or recruiter could be quite stressful to anyone, but especially for introverts who don't like to receive calls out of the blue. Combined with the introvert's tendency to take time to think things through, and the pressure to give a quick response, things may get quite difficult.

Having a Job Search Spreadsheet handy while an employer or recruiter calls could speed up the thinking process and decrease the stress. That's why it is useful to have a printed copy of this document handy when you receive that phone call: it will help you quickly remember the important details about the position and what resume you sent, so you can focus on your answers instead of trying to remember what the position is about.

Once I received a phone call from an employer two months after I sent my application. Without this document, I wouldn't have remembered what the position was about.

Such document could also be useful to remind you when you need to do a follow-up, and in what stage each of your applications is (especially if you sent many). It's important to use your mind to figure out the next steps in your job search, not to memorize all the details regarding each application!

Here's what you can capture in your Job Search Spreadsheet:

Job title	Company	Date (when I applied)	How I Applied	Where I Heard About the Position	Comments Follow-Ups

Let me give you an example of someone who was successful with this direct strategy:

When John came to me, he had been looking for a job for about two weeks. His latest position was as a fraud and security specialist in a small bank. He loved that position and wanted to find a similar one in a bigger bank. He already knew for which company he wanted to work: the same bank who handled his personal accounts. He liked their services and how they treated their clients. John showed me a new job posting he found at that exact bank, which matched well his background.

I looked at his resume. It was a chronological resume, but it didn't do a good job of highlighting the great work John did while working in his last position. Some information from his resume (presented at the beginning) was not relevant for the position he was applying, and the resume didn't have a nice flow when he described his work experience. I gave him a few ideas on how to better target his resume to this specific position, based on the job description. For the cover letter, I suggested he include the certificate of appreciation for outstanding performance he received from his previous manager (which was not mentioned at all before). Also, I told him to mention what he discovered during his research (the bank he was interested in received a certificate for Excellence in Customer Service), and how much he would like to work for them to contribute to the company's success.

John was invited to a job interview, and got the job! The bank received over 240 applications for the same position. I'll tell you more about John's story in chapter 13 (Interview Tips to Sell Yourself without Being Salesy), to show you how he was able to stand out and outperform the other candidates.

Indirect Job Search Strategies

Have you heard about the "hidden job market"?

To me, this term means all the positions I couldn't find or that were not created yet (although there is a need for someone with those skills). These could be those positions advertised only internally or not advertised yet, positions advertised externally but I didn't find them yet, or positions created for those job seekers who were able to demonstrate there was a need for their expertise to overcome company's specific challenge (and the companies figured out a way to get them onboard).

Are you surprised to hear that companies could create positions when the right candidate shows up to help them? I've heard about this happening from different credible sources, and I'll give you details in a bit.

Coming back to the indirect job search strategies, these are strategies to help you get access to the hidden job market.

There is a common belief that around 80 percent of jobs are in the hidden job market. If this is true, and the direct strategy is not so effective in a competitive job market (especially for introverts), doesn't it make sense to pay more attention to the indirect job search strategies?

Yet, most of my clients didn't know or didn't try them until they understood their value. There is a lot of information on job search strategies on the Internet, but most sources fail to mention the reason *why* these strategies are effective (especially for introverts).

If you're willing to understand the reason why these strategies could work in your case, let's talk about it now.

12 Employer Points of View on Candidates (From a Job Search Perspective)

After this section, we'll finally get to talk about indirect job search strategies and how to use them more effectively using your introverted strengths.

While reading the following points, think about which job search strategies could be more useful to you to meet employers' needs: the direct or indirect strategies?

1) The recruitment process is lengthy and costly.

Whatever you can do to help the employer shorten this process and decrease the costs is helpful for them and also in your favor (because you will have less competition). Responding to a job opportunity already posted online doesn't shorten their recruitment process nor decrease their costs.

2) Hiring someone comes with certain risks.

Many employers have experienced new hires who didn't perform as expected or left soon after being hired. So they are more cautious when reviewing applications from unknown candidates, to decrease the risk and save money. Starting a new recruitment process is costly, and the overall productivity is affected for a longer period of time (until the new person is hired).

3) If I trust you and I need your expertise in my company, I am willing to hire you.

Employers are more willing to hire someone they already trust (who works in another company) or who has been referred by someone they trust (like one of their employees, or a recruitment agency who worked with them before and provided good candidates). This way they expect to decrease the risks and costs involved in the recruitment process.

4) A manager always knows what's going on in his department.

A manager usually knows before HR when someone will be on maternity leave, take a non-paid vacation, or go back to school, or when new staff is needed for a project. Compared to an HR specialist (who is not a specialist in your field), your potential manager can better evaluate your skills and expertise because they are directly related to the work in his or her department. If the manager considers you a great candidate, your resume is then sent to HR letting them know he or she is interested in your application (which weighs much more than an application from other unknown candidates).

That's why using indirect strategies to reach your potential manager before the job positing reaches HR could give you more chances than replying to a job opportunity advertised by HR (which is already visible to other potential candidates).

5) If I trust the person who referred you, I might be willing to give you a try.

Their own employees know the company needs and culture better. Also, they don't want to jeopardize their own reputation within the company. That's why employers are willing to consider candidates for a job interview that are referred by their own employees. Some companies even take it a step further, giving a bonus to an employee who referred a candidate who was hired and passed the probation period. Using indirect job strategies effectively could help you find such employees and gain their trust.

6) If your values match our company's culture and values, I am more inclined to hire you than someone else.

Being a good fit for the company's culture and values usually leads to increased motivation and productivity from that employee. That's what the company is interested in, after all. Employers appreciate such candidates.

7) You may have the best expertise, but I won't go over this salary range.

Employers expect that candidates with the best expertise will ask for a high salary, and they might not have that budget. That's why even candidates with less expertise get hired.

If a very experienced professional would be willing to accept a lower paying position, it raises a red flag for the employer. You'll need to make an extra effort to explain to the employer why you will accept a lower salary. You'll also need to reassure the employer that you will not leave soon after you get the position (because you find a better paying one). For them, an overqualified candidate is considered a risk. That's why a targeted resume that leaves behind some of your experience might pass better if you're willing to accept a lower paying position.

8) I like how passionate you are about our projects/products/services/company's culture. I know you can learn the missing technical skills.

Such candidate will project enthusiasm and positive energy during the job interview, qualities appreciated by employers and seen as leading to increased productivity. They know technical skills can be learned if you made it to this phase, but improving soft skills takes more time to learn (if the candidate is willing to change)! An assertive, proactive employee will positively contribute to the team morale and will be able to integrate much faster in a team than someone who complains often, for example. Employers are skillful in reading "between the lines" and assessing if your behavior is a good fit for their company.

9) Tell me why I should hire you instead of someone else (I don't know you, after all). What's in it for me?

This is a common interview question. The reason for asking it is to understand why the candidate is motivated to work for their specific company, instead of any similar position in no matter what company. It ties in with point 8 above. Employers love to hire candidates who want to partner with them for a bigger purpose. Wanting to just pay the bills doesn't lead to high productivity long term like having a more meaningful reason does.

10) Be concise and provide relevant information if you want to keep my attention long enough.

These are great skills to have whether you send a job application, go to a job interview, or speak with another professional. People (including employers) are already busy with their own stuff and you can quickly lose their attention if you don't provide interesting information or you take too long to deliver it. In a professional setting, where time is considered money, first highlighting "what's in it for me" (the person doing the hiring) is a way to keep their attention long enough to make your point come across (to help them understand who you are and what you can offer).

12) I prefer candidates with recent experience related to the position because they have used the skills recently and will be quick starters.

Keeping this is mind will help you craft a better resume, by using the appropriate resume type. Get the relevant information at the top of your resume to grab their attention quickly and make them understand you have the required skills. This point could also help you better prepare for the job interview (more on this in chapter 13).

Now you understand the whys of indirect job search strategies (IS). Let's move on and talk about the indirect job search strategies (IS).

You might recognize some of these strategies, but you'll also see why they are more effective for introverts and how your strengths could play in your favor. I mentioned some of these strategies here to have a more comprehensive list in this chapter, but I'll get into more details in the following chapters.

IS 2) **Define Your Project**

As I mentioned earlier in this book, you can consider this job search process your own project.

Even if you don't know the project due date (it depends on many factors, some of which you can't control), you can still organize your job search

project in a way that makes the most of the time and resources you have, to get the desired results faster.

Why could this perspective be useful for an introvert like you?

• Introverts are good at solving complex problems, so you'll use at least one of your strengths! :-) Job hunting is quite a complex process: It involves many variables (your background and goals, what the offer/demand is in your field, the competitors, gaining employers' trust, costs of living while you're job hunting, time and social pressure, etc.). It also presents certain risks: If there's too much competition, if you run out of money, if the process gets too long you might not be considered "employable" at your level, etc.

• By regarding your job search as a project, you can dissociate who you really are (as a person) from the role (the job seeker). This way, you can get a more objective perspective on what you can do to make the project more successful: What are the weak points? What strategies could work best in your situation and how can you mix them for better results? How can you maximize the results and minimize the risks within the given constraints? Etc. You become more in charge of your job hunting (your project) than feeling at the mercy of employers and the job market tendencies.

• Is your job search project meaningful enough to you? I hope it is. By choosing your own short-term goals and long-term objective, motivation and persistence should be on your side. Introverts can be focused and tenacious when they work on a meaningful project to them.

In chapter 14 ("Put It All Together") you'll get more tools to help your job search project run smoothly, to minimize the risks and maximize the results in the given circumstances! Until you get there, keep in mind the introverts' job search skills mentioned in chapter 6 ("Skill Set Inventory"), you'll need them for the following strategies.

IS 3) **Reframe Your Background According to the New Position**

I've seen many applications where the job seekers focused literally on their background, hoping that employers would understand how great they are. Introverts are no exception. In fact, it's even worse because they tend to not speak about themselves in the same impressive ways as extroverts do.

By literally I mean: listing the exact title of the previous positions, the tasks performed, etc.

Keep in mind that employers have a limited amount of time to filter the applications they receive. So make yourself a service: reframe (if necessary) and reorganize the skills and experience you mention in your resume in a way that makes it easier to be understood by the employer. That's why I spend so much time talking about targeted resumes and employer's perspective in chapter 8.

What do I mean by reframing? Depending on the new position you're interested in, the title of the previous position(s) might not quickly indicate that you're a good fit for the new position. To decide if your application ends up in the shorter list or not, the employer takes a quick look at your previous positions without reading the details. In which case, the position titles listed on your resume are important!

I don't encourage you to lie. All I say is to present your background in a way that grabs the employer's attention.

Examples of reframing a position title:

1. Let's say you target a position that requires leadership skills and you mention "administrative assistant" as your previous position on your resume. This title might not suggest that you actually have and used your leadership skills in that position. Maybe you've organized several events, managing a small team to make things happen, but the title "administrative assistant" won't project this image. Presenting this position as "administrative assistant/event organizer" will better serve your purpose of applying for a position requiring leadership skills.

Let's say you choose a second short-term option to work in a financial department. And you previously worked as an administrant assistant, took accounting courses, and handled financial documents in a small company. Your resume could mention your previous position as an administrant assistant/bookkeeper.

2. Here's a real example, from a message posted on LinkedIn: An administrative assistant was complaining that a recruiter considered her unemployable because her resume showed a gap in work experience. She took a year off to take care of her fiancé, who was battling cancer. At a first glance, this might seem like a gap of experience in her field. But then she gave more details: this whole year she helped her fiancé handle his business as an executive assistant because he was too weak to do all those tasks. Hey, this *is* professional experience! So my suggestion to her was to reframe the "gap" in her resume to mention she worked for his business as a freelance or virtual assistant, because she actually did work and used her skills recently, even stepping up to the next level. She didn't have executive administrative experience before.

An employer or recruiter is interested in seeing that you've applied those skills recently (which was her case), not if you consider this as a year off. A gap in the resume looks exactly like that if you don't make an extra effort to show that you actually applied your skills recently. Taking care of someone who has a business requires a lot of skills very useful in the professional environment:

scheduling appointments, doing follow-ups, handling documents, taking care of the financial transactions, etc. Aren't these administrative tasks?

Instead of letting the employer guess, it's your job to present your background in a way that shows your value best. Otherwise you might be in for a unpleasant surprise.

IS 4) **Information Interview**

If you aren't familiar with this strategy, I highly encourage you to embrace it. This is one of the most effective job search strategies for introverts! And it's not only my opinion.

I asked an HR manager from a well-known bank what job search strategy she would recommend to an introvert like me (not a beginner, but not interested in top management positions either). "Information interviews!" she answered without hesitation.

This is also a job search strategy recommended by Ryerson University to their students when they want to enter the workforce, so if fits the beginners too.

So what's an information interview?

It is a way to get information from people who are not your potential new manager. I would recommend asking people who already hold a position similar to what you're looking for, someone in the same industry or working for a company you're interested in.

An information interview might not look like a job search strategy, because it's focused on gathering information, not targeting a job, but from my experience (and others') it's an effective job search strategy to actually land a job (even if that's not what you're asking when you meet those people in person).

What kind of information can you get from them?

In a book like this one, I can only give you general information. But when you talk with people already working in the field you're interested in, they can give you tips and suggestions for a job search specific to the their field/position and about the specifics of the recruitment process in their field, or information about the company they're working for (culture, values, recruitment process, and how they source candidates, etc.).There's a high chance they know other companies and recruiters looking for candidates like you, and they can also share how they got where they are.

"But, Gabriela, I'm an introvert. I don't like to talk to strangers!"

I know, I'm an introvert too. But I'd rather focus on, "I need more information and ideas to take me further," than on, "I don't like to talk to strangers."

The first one puts me in the "curiosity" mood and gives me motivation and energy to reach out to someone, while the latter makes me hide in my own bubble (in which case companies probably won't reach out to me because they don't even know I exist, or I won't be assertive enough to find what I want).

What about you? Do you still want to stay comfortable in your bubble finding reasons not to reach out to others and blaming the system? Or are you ready to tap into your strength (your ability to have meaningful one-on-one conversations) and connect with people who might have information to help your job search and are maybe even be willing to help?

Here's one more thing to make you more comfortable reaching out: If you exchange a few messages with this person before you talk in the real world, and you also check their LinkedIn profile, you will know a little more about that person. Wouldn't that make you feel more at ease to open up and have a discussion?

At least that's what I've noticed, as well as my clients who used this method. Does this strategy make enough sense now to give it a try?

If you noticed, I approached my own introvert barrier about information interviews the same way I asked you to change a barrier in chapter 5 (about mindset). Instead of sticking with a belief that didn't serve me during the job search ("I'm an introvert, I don't like talking with strangers"), I switched to a more empowering belief that made me pursue my goals more assertively ("I'm curious what information this person has for me, to help my job search").

"Why ask for information interviews when I'm actually look for a job?," you might ask.

Oh, that's a great question!

Here's why:

• Employers tend to hire the candidate they trust more. So you have to do something to gain their trust, right? A resume might not be enough, especially if other candidates have great resumes too or are able to build trust by reaching out to employers before you.

• If you don't increase your visibility, no one will knock at your door to offer you a job if they don't know you exist! If you just send applications in response to job offers found using the direct job search strategy, they might not notice you if they get too many applications or other candidates stand out in one way or another. Information interviews are way to effectively increase your visibility, because you'll be less stressed than in a job interview. You'll be more at ease and show up more confident because you can prepare your own questions in advance — which will make you feel in control of how this information interview unfolds. All these will help you project the real image of who you are and your strengths, leaving a better impression than in a job interview.

• Through information interviews you help people in your field understand your background. And if they like you and the conversation you had together, they might be willing to take an extra step to help you: like sending you useful information they come across several days later (including job postings), referring you to someone else, etc. This is a great way to increase your visibility, because it could go beyond one simple discussion.

• The human factor plays well in this context too: They will know more about you, and if you made a good impression, they could be better ambassadors than your resume while referring you to someone else.

• Remember the hidden job market? Talking with people can give you access to information you otherwise might not discover or have access to, like positions advertised internally or direct referrals to managers (bypassing HR) who might need someone with your background, or will soon.

"Why would people bother to spend fifteen to twenty minutes of their busy time with me? Even more, giving me information?"

This is a valid question, and it came up a lot in my workshops when I talked about this strategy. It's even more relevant coming from introverts who want to limit their social interactions as much as they can.

Let's look from the other person's perspective:

Take a moment to put yourself in their shoes: You are at that moment of your career where you've been working on this position for a while. Whether you like it or not, you know how you got here and what's happening in your field, you're aware of at least a few companies that have similar positions, and you're still connected with some of your peers (people working in similar positions in other companies).

If someone approaches you to ask for advice on how to get a similar position as yours, how would you feel?

You're not threatened by this person (because you already have your job). Doesn't it feel good when someone asks you for advice? Doesn't it make you feel valued? Even more, doesn't this request remind you of your own struggles when looking for a new position before?

In such conditions, are you willing to help someone asking for your advice?

Now back to you:

If you answer yes to my last question, you understand why others might also accept your request. So go ahead, start asking for information interviews! Not everyone will accept or answer your request, but what can you lose? A few seconds writing and sending a message? When you don't get answers, say, "NEXT!" and send another one — or more — until you get people who do accept your invitation to talk with you!

If you answered no, I have another question for you: Why would you expect others to help you if you're not willing to help someone else? As I mentioned earlier in this chapter, the more you help others, the more help you get. If you're a generous person, expect others to be as well, and reach out to them.

Just keep in mind to not lose track of your job search while spending too much time helping others.

Things to consider for an information interview:

• Reach out to other professionals who already hold a position similar to what you're looking for (ask your friends if they know someone, use LinkedIn to find them, contact professional associations, etc.). More on how to use LinkedIn for this in the chapter about social media.

• Remember: You're the project manager of your job search project. Would you like to delegate some of the tasks to others? :-) Look at information interviews as a way to delegate to others part of the research you need to do to find companies and other useful information you need for your job hunt. Consider every person you meet via an information interview as a resource person, because they have information and connections you don't have yet.

• Ask for a fifteen to twenty minute information interview on the phone or in-person, mentioning why you approached the person (say something positive about their background), what you're looking for, and that you'd like to ask a few questions/their advice.

• Before sending, check your message for spelling and grammar, to make a good first impression!

• The message should be short and contain enough information, but not overwhelm the reader or take too much time away from their busy schedule.

• The tone of your message should be professional, like you're talking with someone in your field working in another company.

• If people accept your requests, be flexible: ask what's the best time for them, if they prefer to talk with you on the phone or in-person (ask where, when). Be ready to offer an alternative if what they suggest doesn't work for you, but make it easy for them (meeting during their lunch break or near their workplace, for example).

• Prepare a list of questions in advance to ask during the information interview. Below you'll find examples of questions to get you started.

• At the beginning of the information interview, start with the most important question (to you). If you need more details about the answer received, ask more specific questions to get them. Then go to the next question from you list, and so on. You might not have time to go through all your questions, but at least you'll have the most important one answered.

• Don't ask to be referred to someone else or if there are similar positions available in their company. This is a NO-NO! Because the person (who was generous enough to give you fifteen to twenty minutes of their time) will feel pressured. This is not a pleasant feeling, and they will probably back off because you're asking too much! Stay with questions that feed your curiosity about the job search process, and receive their answers gratefully. If they like you and if they feel good talking with you, they might offer to help by sending your resume to their manager or a colleague from another company, or they might not. Don't put any pressure on them! Let them decide if they want to help you further or not. Remember, this is only an information interview. You're just there to gather information and advice, not to request that someone endorse or refer you!

• Take notes, to show that you're interested in what they're saying. Let them do most of the talking. That's why you're there, right? Not to show what you already know about job hunting.

• Respect their opinions, even if you don't agree with them. You'll decide later what you'll take away from this interview and apply to your job search.

• Don't worry if you don't have time to go through all the questions from your list, but do pay attention to time.

• When it's time to end the information interview (according to what you both agreed upfront), jump directly to this question: Do you know someone else in this field I could ask for advice or companies I could reach out to? This is the most important question you can ask, but leave it until the end. I'll explain in a bit why it is so important.

• Don't get over the time you both agreed from the beginning. This shows you're professional and respectful, both qualities that play in your favor to leave a good impression.

• Follow up with a thank you note within twenty-four hours, and send your resume if you were asked to. Don't send your resume before you meet/discuss with the person (unless you're asked for it).

• If you contact the people you were directed to, follow up with another email to let them know the outcome and thank them again. Grateful people are well viewed, and others tend to help them more.

• Following through on their advice also shows your willingness to learn, a great trait any employer is looking for. See, these are the little personality traits we don't usually mention in a job application, but they can play an important role in gaining trust! This is the human factor I keep talking about, and you need to tap into it more! I'm quite sure that many introverts have these traits, including you, so you just need a way to let them speak on your behalf . . . and the information interview is a great way to do that!

• If an information interview leads to an invitation to a job interview, don't expect that all is set up. The employer will still assess if you're the right candidate for their position and company. So take time to prepare as you normally prepare for a job interview. More on this in chapter 13 ("Interview Tips to Sell Yourself without Being Salesy").

• If a person you interviewed for information and advice ends up referring you to a manager or HR, they're putting their reputation at stake. That's why these people might be willing to refer you only if you made a good impression, and if they believe that your profile matches what the employer is looking for. Don't expect nepotism or favoritism just because you met someone and talked for fifteen or twenty minutes!

Examples of questions you can ask during an information interview:

- In your opinion, what's the most effective way to get a job in this field?
- What worked for you?
- Would you like to tell me more about your role in this company? (tasks, challenges, etc.)
- What are some dos and don'ts for job searches and job interviews in this field?
- What would you suggest doing in my case?
- Would you mind looking at my resume and giving me some feedback?
- (*Toward the end of the interview*) "How may I help you?"
- Sometimes people don't ask for anything back, but if they do and you have no idea how you can help them at the moment, mention that you'll keep their request in mind and let them know if you come across what they need. If you can help, let them know how.
- (*This last question is the most important!*) Do you know someone else in this field I could ask for advice, or companies I could reach out to?

The answer you receive for this last question will guide your next step. If that's a no, it's okay. Say, "Thank you for the great advice and information you shared with me!" and leave the room. You'll figure out later what your next step is.

But if it's a yes and you get information about new people to contact and new companies to approach, that's GOLD! This will help you dig further into the hidden job market! Because your next step will be to research those companies. Maybe they have job openings or you can find someone to ask for an information interview. And for the new connections you get, you can contact them asking for information interviews! This time you will mention who gave you their coordinates — the person you just interviewed! These people will be even more willing to open up, because you come from a trusted connection. And, toward the end of the information interview with them, you'll ask the same magic question: Do you know someone else in this field I could ask for advice, or companies I could reach out to?

This way, you have access to new people and companies you didn't know before. And you repeat the interviewing process again and again until the magic happens!

Chances are that while you're doing information interview after information interview, you'll end up getting the job you want!

Remember in chapter 2 I talked about a workshop participant who realized what was missing in her job search? It was a workshop on attitudes for effective communication, similar to what you'll discover in chapter 11. While doing one of the experiential exercises, Lili realized she was not assertive enough in her job search! As soon she realized that, she started using information interviews. She was a recent graduate with a degree in market research, and she moved to a new city where she knew no one. Lili used LinkedIn to approach people in her field. She didn't have the courage to approach someone in a VP of marketing role, so she started asking less experienced people for information interviews. From the first interview she got the name of a second person, and from there she was directed to someone else, and she was even referred to a VP of marketing at one point. Continuing this way, Lili got a position in her exact field in — two and a half weeks since she started the information interview process! And even more interesting, they created the position for her! When I asked her more details about her experience, she said 60 percent of the people she interviewed got their positions through information interviews! She was quite surprised, because she didn't know if people would understand what she was asking for (an information interview). And the last time she asked for an information interview, the person on the other end invited her directly to a job interview because they liked her background. After passing some tests and a five-hour interview, she got the position!

Now do you understand why I consider information interviews so effective?

If you meet Lili in person, you'll notice how quiet she is, preferring to observe more than talk. Doesn't this sound like an introvert? And if she was able to get a job without any experience in her field, you can too!

I cannot guarantee that you'll get the job in the same amount of time, but keep trying and learn from each experience. Remember what the HR manager from the bank said: The information interview is an effective way to find a job!

Here's why I like this job search strategy:

• If you stay at home, sending application after application, how will you feel after a while if you don't hear back from any of the companies? I know how I felt before using information interviews: tired, frustrated because I didn't know what happened and what to improve to get companies to contact me.

The information interview will help you talk with real people and get feedback on what you do well and what else can you do. And this alone will give you hope and motivation to put aside the frustration and get more motivated for your job search.

• Besides getting people's opinion about how your background is perceived in the job market (especially in your field), talking to people could also help you understand how others perceive you as a person, and clarify your own thoughts.

I was quite surprised noticing that people's impression of me and my background was better than mine! It's so great to see this difference, because once you become more aware of it, you'll know (or find out) what to do to reduce or eliminate the difference.

• I really appreciated how people opened up when I asked those questions I was really interested in. I didn't realize before that some people actually are willing to give me advice! Totally worth to try!

• As an introvert, I was not willing to use this strategy at the beginning because it takes more energy to put it in practice than sending job applications online.

By focusing on my short-term options and long-term objective, I found the courage to use it. And I'm glad I did! The next positions I got in my career came from using this strategy. Yes, it's effective, even for introverts!

The positive feedback received at each information interview gave me more energy. These types of interviews are not so draining like job interviews, and you can spread them out as you wish to have enough breaks to recharge your batteries if you need to.

• It gives you a sense that you're more in control of your job search process!

You decide who you'd like to contact, when you talk with them, what you want to say, who to follow up with, etc.

You're more at ease in an information interview, which makes you show up how you really are, not the stressful you (which is to your advantage)!

Isn't being in control a more pleasant feeling than being at the mercy of an employer or another to call you for a job interview?

• The ripple effect of that last question is quite interesting! How else can you get to meet those new people in your field? This method increases your visibility on the job market while you stay focused on what you want.

• I also found surprising the fact that some people are willing to help even after you meet them. The connection you make, the report you build with them lasts longer than you might initially think. Which is again to your advantage, because people do get new information, which can be passed to you even after the initial discussion. When these are job postings or job opportunities from the hidden job market, you're one step ahead of your competitors — or even have no competition at all! Couldn't this increase your chance of getting that position?

• As an introvert, hiding behind a computer during your job search might not be the best strategy, because it's hard for others to understand who you are. Reaching out to people (to help them get a better idea of who you are), taking time to get your energy back in between, might take you further.

• The information interview is not a job search strategy that opens doors for you just because you happen to meet someone. This strategy helps only if you're a good fit for the position someone else helps you find (which otherwise you might not discover). That's why you need to continue the information interviews until something clicks.

• It's also a valuable strategy from the time perspective, sorting out the job openings that might not be a good fit for you and exposing you to those that would.

• One more thing: When you meet someone for an information interview, go there relaxed, leaving your stress at the door. This is a more casual discussion, not a job interview. The person who accepted your invitation to talk is usually on your side . . . unless you put pressure by asking to send your resume to someone else or to refer you internally. Again, let them offer to do this, if they want to. It's better to just leave the discussion with some advice, rather than cutting the bridge by asking too much. The last question (Do you know someone else in this field I could ask for advice or companies I could reach out to?) gives them the choice to help you further, so it's still up to them if they want to help. You can leave your business card, to make it easy for them to reach out to you if they have some information for you later.

Here are two more examples:

1. This situation was shared on LinkedIn by a university professor:

One of his students asked him if he would be willing to take a look at her resume and provide some feedback. Since he knew her from one of the classes he teaches, he agreed. Her resume didn't show much work experience, but from what he noticed about her during his class, he wouldn't hesitate to hire her if he was in a position of hiring someone for the position she was looking for. A few days after, one of the professor's friends shared a job opportunity on LinkedIn, and it was a position well suited for this student. The professor forwarded the student's resume to his friend, and she got the position!

Notice how the power of asking for feedback increased her visibility as a potential candidate for the position? She probably wouldn't have had the chance to get that position if she hadn't asked her professor for feedback on her resume.

The "human factor" (direct connection) can build trust, even if it's not directly related to job search: Through her behavior during the class, she gained the professor's trust, leading later to being referred for that position. Talking about trust, the professor's friend took a look at her resume because it was referred by someone he trusts.

Again, things happen behind the scenes! The student didn't move a muscle after the discussion with her professor. But he kept her in mind, and when the opportunity showed up, he put a word in for her.

2. I got my second job in Canada three months after I started the first one. This time it was a job related to my background, and almost doubled my salary. How did I get it?

Relaxed that I finally had a job, I decided to contact someone I had been avoiding for quite some time. I hadn't met this person before, but I had gotten her coordinates from someone else. We had a nice, laid-back discussion about my job search approach since I had gotten to Canada. Impressed that I had found a job so quickly compared to a friend of hers, she asked more about my background. Then she turned to her computer and checked the job opportunities at the company she was working for. She sent me a couple of job postings, encouraging me to apply. And I did.

Two months passed by, and one day I received a phone call inviting me to a job interview with that company. I passed the interview, and worked with that company for three years.

As you see, by finding the courage to meet this person, I was able to tap into the hidden job market (otherwise I wouldn't know about that company and their job openings). While working there I noticed that the company gave an incentive of $2,000 to the employees who refer candidates who are not only hired, but also pass the six-month probation period. That was the way this company approached their recruitment process, to decrease the costs and the risks by getting pre-qualified candidates referred by their own employees.

While working there I referred someone too, but the person was not invited to a job interview. Later on, when someone else approached me, I suggested they contact the HR department directly (without me referring her), and she was invited to a job interview.

These examples show that a company who cares about its success hires people who are referred only if they are a good fit. Would you like to work for such companies? Then use information interviews to increase your chances of getting hired by tapping into the hidden job market!

IS 5) **Pain Letter**

You've already heard me talking about the pain letter several times. Liz Ryan coined this term, and it's one of the main job search strategies she recommends. She is the founder and CEO of the Human Workplace, and author of *Reinvention Roadmap: Break the Rules to Get the Job You Want and Career You Deserve.*

Liz's pain letter approach is quite simple:

1. Do your research to find companies you want to work for, and get more details about them.

2. For each company, identify the manager of the department you'd like to work for. If you're an experienced professional, identify what could be the biggest business challenge the manager has, and how your expertise could help in overcoming this challenge. This is the "pain" you'd like to address in your pain letter. If you are changing your career direction or you don't have much experience, think about what feeds your motivation to work for that department in this specific company. For example, is it a field you've always been interested in? Are you passionate about the difference this company makes?

3. Based on your research and what you identified at step 2, create a one-page pain letter addressed to the manager of that specific department:

- If you're an experienced professional, mention you have the expertise to help in overcoming that challenge. If you don't have much experience, mention why you'd really love to be part of the manager's team and work for that company.
- Ask if there's a need for your skills and expertise on the manager's team, and for a few minutes to talk about the company and share a bit of your story.

4. Send the pain letter and your resume via snail mail (not email) directly to the manager you're interested in working for. To better understand the elements of such a letter, check out Liz Ryan's article on Forbes.com "How To Write Your First Pain Letter":

https://www.forbes.com/sites/lizryan/2015/03/01/how-to-write-your-first-pain-letter/#4ae2b3162546.

Reasons why I consider this a very useful strategy for introverts:

• Introverts are quite good at solving complex problems. If you already have the expertise, using this strength and some research can help you identify what could be the biggest challenge for that manager.

• Managers like to have motivated people on their team. This makes the work environment more positive and increases productivity. That's why you can use this strategy even if you have little or even no experience. And because you're sending the letter to the manager, it will get directly in front of the person who might need you on his team.

• Approaching a manager directly this way will bypass the HR department. So you'll directly reach the person who has the expertise to understand your background and what you're saying in the pain letter (how your expertise could help overcoming that specific challenge). Such a letter sent to HR will probably end up in the garbage bin, because the HR department might not look at an application without an existing job opening. And they probably won't understand your background so well either (they're not in your field).

• Employers appreciate assertiveness, and by using this method you show (indirectly) that you have this quality that is associated with keeping an eye on the objective, and that you get things done. Doesn't this sound like an introvert trait too? Introverts are very good at staying focused, not allowing themselves to get distracted if they have an objective in mind. So the pain letter is an effective job search strategy for you! And you can do the first steps (research, crafting the pain letter and resume) at your own pace.

• "Hey, Gabriela, I'm an introvert, but I'm not comfortable with authority figures!" That's okay, because you don't need to focus on that. If this keeps bugging you, use the exercise from chapter 5 (on mindset) to change your perspective. Managers are people too, and if they need your expertise and motivation on their team, they will be open to having a conversation with you. This will be a less formal discussion than a job interview. You'll just need to do your homework, to be prepared for the discussion. And you can do that by researching information about the company and by preparing a few questions to ask. You don't need to give solutions at this point. Let them hire you first. :-) By asking good questions to better understand their business challenge, you help the manager understand your value and if they need you.

• How do you handle the discussion with the manager? Beside preparing yourself, keep in mind the manager decided to speak with you because he's interested in what you have to say. So the power is on your side! That manager saw some value in what you mentioned in the pain letter and resume and is willing to spend a few minutes with you to hear more. You're not there to sell anything! You have the skills, expertise, and motivation to help THEM! Put on your confidence posture, relax, step into the office, and let the manager start the conversation (if that feels more comfortable for you). Go with the conversation flow, ask questions to better understand what they need, mention how you helped in a similar situation. Then let go of everything else. Focus on this one-on-one discussion with another human being, instead of your own fears and doubts. Stick with the time you've agreed upon. Managers are busy and will not appreciate going over that time (unless they ask for it).

• The beauty of this strategy? You probably have NO competition by reaching out directly to the manager, no need to wait for a job opening to be advertised. With email communication being so easy these days, how many letters like this do you think a manager gets? Get the surprise factor on your side! If you reach managers who don't like to be approached this way, they probably won't answer. I guess you wouldn't like to work for a manager who doesn't appreciate a motivated, proactive candidate who could contribute to achieving the company's objectives, would you?

I would not suggest using the pain letter strategy for a job posting that's already advertised, because the manager could simply send your letter to HR without reading it, and it will end up in a pile with many other applications for the same position.

IS 6) **Research**

I have a hunch you already like this job search strategy, since it speaks to your introverted nature. But what makes it more powerful is when you target your research, keeping your short-term options in mind aligned with your long-term objective (the ones you identified in chapter 4 — "What I Want" — if you did your homework). If you have not yet identified your short-term options and long-term objective, I highly suggest you get back to it to get a better understanding about what  you want. It'll make your job search much easier because you'll be focusing on something meaningful to you, instead of just a job!

I've met many job seekers who rely only on this strategy, and even worse, they only do a fraction of what they could do using this method (only searching online job boards).

Research is part of your job hunting process, but combined with other strategies it becomes more powerful! And even more, it's something you can do on your own time (at home, coffee shop, library), so it suits your introverted personality very well.

Combined with the introvert's power of unusual concentration when focused on a meaningful project, it could serve you very well. After all, your job search project is a meaningful one, isn't it? It helps you move forward toward something you really want, not imposed by anyone else.

What Can You Research About?

• Companies who could benefit from your skills and background, even if they didn't advertise a job opening yet.

• Job postings corresponding to what you want short term but serve your long term as well.

• Companies who might have such job openings.

• Recruitment agencies with job postings in your field, or who will keep your resume on file for future opportunities.

• Some companies use external recruitment agencies to fill out their vacant positions. So you'll need to find out what works in your field and the recruitment process of the companies you're interested in.

• People you can ask for information interviews.

• Information about the new companies and people you heard about through an information interview.

• Information and news specific to your field that could inform your job search.

• Advice related to the position you're interested in, and specific interview questions for such a position.

• Professional associations to get in touch with your peers.

• Events where you can meet new people. Anyone could be a resource person if you ask the right questions!

• General publications or publications specific to your field that could provide useful information for your job search.

A word of caution though:

• Since research comes naturally to an introvert, you can get lost in the massive world of information out there! Target your research, stay focused, and allot a certain amount of time per day to do your research. This way you will also have time for the other aspects of your job search (sending applications, going to information interviews, doing follow-ups, taking breaks to recharge your batteries, etc.) so you can actually move your job search project forward — faster!

• Something I learned while writing this book is this: You can get eye strain and fatigue by looking at the computer screen too long without breaks. And when we're focused on something, we can easily lose track of time. There are a few apps out there to minimize eye strain. I like the Chrome extension EyeCare, which reminds me to take a brief break every twenty minutes and do some eye exercises to reduce eye strain. You can adjust the time settings if you want.

Now we'll get into more details about each of the above-mentioned research topics, but keep in mind that this list is not exhaustive. Use your intuition and creativity to find new ways of getting the information you need.

Where Can You Research Information about Companies?

Research Companies who could benefit from your skills and background, even if you didn't find their advertised jobs yet. By now you should have a list of companies you're interested in that correspond to your short-term options (identified in the previous chapters). Information interviews will help you get new company names to add to your list.

• Start searching more information about each of these companies: check their website for a section like Careers or Jobs, read their "About Us" to understand more about the company and its culture/mission/values, familiarize yourself with their products and services, look at company's profile on LinkedIn, find out who works for the company (via your network and LinkedIn), contact some of their employees and ask for information interviews, etc. All the information you gather through this research will help you create and send targeted applications that are more attractive to the potential employers, since you can capture what's specific to them. It will also help you prepare for the job interview, if you're invited.

• If you find an advertised job posting through this research, send your targeted application (resume and cover letter).

• If there is no job opportunity listed you could send a direct inquiry (resume and pain letter) to your potential manager. You'll find the coordinates of this manager via research as well (LinkedIn could be a good resource). You might be surprised, but very few people use this method, although you could have less competition or none at all by using it. How does that sound to you? :-) More about the pain letter in the next strategy section (IS 5).

How do you find more companies?

• Check for company directories at your local library. They usually have printed company directories and can give you free access to several online directories. Scott's Directories, for example, give you company details like website, number of employees, and phone and fax numbers, and you can search by industry or geographical area.

• Speak with a librarian to find out what other useful resources they have available for clients like you. They usually have a whole section with information regarding job search, but also newspapers and specialty magazines where you can find companies. I found the Toronto Library service "Ask a Librarian" very useful.

• Trade shows usually have the exhibitor's list on their websites. Research trade shows specific for your industry.

• On government websites you can also find company directories. If you're interested in Canadian companies, Industry Canada is a great resource for finding companies by industry or location: https://www.ic.gc.ca. (When you're in, click on Just for Businesses, then Find Canadian Companies.)

• Online directories like the Yellow Pages can help you find companies as well. A simple search for "engineering Toronto" returned 342 results, a good start for someone looking for such a position, right? :-)

Research job postings corresponding to what you want:

• You can find many job boards (websites listing only job postings) on the Internet. Some job boards are specific to a certain field; others list all kinds of jobs opportunities (like Workopolis, Monster). When you talk with other professionals in your field, you can also ask if there are job boards specific to your industry.

• Keep in mind that not all of the job postings you see on the general job boards are real. Some recruitment agencies are looking for candidates to fill out their database, to have a pool of candidates to choose from when they have a real job posting later.

• The job boards Eluta and Indeed are like Google for job postings. Type in keywords related to the position you're looking for, and they source information directly from companies' websites. So they will return more real jobs for you to choose from.

• While you can search for job postings on these job boards, some of them also allow you to upload your resume (after creating a profile). The recruiters take a look at those newly uploaded resumes.

• If you upload your resume and someone calls mentioning finding your resume on a job board, pay attention if the person is from a company (with a job opportunity) or a recruitment agency, or if they are someone offering to help you find a job. The last option is usually in exchange for a fee, which might not be mentioned on the phone, but the person might try to aggressively sell you their services when you accept to meet. I had such an experience, and my introverted side gave up under the pressure and bought the service. When I wanted to cancel the service soon after, their answer was, "There is no option for cancelation in our contract, but you can use our services anytime within five years." Maybe it they could have helped me, but I didn't trust them anymore.

• Keep in mind that many people can find the job postings on the job boards, so the competition can be high.

• Companies who post on job boards might have a longer recruitment process, since they need to wait until the due date of the job posting before taking the next steps in their recruitment process.

• I love my friend Google: Not only does it help with finding job boards, but also in finding current job opportunities if you use keywords specific to the position you're looking for (like "job marketing Toronto", "entry level marketing jobs Toronto").

• Also, keep in mind that smaller companies might not have the financial resources and a specialized HR department to post on various job boards. So you might have fewer competitors if you target smaller companies, and their hiring process is usually faster.

• It's okay to apply to a position even after the due date listed on a job board. Maybe the company didn't receive good enough applications so they are still looking for candidates.

Research recruitment agencies who might have job postings in your field or keep your resume on file for further opportunities:

• Google keywords like "recruitment agencies Toronto"

• Look for professional associations with online directories of their members (recruitment and staffing agencies). For example, the Association of Canadian Search, Employment & Staffing Services (ACSESS) https://acsess.org/.

• Search the job postings you're interested in. Some might be posted by recruitment agencies. Then visit the agency website to see if they have more opportunities in your field.

• Ask at the local library if they have directories of recruiters.

• Job fair websites: chances are you will recruitment agencies there too.

Find people you can ask for an *information interview:*

• Ask your connections if they can direct you toward someone who works in your field or in a company who has employees holding a similar position to what you're looking for. Even if there are no job openings in that company, you can ask the new person to direct you toward their colleagues (working in your field) so you can ask for an information interview. You can use email to contact all these people from the comfort of your home.

• I found that people are more willing to help when you ask for something else than a job opportunity in your field. You can simply say, "I'm looking for someone who works as a _____ or in a company who has such a position, to ask for an information interview. If you know anyone, would you mind putting me in contact with this person? Thank you!"

• Even if those you ask don't know such a person, once they know what you're looking for, they might keep an eye on what information is coming their way and send you what could be useful for your job search.

• LinkedIn is a great resource for finding people and asking for information interviews. I'll show you how in chapter 12 ("Speed Up Your Job Search with Social Media").

• You can also find people in your field (to ask for information interviews) by contacting or getting involved with professional associations specific to your field.

Research information about the *new people* you heard about *via information interviews:*

• This research will help you know more about them before you actually meet or talk. They won't be total strangers anymore, making you more at ease while approaching them and even helping you find a great icebreaker to start the conversation.

• Google and LinkedIn are your best "friends" when it comes to searching such information.

• You'll find that many people are pleased to see that you did your "homework" upfront, and you already know something about them. Think about what you appreciate about them and their career path, and let them know.

This way you make a good impression from the beginning, which could set a positive tone for the whole discussion.

Research information and news specific to your field — it could inform your job search:

• Besides keeping yourself updated with information and news in your field, this research could bring to your awareness companies and opportunities you were not aware of.

• You can also share (via your social media profiles) interesting resources and articles you find through this research, to keep your name coming up in your contacts' feed. It helps as a reminder to keep you in mind, especially if your profile already shows that you're looking for new opportunities. And if they share these articles, your name and profile will be visible to other people you don't know yet, also increasing your visibility.

Research advice and interview questions specific to the position:

• Research what could be the best way to answer the common questions that show up in most job interviews. Books and the Internet are great resources for this.

• Doing this research before a specific job interview will help you prepare more thoroughly, because you might find questions specific to that type of position. It also helps with decreasing the interview-related stress. Being more relaxed during the job interview will help you come up with better answers, especially to those questions you didn't anticipate coming.

Research events where you can meet new people. Anyone has connections, ideas, and information, becoming a great resource person for your job search when you ask the right questions. Chapter 10 (Networking the Introvert's Way) will give you more information about how to approach such events and how to genuinely connect with others.

IS 7) **Networking and Introverts**

Let me guess how you're thinking about network-ing: "I heard it's a good job search strategy, but I'm not interested! Networking drains my energy and I feel awkward to be around so many people. I don't even know what to say and do while I'm there."

I totally get it! Not only I have been in your shoes, being an introvert myself, but I still get the same feeling when I go to networking events . . . if I don't apply what I've captured in chapter 10 ("Networking the Introvert's Way"). And when I do apply these techniques, I find the outcomes quite beneficial.

Why do I believe networking is a good job search strategy for introverts as well?

• You already have a meaningful objective (the position that'll serve you short term), which is quite motivating for an introvert. When you go to events and places, use the opportunity to ask people if they have any advice on how to reach your objective. You don't have to speak with many people; even one or two per event will help you.

• Speaking with new people helps you get out of your comfort zone, which will expand with each conversation you have. If you use the pain letter strategy, for example, and a manager would like to talk with you, guess what will happen if you go there feeling intimidated and lacking confidence? Yep, it will affect your ability to carry on a normal conversation and how the manager will perceive you. Wanna take the risk? Practicing often, speaking with people in circumstances less risky, will help you expand your comfort zone and get ready for more important situations.

• Would you like to speak with more confidence in a job interview? Then practice speaking with unknown people at any event you participate. Doing so will build your communication "muscle", which is very helpful at any level of the professional world.

• Like the information interview strategy, networking can help you get useful information for your job search. It might lead to new connections as well, and you can follow up with a request for an information interview.

If this section has made you a little bit more curious about using networking as a job search strategy for introverts, you'll find more how-to ideas and suggestions in chapter 10 ("Networking the Introvert's Way").

IS 8) **Job Fairs**

Why are job fairs an effective job search strategy to consider, even if you are an introvert?

• These events are put together to help employers and potential candidates meet. It's a way for you to get a closer view about the companies, recruitment agencies, and other participating organizations, even if they don't have current job openings. They might have one soon! If you don't show up, you lose some opportunities to tap into the hidden job market.

• Job fairs are also a way to connect with other job seekers, whether you are looking for the same type of position or not. Since you have something in common (you both are job hunting), it is easier to connect and start a conversation. This could be as simple as, "Hi, I'm Gabriela. What kind of position are you looking for?" Have a brief conversation, and offer to exchange coordinates to stay in touch if you'd like to. Keep in mind that every person, including someone looking for a job, has (or will have) access to information that you don't have and knows other people. Why not tap into their resources to multiply your chances of finding what you want? And you can do the same for them, sharing information you've already gathered, offering to put them in contact with someone you know (if they're interested), and keeping them in mind if you get useful information for them later. Chances are, they'll do the same! Helping others makes you feel good, which gives you a boost of energy for your own job search. Yet if you find yourself putting too much energy into helping someone else and the person is only in "receiving" mode (without being grateful and willing to help), focus more of your energy on your own job search and helping those with the same generous heart as yours.

• If you do your research before going to a job fair, you'll know what companies will be there. Some job fair websites also list the job opportunities that'll be available. So you'll know which companies you want to approach. Create targeted resumes specific to the positions/ companies you're interested in, and attach a sticky note to each resume as a reminder for which company/position it is for. This way, when you visit a company booth, you'll find the targeted resume quickly, and you'll make a good first impression (before even saying anything) by being so organized and assertive!

• While you are at a job fair, take the time to stop at the booths where no other candidates do. Chances are those company representatives are bored and would welcome anyone stopping to talk with them. :-) If you consider anyone as resourceful, talking with them might lead to advice and useful information for your job search. That's how I found out that companies can create jobs for candidates who approach them directly, if there is a need for their expertise: I stopped at a booth of a training institution with very expensive courses, and no job seekers were interested in getting information from them. The representative was quite happy that I stopped by, and we chatted a little bit. I even asked for his opinion on something I was interested in (related to my objective). So . . . I did an information interview on the spot! :-)

I've noticed that many introverted job seekers avoid going to job fairs (based on their previous experience with such events) or take a quick tour and leave disappointed. This certainly has something to do with their expectations about job fairs. If they go with the expectation of getting a job in their field and they don't, they set themselves up for disappointment.

My question for you is this: What do YOU expect from a job fair?

I organized three bilingual job fairs within two years, and I was in direct contact with employers and recruiters before, during, and after these events. I also attended several job fairs as a job seeker or service provider. Here's what I learned:

• The main purpose of employers and recruiting agencies being present at a job fair is to see and talk with candidates in person and to increase the visibility of their company. They are looking to attract great candidates, while you are looking for a great job. So it's good for both you and employers to be present at job fairs to increase your visibility and see if you find the right fit.

• Not all employers come to a job fair with current job opportunities. Some might direct you to their website to apply online, some might be there to collect resumes and select them later, while some might be so busy talking briefly with each candidate that they won't have time to interview them on the spot. Yet there are employers who conduct pre-selection interviews during the job fair if the organizer offers a space that ensures privacy, and the employer has enough staff to stay at the booth and conduct the interviews. You might not know what's going on there unless you check it out yourself!

• In today's competitive job market, where many applications are sent online, employers want to get a quick idea about the candidates' attitude and personality before even considering their resumes. Remember when I talked about soft skills and why employers appreciate them? A job fair gives them the opportunity to evaluate the candidates' soft skills. They are well trained in "reading" people and have a good idea of what candidates could be a good fit for their company culture. Whether they have current job opportunities or not, they might add a note on the resumes as a reminder of what candidate they'd be interested in (now or for future job opportunities). They are aware that resumes don't represent the person well. To minimize their risks, they take the time to attend job fairs to pre-select candidates. If you don't show up, you might lose this opportunity!

• Since a job fair is a professional event, employers expect candidates to present themselves in a professional way and dress accordingly. If you don't, you might miss a chance to make a good impression! This impression counts a lot, because it takes employers only a few seconds to realize if they want to give you more attention or not.

• Employers don't like to be asked questions like, "What is your company about?" They expect you to check the job fair website in advance to learn what exhibitors will be there and to visit their company website for more information. They don't have much time to talk about their company (especially if there are many candidates waiting), and it's not pleasant to repeat the same thing to each person either. So do your research in advance if you want to increase your chances!

• After a few hours, the employer representatives get tired. It's best to go to a job fair at the beginning, when they are still fresh and open to discussion. Some representatives don't even stay until the end if they get enough resumes or are too fatigued.

• Talking about being tired, have you noticed the difference between your attitude and communication style when you're relaxed compared to when you're tired? Introverts' energy gets drained quickly in events attended by many people, like a job fair. You don't want to show up already tired and frustrated when you get the chance to speak with an employer, do you? So take the time to relax and recharge your batteries before going to the job fair. Also keep a bottle of water with you. It helps decrease your stress and keeps your mouth from getting dry when talking with other people.

IS 9) **Social Media for Job Search**

I've done many workshops on this topic, and many participants seemed surprised that social media can be used for job search. Those who already used websites like LinkedIn thought they knew how to use it. Yet they find out they were using LinkedIn in a more passive way instead of a targeted, proactive way to achieve what they want. They were not tapping into the many other benefits of using these platforms. Having a social media profile is one thing; using it strategically to achieve your goals is a totally different thing.

You'll find suggestions on HOW to use social media more effectively in chapter 12 ("Speed Up Your Job Search with Social Media"). So here I'd like to mention why I consider social media a great job search strategy for introverts:

• Studies show that introverts are more willing to open up and share ideas online. Why not use social media in the context of job search to increase your visibility, so others learn more about you and your expertise?

• I agree that some information shared on social media is not useful, and it could be a waste of time. But you can also be selective while using social media, and stay focused on what you need and want. Even if you don't like social media, please don't throw the baby out with the bathwater — at least not before reading the chapter 12! :-)

• Social media is easy to use and doesn't require as much energy from you as the other job search techniques mentioned in this chapter. It could even be fun! For me, social media is my preferred way to socialize, and I use it for professional purposes as well.

• It works really well combined with the other strategies, for a more effective job search.

• Social media has been here for quite a while, and there are no signs it will go away in the future. You better get on this trend if you want to show that you are keeping up with the professional world. Many companies are using social media, including for their recruitment needs.

• You can find job postings using social media, and even employers and recruiters who are looking for candidates like you. It's another way to tap into the hidden job market.

• For certain professions (event planners and marketing professionals, for example), not using social media is a sign they're not up to date with what's happening in their field and might be less attractive to a potential employer.

• Yes, using social media requires time and can be addictive. The question is, are you investing your time, using appropriate social media strategies to achieve your short-term goal and long-term objective?

• Social media sites are online platforms where users add their content. You can be laser focused on your end goal and use appropriate social media strategies to help you get there. More on that in chapter 12, and examples.

I hope I have you interested in using social media for your job search, because I have focused chapter 12 entirely on effective strategies for social media while you're job hunting.

IS 10) **Cold Calls/Warm Calls**

If you are an introvert who doesn't mind picking up the phone and calling someone out of the blue (not knowing the other person), this strategy might work for you. I know I won't use it, but I've met people who have used this strategy successfully. Yet I successfully used a warm version of this strategy when I needed a job quickly. The situation was so urgent, it pushed me out of my comfort zone, and I simply picked up the phone and called.

Cold calls is a term used by sales representatives meaning they pick up the phone and call people (sales prospects) from a list they created by doing some research. They don't know these people, but they approach them hoping they're interested in buying the products and services they sell. That's a *cold call*. A *warm call* would be if you already have some information about that person or you've met before.

With the information interview strategy, you ask for advice from someone who already works in a position similar to what you're looking. For the cold call strategy, you're directly targeting the managers who might need your expertise in their team, presenting your background and asking if they are interested in hiring you!

Yep, it's quite a bold move! If you have the confidence and courage to do it, go for it!

Billionaire Mark Cuban said: "Every no gets me closer to a yes." So don't get discouraged when a manager says no; just call the next person on your prospect list.

If you plan to use the cold call strategy in the context of job hunting, here's what you need to do:

• Research companies who might need your expertise (even if you couldn't find job openings in those companies).

• Find the name and phone number of the hiring managers in your field (not HR managers).

• Create a list with these "sales prospects" (the managers of the departments you'll work for if you're hired).

• Search the Internet for "cold calling script for job seekers," to understand how to handle such calls so you can actually reach the manager (instead of being stopped by the gatekeeper).

• Prepare a targeted resume and cover letter template.

• Prepare what you'd like to say when you speak with the hiring manager. Your intention is to make them aware of your expertise and that you're interested in working for them. Being your potential managers, they will be able to evaluate your skills quickly (or ask for more information) if they're interested in hiring you.

• Start calling the prospects from your list.

• If you find mangers who are interested, while you're still on the call, offer to send them your resume and get/confirm their email address.

• Customize your resume and cover letter and send them as soon as possible. If the managers are interested in hiring you, they will forward your application to the HR department mentioning they're interested. From there on, you'll probably deal with the HR department.

• Don't forget to follow up with a thank you note, even if the manager is not interested in hiring you. Leave a good impression. Who knows, maybe he'll need your expertise in the future!

With a website like LinkedIn around, some experts say there are no more cold calls, there are only warm calls (because you can probably get some information about your prospect via LinkedIn). If that's the case, the only step to add to this strategy is this: Gather this information in advance so you can refer to it when you reach out to the manager. Saying something specific to him will add a more personal touch to the conversation, giving it a good start.

IS 11) **Mentoring**

In the business world, a mentor is someone more experienced who provides information, encouragement, and support to help you move your career forward. Some companies have internal mentoring programs to help employees understand what it takes to go to the next level (moving up to a position that requires more responsibility or moving to another department).

In the job search context, having a mentor does the following for you:

Helps you better understand where you are and what else you need to land the desired job, the dos and don'ts for a successful job search (in his opinion).

Gives you advice and access to new information, resources, and sometimes, the mentor's network.

Offers encouragement and acts as a sounding board to discuss your ideas. Since the job search takes a while, you might get discouraged or frustrated or loose motivation in the process.

Here are a few reasons why busy professionals would accept the request to be your mentor:

• Being more experienced, they remember their past challenges and how they overcame them, and they are willing to smooth the career path of someone less experienced.

• They remember the help received along the way and are willing to pay it forward.

• (*Reasons related to what they want for themselves*) Being of help to someone else increases their self-esteem. They want to feel valued, develop new skills (like leadership), mention volunteering on their resume, meet new professionals to expand their network, learn more about something related to your background, and so on.

Why do I consider mentoring a good job search strategy for introverts?

• One of the challenges we have as introverts is relying too much on our inner world and actions, hoping others will understand us or at least give us a chance. In the job hunting process we don't usually spend enough quality time with others to help them understand our strengths. That's why a mentoring relationship can help, on top of the above listed benefits: Having the time to understand your strengths, the mentor is more willing to help; he or she can relate to your challenges and provide valuable advice to help you succeed.

• Remember we talked about delegating? Having a mentor could help you expand your network and access new opportunities. Usually the mentor is someone more advanced in the field you're in (or you want to get into), and has information about what's going on in that field: relevant professional events or programs and companies who might benefit from your skills. If not, at least a mentor has ideas on how to find and reach those companies, and how to best approach them.

• The time spent with in a mentoring relationship helps build trust, in which case the mentor might be willing to give you a good reference or refer you to people he knows (making it easier for you to meet new people and ask for information interviews).

• I already mentioned that assertiveness is appreciated by employers. What do you think? Does asking someone to be your mentor show this quality (without having to say anything)? Even if the mentor is not your employer, this quality makes a good impression and might be mentioned if the mentor refers you to someone else.

If you'd like to have a mentor assisting you, here are two ways of getting one:

• *Formal:* Research in your area if there are mentoring programs for people looking for jobs. If there are, find out if you meet their eligibility criteria (imposed by the mentoring program funding organization). Call or email to get more information about the mentoring program you're interested in.

• *Informal:* If during your research and information interviews you find someone you'd like to have as a mentor, simply ask! Mention what you like about their profile, and what you're up to (looking for a position in _____), and ask something like, "Would you mind being my mentor?" Give them room to decide, without any pressure. Some people have never thought about being a mentor, so your question might come as a surprise. Be ready to provide some suggestions if they ask what being a mentor would entail. Mention you're open to whatever format works for them, and be ready to let go if they are not interested.

Below are some **tips** from my experience in designing and running a mentoring program for professionals:

• Four months with weekly or biweekly meetings seems to be a good frame-work for a mentoring relationship, but be open to whatever the mentor is willing to accept.

• One hour meetings are enough to discuss what you've done since the last meeting to advance your job search, and what else you need help with. The meeting could be in person, on the phone, or via Skype. Some mentors are too busy and prefer emails.

• Let the mentor know your objective: "I would like some help with _____". For example, how to find job opportunities in my field, feedback on what I'm not doing right and how I can improve, etc.

• Ask for advice, not job postings. The latter makes the mentor feel pressured to find you a job, which could destroy your mentoring relationship.

• During the first meeting also discuss the logistics: How often do we meet/stay in touch? What communication method do you prefer? What could make the mentoring relationship a good experience for each of you? What will you do if you don't agree on something? (It happens!) Is the mentor available only for the scheduled meetings or also to receive emails in between?

• Let the mentor know your progress, and what happens when you implement the advice.

• Ask how you can help the mentor. You might not be at the same professional level, but there are still ways to help if you're open to it.

• Be grateful for the time and advice you get from your mentor, even if sometimes you don't agree with what is said. Ask for more details when you don't understand or agree. There might be a reason behind, that advice that you're not aware of.

• Be open to trying the advice received, even if you don't envision its benefits. It will help you learn something new, and expand your comfort zone. It will also show the mentor that you're open to advice, so you'll get more.

I had a client who, after two mentoring meetings, wanted to stop the mentoring relationship because she didn't agree with anything her mentor said. I encouraged her to try the advice received and see how everything else unfolded. A year after we've met her again, she stopped me with a smile on her face: "Remember when you asked me to be patient and try my mentor's advice? Everything he said was so true, and helpful!"

Sometimes mentoring relationships develop into professional relationships or even friendship, yet sometimes they don't. Let the mentoring relationship take whatever direction feels right for both of you, without trying to push it in one direction or another.

IS 12) **Volunteering**

Some job seekers consider volunteering a waste of their time, since they don't get paid and would rather use that time for job hunting. What they don't realize though is that volunteering has many hidden benefits for the job search.

I'll specify what the ***benefits*** are for introverts, to stay within the topic of this book:

• Volunteering your time helps you meet new people in a less stressful context, and any of them could be resource people (sharing information and opportunities you might find useful to your job search).

• Since introverts don't like talking about themselves, rather than showing what they're capable of, volunteering offers an excellent opportunity to do exactly that.

• You can volunteer the number of hours you want (could be anything from a few hours per month to full time), in person, or online. The interactions with others during the time spent together will help you open up more, so they'll be able to get to know you better. Doing something together will help build trust (if you do a good job and have a pleasant attitude), making them more inclined to help.

• Volunteering with an organization could give you access to their internal job opportunities (hidden job market). If you're interested in any of those positions, knowing people who already work there will give you an advantage: You can ask for information interviews to find out more about the organization and how to better craft your application. Some might even offer to send your resume to HR. (Don't ask, let them suggest.) And, if you're invited to the job interview, your preparation could also rely on what you've learned about this organization while volunteering and from their employees.

• You don't have to talk about how good you are; it will show up while you're volunteering, making people more willing to help. It's not uncommon to find a job by volunteering with an organization first.

• If you're not currently employed, you can mention your volunteering experience as professional experience on your resume because you're using professional skills and expertise while volunteering (even if it might not look like it).

• For your short-term goal and long-term objective, if you want to develop new skills, you can do that through volunteering, and mention them (new skills, experience) on your next resumes. The people you meet there could also provide you a reference if you ask.

• By intentionally choosing where you'd like to volunteer, you can meet the type of professionals you want and get information about a certain field.

Ways to find volunteering positions:

• Search Google with keywords like "volunteering" and your city.

• Many events (presentations, conferences, festivals, and trade shows) run with the help of volunteers. Search them for your geographical area. Also look on event-specific websites like Eventbrite.

• Ask people in your network if they know where to volunteer, and mention if you have something more specific in mind (meeting certain people, what skills you'd like to use, etc.)

• Look on websites with volunteering positions. For example, in Toronto (Canada) there are many non-profit organizations looking for volunteers, and websites like http://www.211toronto.ca, http://www.volunteertoronto.ca or a librarian can help you find the type of organization you'd be interested in.

• Most professional associations are running with the help of volunteers.

• Find the organizations in your area you'd like to help through volunteering, and then approach them directly. Keep in mind that some volunteering positions might have specific conditions that apply.

• Do you know a place or organization you'd like to volunteer? Ask! You don't have to wait for a volunteer position to be advertised.

• Doing something useful and meaningful will give you a boost of confidence, energy, and enthusiasm, with positive effects on your job search (when you show up to a job interview, for example).

• Create your own volunteering opportunity! This is my favorite!

I like to create my own volunteering opportunities, based on what I'm interested in. Here's an example: Being fluent in both English and French (both foreign languages to me), I realized that many people don't understand that using a foreign language well implies more than learning the vocabulary and grammar. Any culture has its own way of expressing something in words: Native English speakers have a more direct communication style than native French speakers (who are more diplomatic), which can cause communication problems if they're not aware of these differences. So I started the English-French Toastmasters Club, the only bilingual EN-FR club in Toronto. In only one month, I went from the idea to enrolling other people (who agreed with my concept) and we've chartered the club with Toastmasters International! This process usually takes four to six months. With me as president, the club received the Distinguished Club Award within six months, and continued to attract new members. After a while I moved on to other projects, but this Toastmasters club continued to function, taking on a life of its own. What did I do with this volunteering experience? I captured it in my resume as an achievement showing my leadership skills for future professional opportunities.

If you didn't know, since introverts are motivated by meaningful goals and are good at motivating others, they can make great leaders and enroll people in achieving those goals together. Seems strange, right? We're either good at working individually or as leaders, not much in between. :-) Being a group or team member feels awkward to me, because I have so many great ideas without the power to implement them. Sound familiar?

For a long time I didn't consider myself a leader, although I had some examples as proof. But when I finally accepted this strength, my cooperative leadership style came naturally to the surface. That's why creating my own volunteering positions works best for me. What about you?

Two more examples:

1. Alina, a young professional specializing in ergonomics, asked me how she could find a volunteer opportunity aligned with her background. She was quite frustrated: She knew what a difference her skills could make, but she couldn't find any volunteering opportunity. She also had two small children, so she was looking for something close to her home.

- "Do you know any place in your neighborhood where you can apply your skills?," I asked.

- "Oh yeah, there's this small store close by with products all over the place. I feel an itch to put them in order every time I go there! I can understand that lady. She's quite busy serving the clients, so she can't keep up, but I'd really love to help her."

- "Why not go and ask!" I answered, to her surprise.

A couple days later I met Alina again. This time she was glowing. "Remember that little store? I followed your advice: I asked that lady and she allowed me to volunteer, to help her arrange the products!"

2. Several days after giving a workshop on volunteering, Lise (a participant) sent me an email, happy that she found a place to volunteer following my advice.

The day after my workshop, she attended a presentation. She liked the speaker so much that, on the wings of her excitement, she went directly to the speaker at the end of the presentation and asked if she would accept a volunteer to help with any tasks! To Lise's pleasant surprise, the speaker accepted! Lise was interested in the speaker's profession, and she hoped this volunteering opportunity would allow her to understand the ins and outs of that profession.

IS 13) **Local Newspapers**

In the research section, I talked about the useful information you can find in specialty magazines and newspapers.

The local newspapers deserve a special section in this chapter about effective strategies for introverts.

With the Internet so easily accessible these days, many job seekers rely on information found online. Yet the local newspapers could also help you reach companies you might not otherwise find. Not many people are checking local printed newspapers these days, so chances are there is less competition for the positions advertised in these newspapers. Give them a try!

Check the free and paid newspapers in your area (daily, weekly, biweekly, monthly). They usually have sections about jobs and advertising, and there is also news about local companies. If you don't want to buy newspapers, go to the local library from time to time to read those sections.

In Toronto, the newspapers *The Guardian* and the *Toronto Star* have the Jobs section on Tuesdays and Thursdays.

This strategy will take you out of the house, but you deserve some fresh air during job hunting — it's good for your health! :-) And libraries are quiet places where introverts feel at ease.

IS 14) **Spontaneous Application**

Want more chances on your side? It's easy to send spontaneous applications from the comfort of your home, using a computer. What do you have to lose? Yet it might not be so effective as the other strategies mentioned in this chapter.

If you get the attention of a company and get hired, you just saved them money and time by avoiding a stressful recruitment process. It's a win-win!

Managers are aware of what's going on in their department: who will leave soon or take a longer time-off, or what new projects are coming. If your application is received at the right moment, you'll have luck on your side! Well, in fact you made that luck, because it wouldn't have shown up in your life if you hadn't taken action (by sending your application).

Research information about the companies to which you're sending your application, so they can relate to what you're saying (and not see your application as general application and discount it before even reading it).

Also contact companies that had similar job openings in the past. Who knows, maybe the hired employee didn't pass the probation period or has moved to another department (or company).

You can also contact companies where you previously worked, if you liked them. Coming back with more experience might translate into a larger salary. Or, if you changed direction, the trust you've built while working there in the past could open the door for you to get the position you're interested in now.

Companies who have moved to a new location or opened a new branch will need new employees too. Sending your application before they open the positions could make a difference because you are ahead of the competition.

Spontaneous applications work quite well if you're interested in working in a brick-and-mortar retail store (grocery, clothing, etc.) or in food services (coffee shops, restaurants, fast food chains, etc.). Here's how you can approach them: Put your curiosity hat on and walk in, asking to talk with the manager. You'll probably be asked what you're looking for. If you can reach the manager, let him or her know what you're good at and that you'd like to work there. Have a resume handy, in case he or she asks for it. If you can't reach the manager, ask when you can find him or her. Or ask one of the staff members to pass your resume to the manager, and do a follow up if you don't hear back within a few days.

For the positions requiring direct contact with clients, in retail stores and the food industry, they prefer to see the applicants even before inviting to them to an interview. Showing up like this will help! These sectors usually have a high employee turnover, so it might be easier and faster to get a job this way — especially if you're interested in starting with a retail job.

The fact that you can go in with your resume makes it easy to leave a spontaneous application.

That's what Jules did, after moving to a new country with a temporary work permit. With his background in HR, he assumed companies would not be interested in hiring someone without a permanent status. He planned to find a company who would support him in becoming a permanent resident, but until then he needed to find a job. So he started using spontaneous applications, and found work in a fast food chain. After a while, learning more about him, the company offered him the HR manager role when the position became available. If he was able to find his way to achieve his dream, I'm confident that you can too!

IS 15) **Now Hiring/Need Help**

I love to walk around, in the neighborhood or in nature when I need new ideas. And it always works.

You can do the same if you want to quickly find a job in a brick-and-mortar retail store (grocery, clothing, etc.) or in the food services sector (coffee shops, restaurants, fast food chains, etc.). When they need new employees, they post signs like "Now Hiring" or "Need Help" in visible places

(like the entrance door). When you see such a sign, walk in and ask what positions they have available and how you can apply. Then go home, prepare a targeted application, and send it! Don't forget to get the business card while you're there so you have an email address to send it to. Or you can come back to bring it yourself.

Don't be fooled thinking you could get stuck in these low-level positions.

They could be the entrance door for you in a company. You can move up the ladder or in a different department of the head office once you're inside.

Many companies, including corporations (like banks), have high employee turnover in the low-level positions, so they are used to seeing people leave.

Sometimes they even prefer to hire people in entrance-level positions and give them the opportunity to evolve within the company. This way they can reduce the risk involved with the recruitment process for more advanced positions and have employees who understand the different aspects of their operations — leading to more productive and loyal employees. If you wonder how I know that, I assisted at a presentation about the recruitment process for one of the biggest Canadian banks. Not only was the speaker a credible source (she was working in the HR department of that bank), but also she shared that she too started to work at that bank in a customer service position.

IS 16) **Walk Your Talk**

If you're not familiar with the expression, "Walk Your Talk," it means that someone actually does what he's saying. Why could this be an effective job search strategy for introverts?

Let me give you an example: Danny, a marketing specialist, found an interesting job posting at a beer company. Since he liked beer, he was quite excited at the idea of working there. He prepared his application, and sent it to the HR department in a . . . beer bottle! Did Danny walk his talk? Do his actions show that he's good at marketing, especially to quickly grab the client's attention? Of course they do! Danny knew how to walk his talk; his actions spoke by themselves about Danny's expertise in marketing. His reputation preceded him, making a good impression before they even read his resume or saw him in a job interview.

Depending on what type of job you're looking for, pay attention to walk your talk!

Okay, maybe you're not a marketing specialist.

If you're applying for a position in the financial department and you send a well-targeted resume, which is concise and well organized, wouldn't that prove that you have good analytical and reporting skills (which are appreciated in that industry)?

If you apply for a customer service position and during the job interview you're listening carefully to what it is said (to not miss the point) and your answers are to the point and well organized, doesn't that prove you have the skills required for the position?

In one of my workshops, I had a client so frustrated from not finding a job during the last five months that it affected the way she interacted with others. Angela came to the workshop because her employment counselor insisted she be there, not because she wanted to. She was very negative and cut my words off often with that "I know it all" attitude: "I tried all these strategies, but they don't work. There are no jobs in my field!" When I asked what kind of position she was looking for and what strategies she had used, she said she was looking to work with elementary school students and she had approached the schools.

My question for you is this: if you're in the position of hiring someone to work with elementary school students, would you accept someone with a negative attitude and without patience? I assume you wouldn't. Since Angela was not walking her talk (projecting the skills required for working in her field), she had a hard time finding a job.

I was able to turn her attitude around by asking if she had contacted all the schools in the city. No! Did she contact other centers where she could work with children in the same age group, so she could use her expertise? No! Was she aware that she had transferable skills to use in other sectors? No! She finally opened up, stopped cutting me off, and listened more. She looked like a totally different person by the end of the workshop. And she came to the rest of the workshops as well, with an open mind. By changing her attitude, she was able to find a position soon, and after several months she was already ready to proactively look for a position at the next level.

I did several simulation interviews with clients, preparing them for job interviews. Some of them did not project the qualities required for the position they were interviewing. They could be experts in their field, but if they missed the chance to show their skills (instead of talking about them) they would not gain the employer's trust. Employers are skilled to read between the lines: If they notice a contradiction between what you say (verbally or in your application), and your attitude or actions, it will raise a red flag and will influence their decision.

I talked about Nancy before, the marketing specialist in Google Analytics. When she mentioned she was looking for a position in her field, I invited her to the workshop about LinkedIn. To me, someone with expertise in increasing a company's online visibility must be at the top of the game in their field (online marketing in her case). LinkedIn is a platform used by both professionals and companies, so it would make sense to know what this platform is about at least. "I'm not interested", Nancy answered passively.

"This means," I followed, "that you're not walking your talk! Someone with an online marketing background has to be aware and use a professional online platform like LinkedIn, for both self and company promotion". She finally came to that workshop, which made such a positive impact on her job search!

As you noticed, job hunting is not only about your resume and what to do to get an interview; it is a much more complex process.

What do you need to walk your talk during your job search?

Walking your talk is associated with integrity, a quality appreciated at both personal and professional levels, not only in the context of job hunting.

IS 17) **Stand Out**

Being an introvert, you might not like to stand out. If you associate "standing out" with too much effort needed to achieve that state, or using unorthodox ways to get in front of others, that's not what I mean.

In a competitive job market, it's quite important to know how to differentiate yourself from the other candidates. Otherwise the employer might not see your true value, and hire someone who masters this technique better.

I'm including this as a separate strategy to highlight the importance of asking yourself questions like, "How am I different from other candidates who might apply for the same position?" "What makes me so unique that the company will benefit the most by hiring me?"

Have you thought about this already?

People tend to think in terms of what skills and experience they have compared to what's required for the position. But besides doing that, I also invite you to think outside the box: what other skills and expertise do you have that could be benefit to the company if YOU are hired for this position? How you can you also make these benefits visible to the employer?

For example: My engineering background might not seem to be a good fit for a position designing and implementing a new mentoring program in the non-profit sector for professional newcomers. Now, I could have left that expertise aside and focused my application only on the skills and experience I had that was pertinent to the position. If I had simply listed "engineering" somewhere on my resume, I'd have risked being considered overqualified or having non-relevant expertise.

Instead, I chose to include this experience in the Summary of Qualifications section of my resume. Although the position was in the non-profit sector (which has a different culture and objectives than the private sector), having engineering experience reflects my ability to relate to professionals' challenges and communicate in their "language" to build trust. These are both great assets when recruiting mentors (experienced professionals) for this new program and building credibility in front of the mentees (professional newcomers). Being a new program, the recruitment of mentors and mentees was a key factor in the success of the program. So I framed my engineering background as being beneficial to this program, along with my ability to handle diversity (I speak three languages) and having experienced a professional newcomer's challenges myself.

Was I able to stand out with this approach? I think I was, because I got the job! And with that step, I was also getting closer to my long-term objective of shifting careers! :-)

Thinking about what's unique to your background, which could bring added value to the company (helping it achieving its goals faster), will also help your application stand out and make a difference during the job interview.

I talked about John in the direct strategy section, who outperformed more than 240 candidates for the same position. His unique response to the question, "Why should we hire you?" helped him stand out and get hired.

If you think you have something valuable to offer not mentioned in the job posting, include it in your application in a way that creates a bridge between the company's objective and the added value you offer. Don't just put it there hoping the employer will figure it out. *Don't Make Me Think: A Common Sense Approach to Web Usability*, by Steve Krug is a book highlighting the importance of presenting things in a simple way, to be more effective. The same approach applies to employers: Make it simple for them to understand the benefit of hiring you. If they receive many applications and scan each only a few seconds in the first round, they might miss your point if you don't make it simply for them to grab it.

Another way to stand out is to let your reputation precede you: Publish articles showing your expertise, have a well-crafted LinkedIn profile and recommendations, participate in LinkedIn group discussions, have a website (highlighting your previous work, accomplishments, testimonials), etc.

This is the type of promotion that suits an introvert well, since you can rely on your expertise and accomplishments to do the "talk" for you before employers even meet you in person.

IS 18) **Recruitment Agencies**

Contacting recruitment agencies is another way to increase your visibility on the job market and access job opportunities you otherwise might not find. Plus, the trust built by recruiters with the companies they serve could work in your favor.

Since they act like a buffer between you and companies, your approach should be a little different than sending an application directly to a company.

Think of a recruitment agency as a distribution center: They do not produce anything. They bring in products from different factories (job openings from various companies) and distribute them to stores (job seekers). The recruitment agencies want to build great relationships with the companies they serve (considered as their clients), because that's where their income comes from. If a company (client) is not satisfied with the candidates sent by a recruitment agency, they might not use their services in the future.

Job seekers, on the other side, help the recruitment agencies "distribute" the job openings. The relationship with job seekers is important for them too, but in a job market where the offer (job seekers) is bigger than the demand (job openings), it's easier for recruiters to find candidates. Plus, they have a database with all the job seekers who previously reached out to them, who can be contacted if needed (and are still available). So recruiters usually have candidates (job seekers) when they get new job openings. And if they don't, they know how to go "hunting" to find good candidates. :-)

Recruiters also pay attention with whom they spend their time, because they also need to prepare the candidates before sending them to job interviews. A recruiter will not spend time with a job seeker whose background doesn't correspond with the job description or who doesn't seem coachable. By coachable, I mean being open to receiving constructive feedback and advice on how to make the most of the job interview — because the recruiter usually has additional information about the company and the position (not specified in the job description).

Here are a few things I learned from my experience with recruitment agencies, talking with recruiters and clients who used their services successfully:

• If you get the chance to get a job interview via a recruitment agency, keep in mind the recruiter is on your side. If you're considered a good candidate for the position, they want to help you succeed (during the job interview and even after) so they get the commission. Their reputation is at stake if a new hire is fired or leaves the position too soon, so they are quite cautious about who they send to a job interview.

• Share your concerns, and be open to absorbing the recruiters' suggestions. They have more experience than you regarding the hiring process. There are exceptions too. :-)

• If you're interested in a position advertised on their website, send a targeted resume corresponding to this position (not a general resume). Recruiters are busy trying to find the right candidate, and a general resume might not help you stand out from other candidates.

• Some recruitment agencies accept resumes not related to the job openings they currently have. This helps them fill their database with potential candidates, and they'll keep your resume on file for further opportunities. Check out their website if that's the case.

• Contact several recruitment agencies, not only one or two. Check your local library and online for directories of recruiters. At the Toronto Library I found *The Directory of Canadian Recruiters*, which lists recruitment agencies specialized by industry, salary range, and geographical area. This directory recommends contacting at least twenty recruiters, to increase your visibility.

• If you send your resume to a recruitment agency for the first time and a recruiter invites you in, it might not be for a job interview. In this initial discussion you're asked questions related to your background and your objective. It's okay if you want to talk about your whole background (if the recruiter is open), to help them understand where you're coming from and how you can fit into the job openings they currently have.

• Depending on the position you're interested in, the recruitment agencies might ask you to pass some tests. Ask how much time you'll have to spend there, and plan your time accordingly.

• Think of a meeting with a recruiter like a professional meeting. Dress appropriately, behave professionally (including getting there at least ten minutes in advance). If asked, come earlier to have time to fill out their registration form before the actual discussion starts.

Some recruiters might ask that you keep them informed, weekly, if you're actively looking for a job. Otherwise they might not keep you on their radar for upcoming positions.

There are different types of contracts, depending on how the agency works and their relationship with the employers. Your salary may be paid by the recruitment agency or by the company you work for (which also pays the agency a fee for bringing you onboard). If it's a temporary contract, start looking for another position before the contract ends, so you don't find yourself unemployed again (if the company didn't hire you or the recruiter doesn't help you with another contract).

• Treat recruiters with respect, not as someone who's paid to serve you. Building great relationships with recruiters will help your career. You might need them again at the end of your contract, or even later. If impressed with your work and professional behavior, they might take an extra step to help you.

Here are some places to ***find recruitment agencies***:

• Google with keywords (for example "recruitment agencies Toronto")

• Look for professional associations like the Association of Canadian Search, Employment & Staffing Services (ACSESS) with online directories of their members (recruitment and staffing agencies) https://acsess.org/.

• While you browse job boards, pay attention to the job postings. Some might be posted by recruitment agencies. They have real job opportunities too.

• Ask at the local library if they have directories of recruiters.

• Through information interviews

• Job fairs

IS 19) **Employment Services**

There are many employment agencies functioning on funding received from the federal, provincial, or local government, or a combination of different funding sources. Some of them serve the population from a specific geographical area, some are city wide.

This is another way to delegate some of the work you need to do for your job search project.

Their services are free for unemployed people and could include access to an employment counselor, government programs for job seekers, information and access to a resource center (books, computers, printers, fax), job opportunities, and a variety of job search specific workshops. Keep in mind that some of their services might have eligibility criteria (imposed by their funding) — they will let you know.

"Sounds great, but . . ."

Here's why approaching an employment agency could also help an introvert like you:

• This is another way to increase your visibility (without much talking or going to events) and get access to job opportunities not available otherwise. Many companies contact these agencies to list their job postings for free and get access to new candidates. Would you like to have access to these job positions?

• The employment counselor and the workshops provided could help you get information specific to your situation, not only general advice found in books or on the Internet. For certain employment services (like having access to an employment counselor) you need to register with only one agency if there are more similar agencies getting funding from the same government agency.

• Some of the government-funded programs offer additional benefits. For example, if you're unemployed and eligible for the Second Career Program (available in Ontario, Canada), the government pays your tuition if you choose to go back to school for a career change. The entire application has to be prepared with the help of an employment counselor, then sent to the government office for approval (which takes time, so the application has to be prepared well before the courses begin).

• If you need a reference, you can ask your employment counselor or the workshop facilitator if they are willing to give you one.

• Sometimes the employment agencies bring in guest speakers who can provide an interesting perspective on the job search and hiring process, or information about the job market. This also gives you the opportunity to ask your own questions on how you can apply what you hear to your own situation. The Internet is not as good as a real human to provide answers to your specific questions. These presentations also offer the opportunity to share your coordinates/business cards with other participants, and even with speakers (to stay in touch or ask for an information interview). It's a less formal way to meet people with whom you have something in common, making it more comfortable for introverts like you to network (the presentation's content is a great icebreaker for a discussion).

I often organized such presentations for one of the employment centers where I facilitated job search workshops. I too have learned new points of view from these speakers, who were either speaking from their own experience or from the perspective of their role in a specific company. Their personal stories were inspiring, to say the least. I also invited many of my clients to come back after landing a job and pay it forward: share with other job seekers what worked for them, what didn't, and anything else they learned from their own job hunting experience. I spread out the information received in the different chapters of this book, according to the topic.

One more thing to keep in mind about employment agencies is this: While you can find some information and support there, it's still on you to conduct an assertive job hunt. If you rely only on their help, you might be in for a surprise. They can't do all the "heavy" work for you, and you're not the only client either. They need to reach their own annual targets, some imposed by their funding, to be able to serve clients year after year.

IS 20) **Mind Map**

Do you like brainstorming? I hope you do, because it's a powerful strategy to use for a more effective job search.

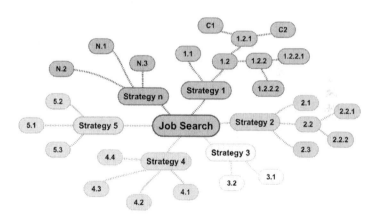

With their focus often within, introverts can easily come up with ideas. I gave you some strategies in this chapter so you can use them as a starting point.

But you can also tap into the power of your own mind!

See the above image? It's called a mind map and is a useful tool used in quality assurance to brainstorm ideas to find solutions. That's what I'll ask you to do, a mind map for your job search project!

Grab a piece of paper, make a circle in the middle, and write "My job search." Then draw circles around each job search strategy you'd like to use (depending on your personality, situation, goals, and objectives). For each strategy, identify what actions you need to take to put it in practice, and add a circle for each action (linking back to the related strategy).

For example, if you choose "information interview" as a strategy, draw circles for each action item: figure out where to search, find people to interview, research each profile, send a message, print resume, meet/discuss, follow up, decide what to do with the advice received, etc.

The purpose of creating a mind map is to brainstorm with yourself: Get out of your head as many ideas as you can to create a bigger view of what you need for your job search. You'll organize these ideas later. For now, just add as many ideas as you can.

You could also add more ideas along the way, but for the moment just put anything you have in mind now about this topic.

You can draw your mind map on paper or using an app or software. I used the SimpleMind+ app for the iPad to create the above mind map, but there are other options as well (search the Internet for free mind map software). There's also a free app, M8! — mind mapping for Windows.

With the app I use, I can even move items around if I want to (from a group of ideas to another, for example). I start every project, big or small, with a mind map like this. It's so useful to get the bigger picture of what I need to do from the beginning. I used the same app to brainstorm the ideas I captured in this book: First I brainstormed the ideas for chapters; then I created a mind map for each chapter.

Why is creating a mind map useful? Because you can easily lose track of the time while searching information on the Internet, for example. A mind map could keep you on track with the actions you want to take, so you can still move forward without getting lost in the process.

After you have your mind map, you'll create a timeline. Some of the actions from one strategy could be done in parallel with those from another strategy. Having all of them in front of you (in the mind map) can help you get more organized and prioritize: What actions could be done the same day? Which one needs to go after another? What are the most important?

Examples of actions for a day are as follows: do three hours of Internet research, send at least two job applications, add one company to my list, send two requests for information interviews, start a discussion in a LinkedIn group (ask for advice on how to get this type of job), etc.

After answering the above questions, put all your actions in a timeline that can look like this the one below.

You can create such a timeline using Excel, Numbers (MAC), or Google Spreadsheets, so you can update and print it whenever you want.

A next step will be to add the actions to your daily agenda or check the time-line often, so you'll remember what you want to do each day. Here's an example:

Day 1	Day 2	Day 3	Day 4
do 3 hours of online research	add 1-2 companies to my list	do 3 hours of online research	update my LinkedIn profile
prepare resume, cover letter	find people and send 4 requests for information interviews	send applications	do research at the library
send 2 job applications	do 3 hours of online research	search companies I'm interested in	prepare and send applications
start a discussion in a LinkedIn group, ask for advice on how to get this type of job	prepare 2 applications	send follow-up emails	send 4 more requests for information interviews
send follow-up emails	ask friends for advice	participate in LinkedIn group	prepare for the job interview

This way, you won't lose time using only one strategy after another, like the guy who sent three hundred resumes in six months then decided to use other strategies. Since you don't know which strategy or combination of strategies will prove more effective for you, your timeline will allow you to make progress while using several strategies in parallel.

In chapter 14, "Put It All Together," you'll get more ideas how this mind map works with other tips to help your job search project be even more effective.

IS 21) **Serendipity and Intuition**

If you're not familiar with the term *serendipity*, the Oxford dictionary defines it as "the occurrence and development of events by chance in a happy or beneficial way."

The job search advice I received or found in books doesn't usually consider serendipity and intuition as job search strategies. But I strongly believe that if you're opening up and take them into considera-tion, you will find them useful.

In a world where we're constantly bombarded with information, and so much also becomes available through your own research, serendipity and intuition could be your guiding compass! You set the goals, now be open and pay attention to what the Universe is sending your way to help you achieve what you want.

I talked at the beginning of this chapter about how I got my first job in a new country, followed by the twenty-one things to consider for your job search. Those are just a few examples showing you how serendipity and intuition played an important role in my job search.

Let me tell you another story. Jimmy is a young professional with an interesting background (spanning various fields), but he needed to find a job quickly. Every day at 9:30 a.m. Jimmy showed up to the resource center to use the computer for his job search. Being a tall guy, he preferred to use the computer at the back of the room, which happened to be closer to my desk. We talked from time to time, and I found out more details about his goals and background than from his resume.

During the same period of time, I invited Nancy (a previous client) to share with the current clients what she had done to find her dream position in about a month. Jimmy was not there when she came, but Nancy followed up with an email sharing the coordinates of a recruiter. When Jimmy told me he'd be interested in working for IBM, I forwarded him the coordinates of this recruiter, and he got hired!

This is what I call, "Things are happening behind the scenes," or serendipity.

And I have many other examples of serendipity at play. I'm quite sure you can find such examples in your life too, if you looking back to how you achieved something in the past. Can you?

As for *intuition*, did you ever have a gut feeling about something you needed to do in order to get what you wanted? You followed through, without quite knowing why, and the result was positive?

Or ...

A thought popped up in your mind, unrelated with anything you were thinking at that moment? You start entertaining this new thought and it gave a lot of energy and enthusiasm?

These gut feelings and sudden thought comes from intuition, your trusted companion if you know how to tap into its wisdom!

I paid attention to my intuition when a company name popped up from the list of over seven hundred while doing a phone survey. I used my intuition to filter the information I came across during the job search, from selecting which brochures I'd be interested in, to what actions to take.

A word of caution: To interpret the messages received via your intuition more accurately, you need to be relaxed. If you're frustrated about how your job search is unfolding or what someone said (or didn't), or tired of doing too much, you might not be able to interpret the messages coming via your intuition channel.

Have you ever gone for a walk and suddenly a great new thought or a solution to a problem you're dealing with popped up in your mind? Or have you ever had a good idea while showering or woken up early in the morning with a new idea for the project you're working on?

These are a few examples of how your intuition channel is less cluttered when you're relaxed, so your interpretation of the message is more accurate.

That's why I highlighted the need to include breaks during your job search, in the Wheel of Life (chapter 2)! Give some time to your hobbies, do something that relaxes you, and get enough hours of sleep when you're looking for a job. Your body and mind will thank you, and they'll reward you with more energy, enthusiasm, and fruitful thoughts. Wouldn't these be beneficial to your job search?

Okay, in this chapter we've covered twenty-one job search strategies that can be effective for introverts to accelerate their job search.

Chapter 10 and 12 will go into more detail about how to use your introvert strengths to also benefit from networking and social media (strategies considered quite effective for job search in general).

Chapter Ten

NETWORKING THE INTROVERT'S WAY

Sometimes it helps to be a pretend extrovert. There will always be time to be quiet later.
~ Susan Cain

I don't know about you, but I used to find networking very challenging . . . until I shifted my perspective!

I'm talking about offline networking, since I'm approaching the online aspect in chapter 12 ("Speed Up Your Job Search with Social Media").

Extroverts are everywhere, and they're doing very well in social situations and professional networking (it energizes them). On the other side, after social interactions, introverts get depleted of energy and need to recharge through solitude. Being an introvert myself, I totally relate to that. Susan Cain also recognizes the challenges introverts face when it comes to networking. She's the well-known author of *Quiet: The Power of Introverts in a World That Can't Stop Talking*, and the TED talk "The Power of Introverts" (fifteen million views).

I still remember how awkward I felt at my first networking event. When I finally got to talk with someone, I asked: "Does everybody here know each other? They seem to be so comfortable talking." The lady smiled: "No, they all are here to meet new people." I was totally blown away! It took me a lot of courage to step out of my comfort zone to just ask her that!

There are and have been successful introverts: J. K. Rowling (*Harry Potter* creator), Bill Gates, Abraham Lincoln, Albert Einstein, Mahatma Gandhi, Warren Buffett, Elon Musk (CEO Tesla Motors, engineer, inventor), Larry

Page (Google co-founder and CEO), Steve Wozniak (co-founder of Apple), Mark Zuckerberg (Facebook founder and CEO), and many more.

If success is not something you're looking for, being content in your own introverted bubble, notice that all the above-mentioned introverts have something in common: They started with a great idea and followed through, and in time, success came as a byproduct. They were passionate about something! How did they get there? For sure they found their way to meeting and associating themselves with the right people that helped them achieve such success. Isn't that networking?

7 Tips for Networking the Introvert's Way

Now, if I piqued your interest about networking, here are some tips for introverts from a blog post I wrote recently on how to approach networking events (or other gatherings you attend):

1. Look at the social event as a way to get where you want.

If there is a networking or social event you're interested in, there might be a reason why you need to participate. To get the courage and motivation to go there, be curious about how that event can help you move toward what you want. You might meet someone who shares that great idea you needed. Maybe you'll find a partner, or get inspired by something happening there.

You'll never find out unless you participate. Get curiosity on your side, and leave any fear at the door. Did you notice that you can't be curious and fearful in the same time?

One thing will happen for sure: Your comfort zone will expand, so you can benefit from that in the future!

2. Set an intention for that specific event. What would you like to get from it?

Before going to an event or meeting set an intention! Think and write down what you'd like to get by participating in that event. As Norman Vincent Peale said: "Shoot for the moon. Even if you miss, you'll land among the stars." :-)

You might not get all you want from that event, but setting that intention will put you into a mindset of inquisitiveness that will help you overcome or at least diminish the fears that could make you feel uncomfortable being there. And that, my friend, will open you up to connecting with people in a more authentic way (that's always appreciated!), having a more pleasant experience, and getting access to some benefits!

3. Decide a minimum time to spend there. Pay attention to your energy level.

As I mentioned earlier, introverts' energy gets drained quite fast in social interactions (whether for business or personal). Thinking of this upfront and deciding on a minimum time to spend there will reassure you that you'll not leave so tired that it will derail your plans for the rest of the day or the week.

It will also give you something to look forward to so you don't look for an exit as soon as you're there. :-) This way, you're giving yourself the chance to get the benefits you're looking for.

While you're there, also pay attention to your own energy level. If it gets too low, you'll not feel good enough to carry on a nice conversation or even to pay attention to what's going on. If that's happening, give yourself the permission to enter "observer mode" (notice what's happening, listen to conversations) until your set time passes. Then feel free to leave knowing that you achieved at least one of your objectives: spending that amount of time there. Yayyyy! :-) Smile, give yourself a pat on the back, and head home knowing that you also achieved something else: You expanded your networking comfort zone! It'll get even better next time.

4. Look for other introverts in the room to connect.

Studies show that introverts make up 30 to 50 percent of the US population. Interesting, isn't it? If there is such a high percentage in a country that appreciates the extroverts' behavior more, chances are in any other country you'll find many intro-verts. And this could apply to a smaller scale too, like a networking or social event.

So look for other introverts in the room! They might hide in the corners or sit near the wall, observing, or you'll hear them speaking with a soft voice. Someone with a composed face might be an intro-vert thinking about a big idea or how to solve a problem. They probably feel as awkward as you do in that environment. Approach one of them and intro-duce yourself. It'll make them very happy that someone reaches out to them! Many introverts like helping others. If that's your case, you just found a way to make yourself feel better in social situations (by helping someone else). This will also increase the chances of making a good connection with other introverts.

For a year I was the organizer of a Meetup group for introverts. What I noticed was this: We (introverts) are much more comfortable starting a discussion with another introvert than with an extrovert. We're even okay with small breaks in conversation, without stressing out about what to say next. :-) After getting more comfortable this way, you can expand your reach to other introverts or extroverts in the room if you want. You can even ask your new connection to introduce you to someone else, or get him or her introduced before you look around to meet someone else or just sink into the environment.

5. Expand your comfort zone: do one thing differently than in other similar situations.

The comfort zone is a psychological state in which a person feels familiar and experiences lower anxiety and stress. It might not be as comfortable as you'd like it to be, but at least you're familiar with it.

Stepping out of your comfort zone, even a little bit, will help you learn something new about yourself, about the environment you're putting yourself into, and about others. When that learning occurs, your comfort zone expands. Next time you're in a similar situation, you'll feel a little bit more comfortable than you felt before.

Use networking and social events as a way to expand your comfort zone. If you do at least one thing differently next time you are in a similar situation, you'll expand your comfort zone. Doing something slightly differently will lead to a more positive long-term impact on your life. Think of this difference in terms of a 2 percent angle. Imagine how much that angle will expand with the passing of time!

Once when I let people know that I enjoy coaching introverts (being one myself), someone asked: "Do you want to transform them into extroverts?" Well, I don't and I can't. Research studies published in several psychology journals (*British Journal of Psychology*, *Journal of Psychological Type*, and *Brain Topography*, to name a few) and by the American Psychological Association talked about psychological differences between introverts and extroverts. These are inborn traits, meaning our brains are just wired differently!

By expanding your comfort zone as an introvert, you too can tap into the benefits of meeting new and interesting people — and fulfill your need for socializing! As human beings, introverts also feel the need to socialize. We just need to find our way into it, while still staying true to ourselves.

6. Choose more wisely what events you'll attend.

Big events are usually overwhelming for introverts, so a good idea would be to choose smaller events or social gatherings that interest you. We're pretty good in one-on-one conversations (especially with people or on topics we love), so smaller events might suit us better. Is there a presentation or workshop you'd be interested in attending? Go for it! You'll have something in common with the other participants, so you can start or join a conversation more easily.

Big events have their own benefits. I personally prefer to choose some of them to test my comfort zone: Did it expanded since I previously attend a similar event? Do I want to try a new networking technique? Will I connect with someone new? Will I get an unexpected surprise? I'll go to check it out, with a curious mind.

I recently attended such an event, and I was quite pleasantly surprised with the results. I was able to focus more on my intention (what I wanted to get from that event) than on how unpleasant such events used to be for an introvert like me. Try it! It felt less awkward to attend such an event the next time. And with curiosity, and keeping my own limiting beliefs at bay, I got out with more energy than I expected. Yayyy! :-) Feeling like I was on mission there, it also gave me the courage to approach some people that otherwise I wouldn't have — like the lady I asked to form a mastermind group together, and, to my surprise, she accepted!

Also pay attention to your intuition when you determine which events to attend and what people to talk with: it could be a good guide for choosing the right events for you.

7. Remember that not all eyes are on you!

I recently coached someone in a public space, a library study room with big glass walls. When we met there, she felt uneasy, believing that all eyes were on her. From a pure coaching perspective, I asked her to challenge her own belief by looking around. To her surprise, everyone else was focused on their own stuff; no one was looking at her! That simple experience got her out of her comfort zone, expanding it!

It's the same in a networking event: People go there with their own agenda, their own insecurities and expectations. They're usually too busy with their own stuff, so you have the freedom to do whatever you want to do there. Keep in mind, by challenging your own beliefs about a specific situation often, you'll discover if they're true or not (and take action accordingly), instead of being driven by what's only in your mind and avoiding other people.

Which of these tips is your favorite? What actions will you take to put them into practice? You never know who might have information for you.

Ask someone to be your accountability buddy, and check in often to talk about your progress and challenges. Another introvert might make a better accountability partner by understanding what you're going through and not pushing you too far out of your comfort zone (which might make you give up). Publicly acknowledging what you want to implement and by when will make you more prone to implementing these tips!

If you want, you can download these tips as a checklist at http://www.gabrielacasineanu.com/jsfilesfree.

Extroverts Can Help Us!

Talking about extroverts and the benefits of knowing them:

- Since they are out there more often than us (introverts), chances are they already know a lot of people and are great connectors. Would you like to tap into their power? They might know someone interesting to connect you with or have an information that can take you further in your job search process.
- Having an extroverted friend is overwhelming sometimes, but going together to networking events could help you get introduced to new people in the room, without you going too much out of your comfort zone to meet new people. Ask your friend to make an introduction, if you're not comfortable approaching someone.
- When you meet extroverts at an event, share that you're an introvert and ask for help in meeting others. Chances are they will be glad to do it, since it makes them feel valuable.

Here are three examples:

1. I told you about how awkward I felt the first time I went to a networking event. An extroverted friend insisted on taking me there, and she's the one who introduced me to the women engineer. My first question was if all these people know each other, they seem quite comfortable talking. The second question I asked her was: "What do you do? How do you approach someone when you want to start a conversation?" "Oh, that's simple!" she answered. "You look the person in the eyes and say: Hello, my name is . . . then ask a question."

Sounds silly, or too simple, but it really made my day! :-) So I walked around and found someone not far away to try the new approach I learned. It worked! And guess what? I asked if he would be available for an information interview! He was a little puzzled by my question, because he didn't have experience in my field, but then I tapped into my strength (finding new perspectives) and told him in what way he could help me: Being an experienced professional, he surely had ideas about how I could approach my job search. And he accepted!

2. I stumbled upon Marie (an extroverted acquaintance) in the subway, and she invited me to one of the events she was organizing in a few days. When I

got there, she happened to be close to the entrance door. She gave me a tour, introduced me to someone, and showed me two other people I should connect with. Half an hour later, I was near the table with snacks when one of those people came to grab some. I approached him, saying that Marie had suggested I should talk with him (great icebreaker, BTW). We had a nice conversation, although he didn't believe that I was an introvert. "I don't like to put people in categories, extroverts and introverts," he said. "Look, you're not an introvert since YOU approached me!" he said. I had to explain that introverts can get out of their comfort zone when they really want something. And I was really curious why Marie suggested I should meet him. :-) The conversation didn't go anyway; he got impatient to move on to someone else, which I found totally okay. What I learned though was a new way to approach someone, and how little extroverts know about us (introverts). I guess it's our duty to educate them, instead of being frustrated by what they think about us.

At the same event I was introduced to someone else. This person, though, became curious about what "coaching" means, so the conversation carried along very well. In fact, his curiosity about my "land" made him open to a coaching session I offered on the spot. Not only was I very comfortable because I was talking about something I like and I have experience with, but it also attracted others to ask questions about what I do.

Are you beginning to grasp how such events can help you too?

3. Don came to me when he was two months deep in his job search, frustrated that he couldn't find one yet. As a social media marketing manager with great accomplishments, he knew his expertise would be valuable to any company. When I asked what strategies he had used, he mentioned applying to positions found online. "Do you network?" I asked.

"Yes," he answered quickly. I had a hunch we were not on the same page, so I asked what he meant by "networking." "Telling all my friends and people I know that I'm looking for a job in my field," he answered.

The Definition of Networking

Well, the definition of "networking" Don had was different than mine. Here's what I mean by networking in the context of this book: having a constant attitude of reaching out, to make new acquaintances, thus enlarging your circle. It's an attitude that many people in North America use to get ahead with their careers.

You can do as much by yourself, but when you leverage your network you can reach out much further. That's why people in North America constantly have this open attitude about meeting new people.

Excuses and More Examples:

"Hey, Gabriela, I'm an introvert!" you might say.

I know, I'm an introvert too. But this didn't stop me from going out and meeting people when I looked for a job. It didn't stop me from meeting new people through volunteering when I wanted to make an impact in a certain area, and so on. Being an introvert is not a handicap; we just need to be more selective and take care of ourselves so we don't get overwhelmed or drained of energy. Taking enough replenishing breaks is helpful.

Look, I'm not asking you to behave like an extrovert if that's not your cup of cake, but I want you to understand that offline networking is a good job search strategy for you too.

We can find all kind of excuses. But they don't help us reach our goals.

George, for example, told me that in his culture it is not normal to talk to strangers.

- "What do you want now, George," I asked.

- "I want a job, and I am having a hard time finding one."

- "Have you heard of a job search strategy called networking?"

- "Yes, my mentor told me. But I don't want to network."

- "George, if you'd be able to find a job faster by using this strategy, would you be willing to try it? You're in a country where networking works well, helping you reach out further than where you can get by yourself."

Only when George was able to connect the dots between the potential of this strategy and his goal was he able to get out of his comfort zone and start networking.

What excuse do you hold on to, that hinders your ability to reach your goal?

If you want to hold on to your excuses, be my guest! But don't be surprised if you don't get the results you want, or not as fast as you wish.

Leverage Your Introvert Strengths

When you get over your own excuses, you'll see there are ways to meet other people and still feel at ease while connecting with them. Some of them you've gotten from the above tips and examples, and here are more to leverage your introvert strengths:

• *Consider the people you meet as potential allies.* Remember your job search project and how you can delegate some of the tasks by gathering information from others? You either learn something new from them or about yourself, so networking is an experience that will benefit your career. You don't have to become friends with anyone you meet, but can send an invite to connect your LinkedIn profiles so you can reach out later if you want to or if you have something interesting to share.

• *Reframe what you name it.* I personally don't think of it as networking when I go to an event I'm interested in. I now trust my ability to connect with others when I find something meaningful to talk about. As you've noticed, it took me time and constantly pushing out of my comfort zone to get here, but I'm confident you can too. Are you? Like me, you can be very selective to which event you put your time into, and prepare yourself before going there.

• *Set a time limit.* Introverts are more sensitive to external stimuli than extroverts, so set a time limit to stay at an event. Pay attention when you lose patience or become overwhelmed, so you can leave when you need to. Give yourself a pat on the back when you're outside, you made it! :-) Also, choose places with less noise if you can.

• *Introverts see more things and perceive them more deeply than extroverts.* Pay attention to your own feelings as a filter to select events and people you'd like to connect with.

• *Claim a specific task.* Introverts get easily overwhelmed in large groups. If you're asked to collaborate, claim a specific task you'd like to take on so you have something to focus on, and shed off the other overwhelming inputs.

• *Introverts have a good ability to analyze others' behavior, and tend to take on an advisor role.* When you talk with someone, tapping into this strength will make you more at ease and take the pressure off of you.

• *As paradoxical as it might seem, introverts make good leaders.* If you can be in charge of organizing an event it will be easier for you to connect with people because you'll be there serving others (instead of focusing on yourself). Then you can follow up with an email or via social media, if you want to stay connected.

• *Introverts have a tendency to observe first, then get involved.* Take your time to familiarize yourself with the what's going on, and choose whatever works for you. Hitting the door might not be the best option. :-) If you've already taken the time to get there, make the most of this experience.

• *Do some research before you go somewhere*, if you can: who will be there, what the event is about, who is organizing it, etc. It'll give you some topics to rely on if you want to start or participate in a conversation.

• *Introverts ask thoughtful questions.* Remember that face-to-face interaction creates more trust than writing or online conversations. Introverts do well in one-on-one conversations, especially when they rely on their capacity to ask thoughtful questions. It's a great way to make a good impression, and you never know who might benefit from your capacity to make others think more deeply.

• *Quality is more important than quantity* when it comes to human interactions. One good connection made at a networking event is better than a handful of business cards collected.

• *Heated conversations?* Introverts have a tendency to avoid conflict, while extroverts (having a more competitive attitude) welcome heated conversations. Instead of avoiding such conversations, express your point of view first (before you withdraw). The others need to hear it; otherwise you leave space for them to make assumptions about you (and feel misunderstood).

• *Explore real-life scenarios in your mind,* to help you be better prepared for an event: How would you like to react when someone approaches you, when someone asks what you do, when you're interested in talking with a specific person present there, etc.?

• *Focus on one task at a time.* Multitasking doesn't fit introverts well. To be more present and avoid being overwhelmed, focus on one task at a time: either active listening or talking.

• *Share your unique point of view.* With your ability to think thoroughly, you might have a unique point of view. Share it! This way, you might be surprised how easy it is to help others understand you better!

• *Self-talk helps!* If you start feeling overwhelmed and you can't leave yet, self-talk helps to calm you down: find something you care about, a reason why it's good to stay there, or start thinking about something you like or you're interested in.

• *Friendly environment.* Introverts open up a little more and like the people they meet in a friendly context. Choose such opportunities to help you feel more at ease. Events where you can meet people who have the same interests and hobbies as you could be a great place to meet new, interesting people. In such environments, you can more easily connect since you share common interests. And the people you'll meet will be more friendly and open to helping you if you have something in common they can relate to.

Where to Network

In my workshops after I mention the benefits of networking and give some tips, I'm often asked, "How do I tap into the power of networking for my job search?" "How do I find events to attend?" "How do I grow my network?"

Here are some suggestions:

• **Personal connections** (family members, friends, neighbors, etc.). Start with the people close to you and ask for any information and advice they have to help you reach your short-term goal. Also mentioning your long-term goal will help them come up with more ideas and maybe connections that can help you further. This is an indirect way to let them know you're looking for a job, without them feeling pressured to help.

• **Social connections.** People you've met in different situations (like volunteering) and stayed in contact with, members of social clubs you're part of, your doctor, dentist, etc.

• **Professional connections.** Your current or former colleagues (school, university, courses, workshops), members of current or previous professional associations you're part of, employers, clients, other job seekers, etc.

• **Events.** Choose and participate at various events to meet people in your field or who could help you with advice, information, and connections:

- Events organized by professional associations and various organizations

- Conferences, workshops, presentations

- Job fairs

- Becoming member of a committee

- Volunteering your time

- Events organized by Meetup groups

- Various events on the Eventbrite website

- Activities and events based on your interests

Want more examples?

1. I met Zara when I joined a hike organized by a local hiking club. She approached me during one break. We talked a little, only to find out that she was looking for a job. She was frustrated by the poor responses she had gotten, and didn't know what else to do. Yet she didn't seem willing to listen to my suggestions, embracing that "I know it all!" attitude. We exchanged coordinates, but I didn't hear from her for a while. When she finally sent me a message via LinkedIn, she was happy about her new position and thanked me for the advice I had given her, mentioning that my advice made all the difference! I was happy for her, reminding myself that people are impacted by what we say even they don't seem like it when we talk with them (remember the 2 percent).

2. If you're not familiar with the Meetup website, check it out. It's a website where you can find groups in your area based on your specific interests. These groups organize events where you can meet other people with whom you share the same interests, making it easier to connect (even for an introvert). That's what Claude did: He went to an event organized by the Try New Things Meetup group. While there, he talked with a few people, and one of them happened to work in a company that need someone bilingual, like Claude. Five days later Claude was already the employee of that engineering company, hoping that in a short time he would be able to step into an internal engineering position according to his background.

3. While visiting a job fair, Aron talked with a recruiter. Impressed by his background, the recruiter referred Aron to another recruiter who needed someone with his experience. Shortly after, Aron start working for the company who was the second recruiter's client!

4. While I organized job fairs, I witnessed similar situations:

- Anton answered my call for volunteers, and he did a great job spreading out flyers in the city. He also came to help us update our social media profiles the day of the job fair, but he didn't want to go to the job fair: "I'm not ready," he said. I insisted he go at least to make a tour, to familiarize himself with such events so he would be better prepared next time. He finally accepted to go, and guess what? While stopping at one of the bank's booths, the company representative liked his attitude and asked a few questions about his background. Two days after, Aron told us that he received an invitation to a job interview; then he was hired as a project manager!

- By the end of a job fair, I talked with a few recruiters and company representatives, asking how their experience was and if they got any good candidates. One of them mentioned that his biggest challenge was hiring an IT professional with a bilingual background. I smiled, asking him to wait a second. Then I introduced Laure (one of our volunteers) to him, she had exactly the background he was looking for. Yes, Laure got hired!

- Clara also answered out call for volunteers. I liked her personality, and I suggested he take on the role of volunteer coordinator. "I'm an introvert; I've never had such role!" she mentioned, a little frightened. I assured her that I was close by and she could reach out to me anytime if she needed help. She ended up enjoying her new role! Even more, soon after that they opened a position in the organization I was working for, and she was one of the first who found out. She was able to stand out among other candidates, and I was happy to give her a good reference because she did a great job while volunteering at that job fair!

5. When Claire came to my workshops, she needed a job as soon as possible. She was shy, and hardly opened up during my workshops, but she was all ears. I liked her personality. She was nice to talk to and a very pleasant person. She was a laboratory technician, but was unsuccessful in finding a job in her field. I encouraged her to take a proactive approach for her job search, to play to her strengths. A week after the last workshop she sent me an email: She had started to work for the salad bar at a hospital. She was hoping to get inside connections, to be able to find a position in her field. Do you notice how she aligned her short-term strategy with her long-term objective?

6. I already told you how Alley was approached at a Starbucks he frequented, just because he went there often and was dressed for the position he was looking for. That Starbucks was in the financial district, and he was able to make some connections this way.

7. Jimmy, the tall guy who happened to use the computer close to my desk, also benefited from enlarging his network (instead of sending applications from home).

And two examples from my own experience:

8. Volunteering my time with an organization helped me find a position with them three years down the road, when I shifted my career to coaching. I reached back out to them, and they offered me the opportunity of a job interview. It was a position that suited my short-term goal well, and I was able to outperform the other candidates.

9. One day I was in the mood to get out of my cocoon, so I checked the Eventbrite website for current events. That's how I found out about the launching event of a new organization. For some reason I was attracted to that event, so I followed my intuition. It was well organized, and I was introduced to a few people until the event started. One of the those who attended that event was a recruiter that I briefly saw at another event. This time we had the chance to chat a little more, and new opportunities came out of that simple discussion.

Now that you understand how effective networking can be, even for introverts, here is one last note about networking: Do your best, and let the opportunities come your way as a bonus, instead of expecting them to come and getting disappointed if they don't. Because not every networking opportunity might lead to situations like the ones I mentioned here.

By now, I hope you understand better that including networking in your job search strategy could be beneficial — even for an introvert!

Let others help you the way they can. It'll make them feel good about themselves by making a difference in someone else's life: yours!

Chapter Eleven

ATTITUDES FOR EFFECTIVE COMMUNICATION

People may hear your words, but they feel your attitude.
~ John C. Maxwell

While listening to someone talking, have you ever been bothered by the person's attitude?

As John C. Maxwell said, people feel your attitude while listening to your words. And when what they feel gives a different message than your words, they trust their feelings more. Communication extends beyond the words we're using!

Do you remember the three levels of communication from the chapter 5, about mindset?

They are communication with yourself, with others, and with the world.

In that chapter we focused on the communication with yourself: how to identify your limiting beliefs and then replace them with more empowering perspectives to avoid sabotaging yourself during the job hunt.

In this chapter we'll focus on the second level: communication with others.

You'll learn eight attitudes for effective communication, and how introverts like you can apply them effectively in the context of your job search.

As Winston Churchill noted, attitude is a little thing that makes a big difference! And it's also true in the context of job hunting.

In a discussion, people usually focus on what they want to say. They rarely pay attention to how they behave while talking. I call this a default behavior. It might serve the person or not in a specific situation, but it is what shows up without thinking.

If you want to be more effective in your communication with others, attitude is a great place to start. In the context of this chapter, I define as "attitude" a stance you **deliberately** take, a way you consciously choose to approach a situation. Think of it as a "jacket" you deliberately put on to help you focus on the desired outcomes while carrying on a conversation.

Below you'll find the eight attitudes I'd like to make you more familiar with, and how I describe them in the context of job hunting. You can get more information in Marita Fridjhon's book *Creating Intelligent Teams: Leading with Relationship Systems Intelligence*. I encourage you to use them often during your job search and in your other relationships and notice what difference they make:

1. **Respect**
2. **Curiosity/Awareness**
3. **Deep Democracy**
4. **Caring**
5. **Collaboration**
6. **Gratefulness**
7. **Commitment**
8. **Lightness**

1. *Respect*

This attitude has two aspects: respect for others and respect for yourself!

Even if you don't agree with someone's opinion, accepting it simply means that you have respect for the person voicing it. This doesn't necessarily mean you agree with it! When people express their opinion, they believe they are right! And they are, but only partially: from their own perspective! :-) And that's all they know, usually.

In the context of an information interview, when you're the one who initiates the discussion, showing respect for your interlocutor's opinion encourages the person to share more. Cutting the person off or having the "I know it all attitude" won't help you get the most of that interview and the time spent there. Even when you disagree on something, it would be more useful to embrace curiosity and ask the reason why the person considers that point useful. You might learn something new!

Respect is also about setting your own boundaries and respecting others'. How many times do you say yes to someone, when what you really wanted to say was no? Respect your time and the other barriers you set for yourself, and others will learn to respect them as well. When it comes to job hunting, you can set boundaries about how much time you allot per day to your job search, to yourself (to replenish your energy), and to those you're in touch with, so you don't become tired and overwhelmed (which will affect your productivity and the way you show up when you need to be at your best, like in job interviews).

2. Curiosity/Awareness

Being curious is an invitation to ask questions. While you can ask the question to yourself, in your communication with others it is useful to ask questions as well. Their answers will increase your awareness about what's going on and what else you can find out, understanding beyond your own personal point of view.

Instead of mulling in your head and assuming, ask questions to let other people share their own point of view. This way you'll also better understand their way of thinking and perspective about the situation.

During a workshop, I noticed two participants talking between themselves in a low voice. Instead of assuming they were not interested in what I was saying, I asked what was going on. When they shared what they were talking about, we all learned something useful and new. Assuming what's going on is not the best way to communicate.

Don't be afraid to ask questions, even in a job interview. It shows your interest for the position, and helps you understand their company better.

BTW, asking a question is a great way to start a conversation, taking the pressure off of you.

3. Deep Democracy

This attitude is about encouraging everyone to voice their ideas and opinions, including yourself!

The negative people might not express themselves in the most skillful way, but the ideas behind their words could be very valuable. The same goes for shy and introverted people: just because they prefer to listen, it doesn't mean they cannot contribute positively to a conversation. Encouraging everyone to voice their opinion is another way to understand the

different aspects of a problem. And with the increased awareness coming from understanding the different opinions, the solutions are easier to find and implement. That's why I often encourage you to understand the employers' and recruiters' points of view.

With this in mind, you have my permission (if you need it) to share your ideas in a conversation, not just stay in your comfort zone (listening, thinking). How would can others understand who you are and how you can contribute if you stay in your cocoon because you're not comfortable talking about yourself)? In the context of job hunting, it is important to open up a bit more in what conditions you choose to. Don't worry, this will not make you an extrovert! You'll still need time to recover, but you'll help the world better understand your wisdom and abilities!

4. Caring

While you're talking with someone, being fully present in the moment shows that you're caring: you're interested in what the other person is saying, even if you don't fully agree with it. You're putting your heart into it, so to speak. I'm sure you've experienced how frustrating it is when you're talking to someone and the person's mind is somewhere else, haven't you?

Being fully present in a conversation means active listening: paying attention to the words being said, and also noticing the nonverbal cues (attitude, tone of voice, body posture, and so on). All these will make you a better listener and help you better understand than just listening to the words — or even worse, letting the words touch your ears while your mind is somewhere else. People notice when you're actively listening. This makes a good impression and shows respect for the other person.

Active listening gives you clues about what's going on with the other person, allowing you to adjust how you'll react to what is being said.

Do you realize how important it is to practice active listening during a job interview, for example? You can get clues about how your answers land with the employer, and adjust your next answers accordingly.

When clients approach me for simulation interviews, they expect me to give them advice. How do I start? By asking what they think they need to improve, based on what they know about themselves and what they've noticed during the previous job interviews (what worked well and what didn't). They don't expect my question, but after pondering it for a few moments, they come up with something they' be interested on working on based on their specific needs.

5. Collaboration

Bringing in the attitude of collaboration increases productivity and gets things done faster. It's a way for team members to communicate that they care about the achievement, and achieving it together. What happens when one of them doesn't collaborate? Or more? The project is affected!

"I don't collaborate with anyone during my job search project," you might say. "I'm on my own!" Really? It might be the case right now, but that doesn't mean you cannot collaborate!

Take an information interview, for example: You collaborate with the interviewee by allowing the other person to give you advice, and helping the way you can — so you both feel good and inspired to continue your own projects!

A job interview can be seen as a collaboration between the employer and the candidate, to assess each other's strengths and willingness to work together. It's a power game only if you allow it to be that way. You might want to land a job as soon as possible, but if the employer considers, based on what YOU are able to show so far, that you cannot help them enough, they will not hire you. How does that feel, knowing that you do play a role in the decision they make? Does it motivate you to project a more accurate image of what you can do and how you can help them?

6. Gratefulness

People often get caught in their own opinion or assumption, and they overlook what's positive about the other and the situation they're in together. Being able to see and be grateful for whatever is an important attitude that can improve communication.

Over a forty-year time span John Gottman, professor emeritus in psychology, conducted research with thousands of couples. What did he discover? A positivity/negativity (PN) ratio of 5 to 1 is beneficial in creating a reliable relationship. Do you understand now why it's hard to be around people with a negative attitude?

During the first meeting between a mentor and mentee, the mentor offered free access to his mentee for his online course (a value of hundreds of dollars). The mentee didn't even say, "Thank you!" How would you feel if you were the mentor? How open would you continue to be with your mentee if you encountered such behavior?

Questions for you to ponder:

• What's the PN ratio of the relationship you have with yourself? That ratio influences your ability to conduct an effective job search. For example: if you don't trust yourself enough, the other will pick that up, and it will affect their trust in you.

• What's the PN ratio of the relationship with your previous employer? If you're too negative, instead of appreciating the opportunity that position brought to you, that will come up in the way you talk about your previous employer. And the potential new employer could think that's an attitude you'll have toward them too, affecting their decision.

• What's the PN ratio you bring to a conversation with someone you've just met? A positive attitude will take you further for sure. People like to be around positive people.

7. Commitment

What does commitment have to do with communi-cation in the context of job hunting? A lot!

From the perspective of your career path, how committed are you to making this path meaningful to you, and enjoying the ride along it? Because if you don't, your communication will suffer, affecting your job search negatively.

From the perspective of communicating with others, being committed to making your job search a successful project will increase your motivation and assertiveness, both of which are appreciated by the people you meet and employers. Are you more drawn into a conversation with someone who's committed, or someone who doesn't care about the topic discussed?

How committed are you to making your job hunting as effective as possible? If you're not, you're sending a message to yourself that it's okay to just respond to online job postings. From what you've read until now, is this really the best way to find a job?

8. Lightness

What I mean by lightness in this context is putting things in perspective and not taking yourself too seriously. In a discussion, you might think you're right and want others to accept your opinion as is, but that's only your perspective about the topic. Others might have a different perspective (based on how they see the world and their previous experiences). By not being open to their opinions, the discussion could stop there making you miss some interesting points that otherwise might broaden your perspective.

How many times have you witnessed people so rigid in the opinions they literally look stiff? How did you feel at that moment? How much were you willing to continue the discussion with such person? If you didn't feel good in the presence of such person, then don't be one of them when you're talking with others.

In the job search context, you should hold your opinions about the job market, for example more lightly, because you don't know everything. Having a negative opinion about your skills and expertise, and why an employer should not hire you, will not serve you either. Because coming from such a perspective, you'll unconsciously project that image and you'll rip the corresponding results! That's why I included a whole chapter about mindset in this book.

In some workplaces, people expect you to smile when meeting others. Some people consider it a fake smile and don't want to play this "game". Actually, studies shows that smiling reduces stress. A work environment could be stressful in itself, with all the deadlines and pressure to perform well. Add to that the stress of each employee's personal life, and you get a better picture how heavy the work environment could be without taking specific measures to reduce its weight. Help yourself and others by smiling more often. If you pay attention, smiling when you're too serious about something reduces that rigidness and makes you more inclined to listen to others' opinions, and they open up more to listen to yours.

I had a colleague from another department who was so serious all the time that people stayed away from him. One day we happened to take the same course, and I asked why I never saw him smile: "I'll smile when I'll achieve my goal!" he answered. "But you achieve small goals every day, so you can find reasons to smile more often," I replied. He nodded his head, and smiled, saying, "You're right!" His face lighted up when he smiled, and he looked much more approachable! Imagine how much he had missed by being so serious all the time?

Just because you're looking for a job doesn't need to make you so serious that you're not approachable anymore. Put things in perspective a little! :-) Introverts tend to stay in their head a lot, mulling things over, but if you take the time to reconnect with the outside world, you discover help and support out there — and smiling will help you connect easier!

Wheel of Attitudes

Okay, by now you have a better idea of these eight attitudes of effective communication. Let's put them in a wheel to do some exercises. Grab your notebook to jot down the answers.

Exercise 1: Quick check, how many of these above attitudes are you already using while you're job hunting?

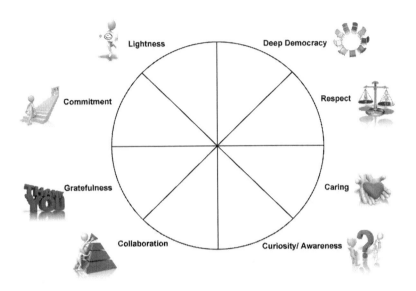

Exercise 2: Now take the time to "walk" the wheel of attitudes, going around and experiencing each of them. Notice the feeling each of them brings in you when you take it on consciously. Think of how you used it in the past and the benefits it brought. Also think of what the benefits of using them more in your job search could be.

Exercise 3: From these eight attitudes, which one do you consider your strength (you're very comfortable with and use it more often)?

If you have more than one, just pick one for now.

Exercise 4: Now take the time to "walk" the wheel of attitudes again, and notice which one you consider your weakness. There are situations when you need to use this attitude, even if it's not your strength. What action can you take to become more skilled at using it? What would remind you to take that action? Put that reminder wherever it needs to be to help you take the required action. You might want to work on this before a situation occurs where this attitude could help you make a difference. Why? If it's a weakness, your default behavior will show up in that situation (where it is needed), and you'll be so caught up in what you're doing you won't remember (unless you practiced it enough before, until it becomes a second nature).

I used this wheel in my workshop called Attitudes for Effective Communication. After putting some tape on the floor to resemble the wheel, and labelling each area, I invite the participants to literally walk the Wheel of Attitudes to get a sense of each of them. Then I invite them to stop in the area corresponding to the biggest strength and say a few words about what that attitude means to them. In one of these workshops, a participant stopped in the Caring area: "This is my strength!" she declared, satisfied. A second after she added: "Oh, this is also my weakness! Because I often give too much heart and forget about myself!"

As you see, in each situation an attitude could be fully present, present to a certain degree, or not at all present. Depending on the situation, you might want to adjust the level of the attitudes you're using, to be able to communicate more effectively.

When participants stop in different areas corresponding to their strengths, I invite them to consider themselves a team and to notice which of the attitudes are present in their team and which are missing. The exercise is quite revealing, helping participants understand each other's strengths.

You can do this exercise with a real team or group you're a part of, to see how interesting it is. After looking at the strengths, each participant can choose the weakness and look around. This way, you can not only understand each other's weaknesses and help each other improve, but you can also leverage each other's strengths!

How does the Wheel of Attitudes and identifying your strengths and weaknesses apply to the job search process?

When you're about to go to an information interview or job interview, for example, go through these attitudes and see how they inform the situation: Which one will you need to use more? Which one less? How you can approach the discussion to be beneficial for both parts? (How could commitment and collaboration play a role in this situation)? What do you need to remind yourself to be in the moment (instead of in your head, judging yourself) and to be grateful for the opportunity? What questions can you prepare in advance, to remove the pressure and stress during the interview? How can you be respectful of the others and yourself? What do you need to say about yourself, and in what way, so the others can better understand you and your abilities? What reminder do you need to not take yourself too seriously and forget that this is only another experience (helping you learn and improve)?

Exercise 5:

a) Assessing a Situation

As with the previous wheel, the Wheel of Attitudes can also be used as an assessment for a situation.

Think of a situation related to your job hunt, that involves at least one more person. Put the situation in the middle of the wheel, and look at it from different perspectives (the attitudes we're talking about). For example, how does the situation look from a deep democracy perspective? Do you allow your voice to be heard? Do you make an effort to understand the other's point of view?

What do you notice? What actions can you take to improve the situation?

Many people take the situations or others' behavior for granted and fall into the victim role: "I can't do anything about this!"

The truth is, you can do something, and you should start by stopping to consider yourself a victim of the system!

I could keep saying things here, but the most important is to find your own answers. Use this tool and the others I present in this book, to make things change in your favor, to find your own solutions! There's a reason I put the captain's hat on the wheel. It's your hat! Take it and your captain role back in the play called your job search project! And as a good captain does, adjust what needs to be adjusted to help you move ahead toward your destination.

b) Assessing a Project

You can also use the Wheel of Attitudes for your job search project, considering the relationship you have with your career. What is the wheel revealing to you in this situation? Which attitudes are present, missing, or not present enough in your job search?

When Lili attended the Attitudes of Effective Communication workshop and walked the wheel thinking of her job search project, she realized that her commitment was not strong enough to her job search. "I'm not as assertive as I should be," she declared, surprised by what she had discovered. Then she "collaborated" with herself to find way to be more assertive, and it paid off: She was hired after two and a half weeks of doing information interviews!

Do the exercise yourself, to see what you discover: What's lacking? What's not enough? Which attitudes do you need to adjust to make your job search project more effective?

This wheel helps you identify what's missing in a situation and apply the attitudes more consciously to increase your chances of success.

Let me give you a few more examples of how poorly used attitudes could affect your job hunting results:

• Curiosity: Take a moment to notice how you feel when you say, "I don't know how to sell myself." How much energy does it give you? Instead of saying this to yourself, switch to curiosity and start asking questions like: "How can I present myself in a way that is true to myself but also projects the right image of my background and what I can offer?" How does this feel? Does it make you get out of your comfort zone to find the answer?

• Respect: Isn't believing that the employer has all the power disrespectful to yourself? What if the employer needs your ability to solve the problem they have? Aren't you doing them and yourself a disservice by not trusting your own power?

• Deep Democracy: Wouldn't looking at the job search only from your (job seeker) perspective limit your ability to understand the bigger picture (including the employers' perspective) and meet them in the middle?

• Heart: In an information interview, wouldn't focusing too much on your inner world make you disconnected from what's really going on? What I mean by "focusing too much on your inner world" is worrying about your mistakes, what you should say next, or focusing on your fears instead of being in the moment so you can notice if your interlocutor is excited, intrigued, or bored by your discussion. Picking up these clues could help you understand what to say next.

• Lightness: Considering yourself a victim of the system (not enough job in my field, there are many candidates better than me, I'm not as good as an extrovert at selling, etc.) will only make you feel worse. Lighten up by putting things in perspective! How many other introverts have found jobs. So will you if you don't hang on to the victim perspective.

• Collaboration: Instead of closing yourself in your cocoon, think of who could collaborate with you, so you could help each other reach your goals? Reach out to them; they might be waiting for someone like you too!

• Gratefulness: Are you counting your blessings every day for what you've learned, what went well, what you already have? An attitude of gratefulness will open your heart so you can receive what you need. Otherwise you might not even recognize an opportunity in disguise.

• Commitment: How committed are you to reaching your goals when you allow yourself to get discouraged during the process of reaching them?

Now, that you know how to improve your interpersonal communication, let's move on to how you can use social media for your job hunting.

Chapter Twelve

SPEED UP YOUR JOB SEARCH WITH SOCIAL MEDIA

Social media is the ultimate equalizer.
It gives a voice and a platform to anyone willing to engage.
~ Amy Jo Martin

I have designed and delivered many workshops on social media along the years, for both small business owners and job seekers.

As a side note, it's interesting how I got into this. :-) A few years ago, I saw a flyer about a workshop on the topic of social media for job seekers. Being a curious person, I wanted to sign up, although I had already been using LinkedIn for about four years (over five hundred connections), had a constant presence on Facebook, and had over four thousand Twitter followers at that time. (I didn't get there overnight, so don't panic if you're not there.) Before the workshop, I started researching information about the presenter, only to find out that she was a communication specialist with only one LinkedIn connection and five Twitter followers. My interest in her workshop dropped suddenly. She might be a great communicator, but I simply didn't trust her expertise in social media. In my eyes, she wasn't credible anymore because she wasn't walking her talk! "How can someone who obviously doesn't use social media understand its potential and pitfalls for job search?" I asked myself. All of a sudden, I realized how much I had to say about this topic based on my experience with social media for professional advancement, so I start delivering workshops on social media! :-)

Later on, I was at a conference with my colleagues, and one of the presenters talked about social media. His background was impressive, years of experience at a well-known computer company, but what he did was walk us (via a Power-Point) through the steps of creating a profile on various social media websites. That was so boring that even my colleagues got annoyed (some looked at me saying that I should be giving a presentation about this topic). :-)

Why did I share these with you? To show you how important it is to walk your talk in a world where people have access to a lot of information via the Internet.

If you're not on social media at all, people might ask why, what do you have to hide? If you are, you should pay attention to what image your social media profiles and activity projects.

Before you roll your eyes because you don't believe in social media as an effective strategy for job search, or you're one of the introverts who don't want to use it at all, please read this chapter first. You can discard this strategy later if you still consider it not useful.

If you're already an experienced social media user, I'm confident you'll learn something new and helpful as many participants at my workshop did. Here's what one said: "For those that don't know LinkedIn, this workshop presented an excellent tool for networking. For the others, we discovered many tips and tricks to better use this website to obtain the information and contacts we need."

As an introvert, my main reason for using these platforms is similar to Guy Kawasaki's: "Social media allows me to pick my times for social interaction."

This way I can increase my visibility, network to meet and interact with people on my own terms and time, from the comfort of my home (coffee shop, library), without directly interacting with a human being. How does that sound to you? :-)

My approach to social media is more strategic: start with your end goal in mind, and "walk" your way toward it. It's a more proactive and effective way to use social media, even for job search.

What struck me when I designed my workshops on social media was the similarities between the needs of small business owners and job seekers, at least how I see them. But then, when I started my workshop by asking small business owners what they need to grow their business, the answers were usually "money and clients," while the job seekers answered they need job postings in order to land a job!

To me, the answers of these two categories look more like the outcomes of what I believe they actually need to get there: a long-term objective (with a short-term goal aligned with it), access to opportunities, a successful mindset, more visibility, trustworthiness, connections, relationships, feedback, recommendations, a good reputation, new ideas, and staying up to date.

Although I touched on these topics in the previous chapters, I'll explain again briefly why I consider these elements important for an effective job search for introverts:

• Long-term objective (with a short-term goal aligned with it): Knowing what you want before you actually start looking is crucial. Otherwise you might get lost in the process.

• Access to opportunities: They might not be direct job postings, but these they could lead to finding the job you want sooner or later. Not paying attention to opportunities other than job postings is a mistake that often makes the job search process longer and more frustrating.

• Successful mindset: What's the point of having access to a job posting if you don't have the right mindset to create a good application, enough confidence to pass the interview, and the belief that you can actually do well at the job?

• More visibility: Being more visible increases your chances of finding what you want.

• Trustworthiness: Even in a world where Internet is easily accessible, people do trust their own opinion about someone else. Taking the time to build trust pays off.

• Connections: How far can you reach by yourself? The jobs you're looking for might not be in your reach, so making connections multiplies your chances of reaching them.

• Cultivate relationships: Both personal and professional relationships benefit from treating people well, as a two-way "street" not a "hit-and-run."

• Feedback: Asking for and receiving feedback is valuable so you can adjust your strategies to better suit your goals.

• Recommendations: What others say about you has more value in someone else's eyes than what you say about yourself.

• Good reputation: Building a good one helps gain someone's trust before actually meeting that person.

• New ideas: Being open to new ideas during your job search makes the process more effective.

• Staying up to date in your field: Being up to date denotes adaptability and being open to learning, both of which are important to gain trust and set you apart from someone who relies only on previous expertise.

What do you think, do you need all these for a more effective job search?

If you think your do, I'll show you how to use social media to get all of them except the first one (only you can define your long-term objective and the aligned short-term goals).

Okay, so let's get started.

First, what do you think social media is?

Many of my clients consider social media a way to network or communicate with people, while I consider these to be benefits of using social media. And there are many others benefits.

I like Joel Comm's definition from his book *Twitter Power*. Imagine you're in Hollywood and a film studio opens its door to allow people from the streets to get in and create their own movies. They are not professionals, but they use the platform (film studio) to add their content and create something.

That's how I see social media too: as platforms that allow users to create their own content. How they use these platforms further makes all the difference. Of course, there are different features from one platform to another, but what makes a real difference is what strategies the users employ while using those platforms: some strategies lead to much better results than others; some don't take them anywhere. One of the best way to use social media for job search is to combine it with the other strategies I presented in chapter 9.

If you search the Internet for "social media landscape", you'll find there are a lot of social media platforms besides those that are well-known (Facebook, Twitter, LinkedIn, Instagram, YouTube). Fred Cavazza groups the social media platforms into categories based on the main benefits users can get by using them: networking, collaborating, discussing, messaging, sharing, publishing. If you check his "social media landscape" you might be surprised by how many social media platforms you are not aware of, and that some of them are used for several benefits.

For your job search, it might be useful to find out which social media platforms are more used in your field By using the same platforms as others in your field, you increase your chances of having access to information specific to what you're looking for, and even to network with peers and recruiters interested in your field.

I'll let you discover which social media platform is used more in your area and in your specific field. And I'll share with you some tips and strategies to use with a few well-known social media platforms.

One word of caution though: If you plan to use these platforms, keep in mind the "social," interactive aspect of social media! While these platforms can be used for marketing to increase your visibility, HOW you will use them (what you do and what you say) will make the difference between people being interested in connecting with you and disconnecting because you're using social media in a traditional marketing way (like a broadcast to promote yourself).

Job Search Approach to Using Social Media

Before giving you more details, here's the approach I suggest when you want to use LinkedIn for job search:

1. Have in mind your short-term goal and long-term objective.
2. Define which strategies (listed in chapter 9) you'd like to use in your strategy mix.
3. Identify what you need (information, connections, advice, build trust, visibility, etc.) to make those strategies more effective.
4. Use LinkedIn to get what you identified at point 3. It's a similar approach with other social media, but you'll need to customize it according to that specific platform's features.

I found the LinkedIn platform very well fitted for making a job search more effective, but I'll also give you some suggestions for other social media platforms.

LinkedIn (linkedin.com)

With over four hundred million professional users all over the world, and growing, LinkedIn is well-known as a professional networking platform. Statistics show also that 85 percent of employers and recruiters are sourcing or verifying their candidates on LinkedIn, which makes it an important platform to consider for your job search.

If you're not familiar with it yet, I highly encourage you to create a profile and explore it a bit. You'll find a lot of professionals in your field to connect with, companies you can approach, job postings, groups, conversations (in groups), and more.

While writing this chapter, I had a big challenge. For my workshops on social media, I didn't have a handout, only a computer with Internet access and a screen. I was showing in real time how the participants could use LinkedIn for job search, and answering their questions on the go (which made me add additional information and customize the workshop according to their needs and level of knowledge on using social media). "Click here, click there to get this" was a simple approach to help them understand the power of social media, especially LinkedIn.

Due to copyright issues, I will not add LinkedIn screenshots to this book, and it might seem more difficult to follow with what I say. I suggest you login into LinkedIn while reading this section and follow along to understand my points.

If you don't yet have a LinkedIn profile, create a basic one quickly with your real name, email address, and a password of your choice.

Recently LinkedIn changed their website completely, the following information applies to the new website version.

What I will find below?

• A walk through a few important features you can use for your job search. LinkedIn keeps making changes to their website, so some of the features might not be easy to find. You can use the Help Center (found on the right side of Home page) to find them.

• Several tips and strategies on how to use LinkedIn in more proactive way (having your objective in mind) instead of a passive way (creating a profile and waiting to see if someone discovers it).

• Examples of how other job seekers successfully used LinkedIn to land a job.

• LinkedIn has different types of membership, but the tips and strategies I'll share can be used with the free membership.

• Below you'll find these points mixed up a bit, because it's hard to separate information about features from tips and strategies and examples without repeating myself. :-)

LinkedIn Profile and Connections

• Because LinkedIn is a networking platform, you'll have the opportunity to invite people to connect with you inside LinkedIn. This is possible right after creating a basic profile or any time after. Click My Network on the top menu, and on the following page you'll see the "Add Personal Contacts" section (on the left). You can either add the email of the person you want to add, or click on More Options to allow LinkedIn do what it knows best: find people who are connected with your email and show which of your email contacts you're not connected to on LinkedIn yet, so you can invite them to connect via LinkedIn as well.

• When Glenn learned this feature, he was so pleasantly surprised to see that he could reconnect with former colleagues and friends he hadn't been in touch for a long time! What a great way to become more aware of your existing network! Although he was an IT network administrator, Glenn didn't go beyond creating a basic LinkedIn profile and had previously thought there was not much else to do on the site.

• When people accept your invitations, they will become first-degree connections for your LinkedIn profile. You'll see a "1st" near their photo or name when you look at their profile or when their profile shows up in one of your searches inside LinkedIn.

• When you send an invite to connect with someone via LinkedIn (to become a first-degree connection), the person might check your profile before deciding to accept your invitation or not. I suggest you add more information to your profile (experience, education, summary, volunteer work, photo) before inviting people to connect, to make a good impression from the beginning with your well-crafted LinkedIn professional profile.

• Why add a photo? It's a common practice on LinkedIn. A professional-looking headshot could be to your advantage, and will also screen out those who might not be interested in connecting or communicating with you. You don't want to waste your time with such people, do you? No need to spend money on a professional photoshoot (unless you want to). Dress professionally and ask a friend to take you a few pictures in a well-lighted place. I bet that a little smile will make you look better in the photo. I also suggest you think about a project dear to your heart when you pose, so your face lights up and the photo projects good energy.

• If you have no idea what to put in your profile, start by adding elements from your resume (experience, education, volunteering). Then add what is the most important for your short-term goal in the Summary section (which will be seen just below your name). I highly encourage you to create your LinkedIn profile similar to a targeted resume, corresponding to what you want to achieve with your job search. Don't forget to include in your profile some keywords specific to your field.

• Some employers and recruiters are not interested in a candidate who is unemployed, because they think their skills are not up to date, or they fear you were fired for a reason not good for their business (and don't want to take the risk). To offset this aspect of being unemployed: based on your expertise, you can consider yourself a consultant during the unemployment period of time, and adjust your resume and LinkedIn profile accordingly.

• If you look at someone's profile and it shows "2nd," it means that both you and that person have a connection in common, but you cannot send a message directly to the second-degree connection (called a "shared connection"). You can also find "3rd" or no number beside a profile, which means there are two or more people between you and them, which makes it harder to reach them.

• If you're currently job hunting and want to make this visible to other people and recruiters, do the following:

> - Add "open to new opportunities" at the beginning of the "Summary" section of your profile.

> - Go to "Account/Settings & Privacy" (by clicking your photo in the top menu). Scroll down to the "Job Seeking" section and turn on the button for "Let recruiters know you're open to opportunities — Share that you're open and appear in recruiter searches matching your career interests".

Why Is Good to Have LinkedIn Connections

• Imagine you're a recruiter or employer and you end up on someone's profile that has only two or three first-degree connections. What would you think about this person? That this is someone who doesn't like to connect with others? Or is not familiar with the importance of the use of LinkedIn in the professional world? Either of these won't shed a good light on that profile, because recruiters are looking for people who want to collaborate with others and are up to date with what's going on in the professional world — and a small number of connections doesn't show any of these.

• For the first-degree connections, you can send them a private message (via LinkedIn) anytime, and you have access to their email address and website (if they add one). That's a great way to let them know you're looking for a new opportunity as (insert here your short-term goal) and ask for an information interview or advice, for example. Some might accept, and some won't even bother to answer. In the latter case it is better to move on, instead of insisting. There are so many others you can approach via LinkedIn, even if they are not direct connections.

• If a first-degree connection allows his own connections to be visible, you can browse those connections, and if you're interested in contacting (or connecting) with one of them you can ask your first-degree connection to introduce you. This is a great way to reach out to people you don't know directly: they might work for a company you're interested in or might accept your request for an information interview. To turn the visibility of your connections on or off, go to "Settings & Privacy" (when you click on your photo in the top menu).

• The more connections you have, the more you multiply your chances of reaching out to people you'd be interested in. For example, if your profile is connected with mine via LinkedIn (first degree), and I have 2,000 connections, you can ask me to put you in contact with any of my connections. And if you have another first-degree connection who has 300 connections, you can reach out to any of these 2,300 connections via us. And that's from only two direct connections! Imagine you have 200 direct connections and they have their own connections . . . Now can you see the power of having more LinkedIn connections?

• There are different ways to connect with people on LinkedIn, and I'll share a few in a bit. When I say "connect" in this context, I mean sending an invitation to someone via LinkedIn to connect your profiles. Keep in mind, if you send too many invitations the same day, LinkedIn might ban your profile considering that you're spamming others. They might ask you to read their policies and contact customer service after, if you want to be able to send invitations again. Been there, done that! :-) The LinkedIn platform was created on the principle that you should connect only with the people you know. With the growth of this platform, being used by many professionals worldwide, they are not so rigid anymore if you do it with moderation.

• Having LinkedIn connections is not like having friends that you have to communicate with all the time. But when you need something, you can reach out politely and ask. With so many professionals on LinkedIn, chances are you'll find people who are willing to connect with you, and even help. As a matter of fact, most of those who have a LinkedIn profile understand the power of networking (and tap into it for their own interest).

Search

By using the Search function (top left corner) you can search LinkedIn by entering keywords corresponding to what you're looking for. When you click on the magnifying glass (inside the Search area), you'll have the option to choose from additional categories (Companies, LinkedIn groups, Schools, Industry, Location, etc.)

• For example, by entering "engineers Toronto" as keyword in the Search area (without clicking on the magnifying glass) LinkedIn returned 64,176 profiles. I can be more specific if I want: "electric engineers Toronto" returned 4,261 results. Still more than enough to get me started, if I were an electric engineer looking for a job.

• What do I do next? I look at the list of profiles LinkedIn shows me. By reviewing each profile I can do the following:

- Find names of companies to add to my list: where they currently work or they worked previously, or companies they follow on LinkedIn.
- Look for a way to send a private message to those I'm I want to ask for an information interview or ask a simple question:

- If I see a "1st" near their name, I can send directly a private message via LinkedIn or an email.

- If it's a "2nd," I can ask the shared connection to forward my message. Another way to do it, is to click on the "…" near the person's profile picture and choose Connect (if LinkedIn shows this option, sometimes it does).

- I can join a group listed on someone's profile and send a private message via the group: If you scroll down the profile, you'll get to the "Interests" section. If "Groups" doesn't show up in that section, clicking on See All (bottom of Interests section) will open a separate window. There you can see what companies the person is following and of which groups is a member. Click on Groups, then on the name of the group you'd be interested in, then on Ask to Join (on the right). After you've been accepted as a member in the group, open the group again. Under the group name you'll see the number of members. Clicking on that number will take you to the search page for the members area. On the right, type the name you're looking for in the Search section, and you'll find a Message button near the name (when it shows up). It might seem difficult to get here, but if you do it once, it'll be much easier next time when you want to reach someone else via a group. At the time I'm writing this book, no paid membership is required to use this method.

- If, in the list of profiles from your initial search (by keyword) I see a "3rd" near the name, I'll click on the profile, then on the Connect button. If LinkedIn allows, I'll click on Add a Note specifying why I'd be interested in connecting with that person before pushing the Send button. A well-written personalized message increases the chances of the invitation being accepted. In that invitation, I would say something brief about their profile, and tell them why I am reaching out to them. If the person answers or accepts my invite, I will follow up with a Thank you message and ask for an information interview or the information I want.

- I could also search Google for more information about that person. Maybe I can find an email address to send my message to, mentioning where I found their email.

- "Send InMail" button near a name means you don't have direct connections or groups in common with that person. A paid membership with LinkedIn will include a number of "InMail" credits you can use each month to reach out to the people you cannot reach out to directly. If one person approached this way doesn't answer, LinkedIn will return that credit to your account so you can reach someone else. I personally was able to create more than two thousand direct connections without using the InMail feature.

- Looking at the profiles returned by the Search feature, I could also get ideas on how to improve my own profile. I was giving the workshop on social media to a group of marketing professionals, when someone asked me to look at her profile and suggest ways for improvement. With her permission, I found her profile and opened it up so all the participants could come up with feedback. Being in the same field (marketing) her peers came up with really great suggestions! She was right: her profile didn't portray her very well and didn't show she walks her talk (as a marketing professional). Don't underestimate the power of your peers or asking for feedback, even from someone not in your field! Another participant at that workshop sent me his website and asked for a review. The website showed several of the big projects he had worked on, with great accomplishments. What I noticed though was this: each project started with a description, followed by his accomplishments (visible only if you were interested enough to scroll down). From an employer perspective, I would be more interested in reading about the accomplishments first, then about the project description! If I'm busy and not willing to scroll down, I wouldn't see what a great candidate he is just by reading a few words at the beginning of each project. So I encourage you to use the ideas learned in the other chapters even when you're using social media. Putting yourself in the reader's shoes and looking from that perspective at your profile; updating it accordingly will help you reap more benefits from using social media!

• Do you know what LION means in this context? Unless it's their name or company's name, LION means LinkedIn Open Networker. Some people love networking so much that they are open to accepting connections from anyone via LinkedIn, and they add LION to their profile. Usually they are the ones with the biggest number of connections as well. And you know what that means? If you connect your profile with them, you'll get many second-degree connections! Sometimes LinkedIn even allows you to send an invite to connect with second-degree connections. And when they accept, you're increasing your number of connections so you can reach more people without going out! :-) I encourage you to use the keyword "LION" in the Search section, and invite those LIONs to connect. You'll never know what other opportunities might open up when you connect with them. Two LIONs helped me understand the power of LinkedIn. It was very beneficial, and I'm very grateful for that! I used to have LION mentioned in my profile, until I reached five hundred connections. Then I took it off, becoming more selective. I usually accept LinkedIn invites, unless the person has minimal information on their profile or less than five to ten connections.

• First invite people you already know, and add more information to your profile before inviting others to connect if you want to increase your chances of having your invitations accepted. Trust is something you need to gain even when using these virtual platforms like social media, especially LinkedIn, which is a platform used for professional purposes.

LinkedIn Recommendations

• Talking about trust, people tend to believe what someone else said about us (a third party) more than what we say about ourselves (directly, in a profile, social media updates, job applications). That's why having recommendations on your LinkedIn profile gives you more credibility and gains you trust more easily.

• You can ask former managers, teachers, colleagues, peers, and clients to give you recommendations, but to make them show up on your LinkedIn profile, you have to ask by using the LinkedIn platform. Go to your profile, and scroll down to see the "Recommendations" section, and on the top side of this section you'll see "Ask to Be Recommended." Click that link, choose who you'd like to ask for a recommendation (someone who already has a LinkedIn profile), add for which position you'd like to be recommended, customize the message for this person, and send! When someone receives your request for a recommendation and will write one, LinkedIn will notify you. At that point, you have the option to accept the recommendation (and show it on your profile or not), or ask for a rectification. Recommendations are a powerful way employers and recruiters can see how other people think about you, before they ever invite you to a job interview. How's that for introverts, who don't like to talk about themselves?

• The recommendations showing up on your profile are linked to the profile of the person who gave you the review. This way, anyone visiting your profile can also check out the profile of the person who recommended you. And if it seems like a trustworthy person, your profile will gain more trust too.

LinkedIn Endorsements

• A LinkedIn endorsement is one click away from anyone who visits your profile, someone who knows you usually, to acknowledge that you have a certain skill.

• Endorsements will show up in your profile in the "Featured Skills & Endorsements" section, which is a list of skills showing how many people acknowledged you have those skills, and a small image that links to their profiles.

• For someone who doesn't want to spend time reading the recommendations from your profile, the list of endorsements could be quite revealing.

• Endorsements are not requested. People choose to give them when they visit your profile. That's why being active on LinkedIn and inviting your own friends and acquaintances to connect via LinkedIn could help you get more endorsements.

LinkedIn Groups

• Anyone can create a LinkedIn group, but making it active requires investing a lot of time and energy.

• The groups can be open or closed, depending on how the group administrator (admin) or manager chooses it to be. Every group has a description, and if your profile doesn't fit with what the closed group is for, your request to join might be rejected. Anyone is accepted to join an open group, but you still have to request it.

• There are many groups already created that could benefit your job search, and even your career: groups related to your field, groups for job seekers, groups in your area, etc.

• The number of members is different from one group to another, and some groups are more active than others. Starting a conversation in an active group will help you get more responses.

• You can use the Search feature to find groups you'd be interested in. For example, if I type "engineer" as a keyword, the results page allows me to choose Groups in the top menu to see what groups have "engineer" in their description. My search returned about ten thousand groups. I could narrow the search by adding more keywords, if I want to be more specific. You can search by any keyword or combination of keywords you want.

• I encourage you to join several groups. You're allowed to be a member of one hundred LinkedIn groups. And if you find another one you're interested in or want to join to reach someone, just leave one of your groups and join the other one. Keep in mind that based on your settings, you might or might not receive email messages with updates from the groups you joined. To change which updates you'd like to receive, click on your image (top menu), go to Account/Setting & Privacy/Communications/Groups.

• To see in which groups you're already a member, click on Work (top right menu), to get to the "Groups" page. There you can see My Groups, and Discover (another way to search for groups).

Benefits of Joining and Being Active in LinkedIn Groups

• As I mentioned earlier, being in the same group allows you to contact another group member via a private message without being directly connected or knowing the email address. LinkedIn allows you to send up to fifteen private messages to group members per month with the free membership.

• You can participate in the conversations that are already created in a group, or start one. When I wanted feedback on the title of this book, I started a conversation in a group and received more than one thousand answers. It was a question that allowed me, indirectly, to make people aware about my upcoming book. This way, besides the great feedback and suggestions received, I also increased the visibility of my profile (some checked it out), and some group members expressed interest in buying my book when it's published.

• You can comment on other conversations to show your expertise, to help, or to provide your ideas and suggestions. It's a way to increase your visibility and share your ideas and opinions in a relaxed way, without feeling the pressure that you have to come up with something quickly (like in a direct conversation). You'll be surprised to see how easy it is to connect with people this way.

• You can start a conversation yourself, like Carl did when he was still in the UK. He started a conversation in a specialty group, mentioning his expertise and asking for advice on how to find a job in his field when he moved to Canada in six months. Not only did he receive great advice from peers and career specialists, but also someone even asked for his resume because she needed someone with his expertise in her company.

• You can't control the outcomes of your presence on LinkedIn, but rest assured there are many people willing to share their opinion and advice if you're genuine in your communication here (and on social media in general). Why not tap into this great resource? By following the advice and directions you get, you might get closer to your goal (getting the position you want). When I started a conversation in a very active group, I got also answers not related to my question. I was asking to choose between a few titles (for this book), and someone suggested that introverts should create a brochure for themselves and give it to managers. I thought it was an interesting job search strategy, so I am passing it along to you if you're interested in using it.

• Unlike the local groups, in the specialty groups you can find people from all over the world, which is okay: the diversity of ideas that pop up are quite interesting and useful, like in Carl's situation. Plus, you never know who is connected with who: Maybe someone from another country is connected with one of your peers in your city. While I'm in Canada, someone from the United States asked me to put him in contact with the person he wanted to reach in Hawaii (because my profile was connected with the Hawaii guy's profile). When a friend of mine wanted to share an idea with a Walmart VP, I used the strategies I have shared with you to reach someone this way: I mentioned why the person wanted to make the connection, and he agreed to discuss with my friend. LinkedIn is a powerful networking tool, as you see.

• Some groups might ask you to introduce yourself when you join the group. This is your opportunity to help others learn more about you (background and what you're looking for).

• All groups have the Conversations tab, but some have also a Jobs tab — check it out!

• There are many HR specialists and recruiters in groups, being very active when they have positions to fill. Many of them have a paid membership that allows you to reach out to people on LinkedIn without having a direct connection with them. Being active in groups (posting, responding) will make your profile more visible, and if someone wants to know more, your profile is only one click away.

LinkedIn "Jobs" Section

• LinkedIn has a special section for jobs. When you're logged in, you'll find it in the top menu.

• When you visit the "Jobs" page, you'll see some job suggestions from LinkedIn based on your profile. If you craft your profile in a way that's targeted toward what you want (not only showing the past), the suggestions will be more relevant to what you're looking for right now.

• When you browse the job suggestions, you'll see how LinkedIn makes it easier for you. I am looking at the "Jobs" page for my profile now, and it shows if I have connections who work for the companies who have these positions, if I'd be one of the first ten candidates to apply, and when the positions were posted. The more LinkedIn connections you have, the more you increase your chances of finding job postings where you have a connection who you can ask for advice and about the company's culture, the recruitment process, etc. And maybe the person will offer to send your application to HR.

• On the "Jobs" page you can also search job postings by title, keyword, company, and location. How cool is that?

• Some of the positions are only listed on LinkedIn, or listed there first, because employers can have direct access to the applicants' LinkedIn profiles.

• If you want the Premium membership, it allows you to see jobs where you'd be a top applicant if you applied.

What I Like the Most about Jobs Listed on LinkedIn

• When you click on the job posting, you'll land on the job page and see how many candidates already applied.

• From the job page, you can visit the company's website or LinkedIn page to see if they have other job openings.

• If you're interested in a job posting, from the job page go to the company's page and you'll see on the top right "See all (company name's) employees." By clicking on that link you'll get to a page that lists the LinkedIn profiles of their employees (who are on this platform). Browse the list to see which ones you're interested in connecting with to ask for information or advice, or about the company culture, company challenges, etc. Wouldn't that be useful for creating a more targeted application? Or to help you prepare for a job interview with that company? Sometimes you can even find the name of the manager of the department you're interested in. From the company's website you can find the address, and you'll have all you need to send your pain letter and resume by mail, if you want to use that strategy.

Find Companies via LinkedIn

• In the previous paragraph I told you how to get information about a company and their employees starting from a job posting listed on LinkedIn.

• You can also find companies directly by using the Search section from the top menu when you're logged in.

Here's an example: Using the keywords "engineer company" LinkedIn returned over seventeen thousand companies. I agree with you that not all might be in the geographical area I would be interested in, but have you considered that international companies might have a branch in your area while their LinkedIn page doesn't mention that? I could also narrow it down: "engineer company Toronto" returned fifty-one companies, quite a good start for a job search, especially since Toronto is not such an industrial area. Then I could visit the websites of these companies and their LinkedIn pages to see what job openings they have, who I can connect with for information interviews, who to send pain letters to, etc.

When Steve was looking for an engineering position in his field (renewable energy), he used these strategies to find companies. To showcase more of his experience, he created a simple website, and added the URL to his resume and LinkedIn profile. Then he was able to connect via LinkedIn with the recruiter of one of the companies he found this way, and the next thing I heard from him was, he got hired!

• Just because I give you examples about engineers doesn't mean you cannot apply the same strategies to whatever type of job you're interested in! I had participants in my workshops with all kind of backgrounds and expertise levels (including managers), who found these LinkedIn strategies very useful. One was Don, the social media marketing manager. The other was Lili, the newly graduated marketing specialist who moved into a new city and got hired within 2.5 weeks using LinkedIn to approach people for information interviews. Lisa found a position as a social worker using the same strategies.

• You can follow the companies you're interested in, by clicking the Follow button on their LinkedIn page, to get news about the companies and when they have new positions available.

LinkedIn "Home" Page and Status Updates

• When you log in on LinkedIn, you land on the "Home" page.

• Here you can see updates from your first-degree connections, like when they move to a new position, if they share something, etc. You can like and reply to these updates if you want, which brings your profile to their attention and helps build relationships.

• At the top of the page there is a section where you can post your updates, which will show up on your first-degree connections' "Home" page. This is a way to let them know what's going on with you or share something useful. For example:

> I'm looking for a position of _____ (fill in the blank). Any suggestions and ideas who I should approach in my job search?
>
> Just attended _____ presentation. What I loved most was _____.
>
> Great article on _____ (then add link).
>
> This company has many job openings for _____.
>
> Interested in _____? Check out this blog post (add link). It could be your own blog post, if you want to share your expertise and bring people to your blog/website.

• Besides reminding people about you, posting updates via your "Home" page will help people better understand who you are, in what you're interested, what you're looking for, etc. You'll project a better image of yourself if you share interesting articles and if people see your positive attitude and how active you are in building your own reputation . . . without even opening your mouth. :-) I received several invitations from my LinkedIn connections to do presentations or workshops, just because I gained their trust by sharing on LinkedIn interesting facts and lessons learned from my experiences each time I did a workshop or presentation. Through my updates, people noticed the progress I made, and they became more willing to invite me into their own networks.

• When I joined LinkedIn, years ago, the status update feature was not there. They created it to be similar to the Facebook profile update, and I have found it very useful as an introvert. It allows me to share things from my professional path without talking directly with a person, to build a reputation without interacting with people so much.

LinkedIn Articles

• This is another LinkedIn feature introduced recently. It allows you to write and post your own articles on LinkedIn, and they will show up on your profile. These articles can also be found through an Internet search by keywords, allowing people outside LinkedIn to find them too.

• In what way could these articles help your job search? They can show your expertise, your own unique point of view on certain topics, thus allowing you to gain the readers' trust more easily. And since they can be found on your profile as well, after the "Summary" section, they show your expertise in an indirect way, without you talking about it.

Messaging

• In the Messaging section (accessible via the top of the "Home" page), you'll see the messages you send to or receive from other LinkedIn members.

• If you send messages to ask for information interviews, I encourage you to not exchange too many messages via LinkedIn. When someone accepts, decide together which way you will go (meeting in person, talking on the phone, emailing) and try to get the discussion outside of LinkedIn (via email, for example) to discuss the details or follow up. You'll notice that after viewing the person's LinkedIn profile and the initial message exchange, you will feel more comfortable actually meeting the person or talking over the phone. They will not be a stranger anymore.

Things to Consider About LinkedIn

• I am aware that I have given you a lot of information, and it could be overwhelming. Take baby steps to understand these features, and use just one or two until you familiarize yourself with them, before adding more. I didn't learn all these overnight either! :-)

• With any social media platform (including LinkedIn) you have to be patient and perseverant to see results. Remember Aesop's fable "The Tortoise and the Hare," which was also portrayed in a famous Disney cartoon? If I were to draw a parallel between social media and traditional sales, I would see it as the race between the tortoise and the hare. With a slow and steady approach to social media, you can gain much more than if you focus only on mastering the sales techniques. That's why I don't agree with those introverts who consider themselves not good at sales: I think they compare themselves with the image of a talkative (maybe even aggressive) salesperson. Susan Cain mentioned in her book "Quiet" very successful introverts who are in sales or successful in negotiations. And that's because they have learned how to rely on their strengths such as researching well, asking thoughtful questions that draw people in, caring about the long term of a business relationship (not just the "hit-and-run" approach), and focusing on something they find meaningful to get the motivation to get out of their comfort zone and meet people, etc.

• Trying to get faster results with social media by using the same channel too much might lead to the opposite effect. Wouldn't you disconnect or unfollow someone who was posting too often, or only about himself, or using your connections too much?

• Varying the way you use LinkedIn and the type of content you share will help you get more out of it. You have several options: status posting, starting/responding to conversations in groups, approaching people (inviting to connect or sending a message), etc.

• LinkedIn does a good job of notifying you when someone accepts your invite to connect, when you get responses to the conversations you start in groups, when someone sees your profile, people you might know (if you want to invite them to connect, etc.). These are accessible through "Notifications" in the top menu. Sometimes you can see who visited your profile, so you can pay back the visit (maybe it's a recruiter you can connect with or someone you'd like to approach).

• Providing value through your posts and being curious are better received by others. If I want to share something about myself, I will choose an indirect way to do it. For example, I will mention what a participant learned from a certain exercise in a workshop, indirectly saying that I delivered that workshop. This way I can add value and talk about myself at the same time, without feeling like I am bragging.

• Commenting or responding to conversations is a way to express your opinion when you want to "socialize" a bit without actually meeting people. Even introverts feel the need to socialize sometimes, right? Why not do so in a professional setting, like LinkedIn, where you can give your input in deep, meaningful conversations. There are various points of view shared in a discussion, which could also be useful to you.

• If you want to list your LinkedIn profile on your resume and business card, it's nicer to get a nice URL. LinkedIn assigns an URL to each profile, but it has a series of numbers which make it longer and less pretty. You can make it shorter and nicer by going to your LinkedIn profile > Edit Profile > "Edit Profile URL" section (on the right side) > clicking the pen icon.

• Being able to edit your profile whenever you want is a useful LinkedIn feature. It allows you to update it when you want to change something (after receiving feedback, for example), or to add more specific keywords in the "Summary and Experience", or when you want to target it to a different position, etc. There are several settings regarding your profile that you can adjust: click on your small profile image (at the top) > Account > Settings & Privacy > Privacy. If you have many changes to make to your profile, I suggest making almost all of them with the "Sharing Profile Edits" off, then turn it on only for the last change. This way, your direct connections won't be bombarded with many updates at once.

• Headline: this is the line that comes under your name. It's more useful to create a punchy headline focused on the benefits of having your onboard, than a classical one listing your profession. For example, which one is more compelling: "Administrative Assistant" or "Decreasing the CEO's pressure to meet deadlines"?

Frequently Asked Questions from My Clients and Workshop Participants

• I'm not interested in LinkedIn.

  - It is your choice, but keep in mind that your competition might be and you might be left behind by not staying up to date with the current trend in recruitment.

  - Remember Nancy, the Google Analytics expert? When she understood the power of LinkedIn, she started to use it. At first she connected with people in her field (peers) for information interviews (feedback on her resume, tips about the job market, and recruitment strategies specific to her field). Then she used it to find companies who needed her expertise.

• What about security and privacy? I'm not at ease sharing information about myself on LinkedIn.

  - You can share as much or as little information as you want. You have total control on what information you put on your LinkedIn profile and what you share. You can also modify the settings & privacy settings to show only what you want.

  - I wouldn't recommend putting your address and phone number on LinkedIn. Information about your background and current updates are okay, because those who want to reach you will find a way to do it.

  - Some people add their email address in the profile description, to make it easier for others to contact them. You'll find some LIONs, recruiters, and even job seekers doing that.

• Do I really need a photo? I don't want people to discriminate me based on my looks.

  - It's a common practice to have a photo on your LinkedIn profile. If you choose not to add one, keep in mind that people could wonder what else you want to hide. A photo on your LinkedIn profile could also mean you're conformable with who you are.

• Why should I make my profile public? I want to let it be visible only to my connections; it's too risky otherwise.

- It's true that you can change the settings, to show only what you want. But I have a question for you too: Would you like to make your profile visible to employers, recruiters, and other people who might be interested in connecting with you? If you do, making your profile public is a more effective way to facilitate that. I saw only profiles of managers who are not public (you can see only their names), probably because they are too busy and not open to other connections.

- You can choose between the risk involved with having your information visible and the risk of your profile not being found or seen by those who might be interested in your expertise. Your choice!

• What happens if . . . ?

- Sometimes I get questions about LinkedIn or other social media platforms that I can't answer for the simple reason that I don't know. In this case, I suggest getting curious and using social media to get answers about . . . social media! :-)

- For example, with the new LinkedIn website, I wasn't sure if the features I was familiar with were still in place or something had changed. I had to use either LinkedIn's Help Center (found on the right side of the "Home" and "Notifications" pages) or Google (using a question like "Where do I find my LinkedIn Recommendations?" and choosing the URL that contains linkedin.com) so I get the most recent and accurate information directly from the source (the LinkedIn website itself).

- If you find a feature or something you don't understand about LinkedIn, you can always open a ticket (search for "contact us" in the "Help Center") and they will respond promptly. That's how I found out that I can send only fifteen messages to group members in a month. If I remember correctly, it wasn't so limited before. My question came from a genuine interest in thanking the over one thousand people who answered my question about this book title, and after a few messages sent, I couldn't send anymore. The link to "Help Center" in on LinkedIn Home page, on the bottom right (when you're signed in).

Before moving to another social media platform, let's recap some of the things you can do with LinkedIn for your job search:

• Keep your short and long term in mind when you're using it, so as not to get distracted by all the features and information you'll find on LinkedIn (so you don't end up spending too much time on this platform, neglecting the other activities that could help your job hunt).

• Increase your LinkedIn network by inviting your own connections first. Then start inviting people to connect (a few each day). This way you increase your chances of reaching out to the people you really want to contact.

• Search for the professionals in your field (peers) and ask for information interviews. From each interview, you'll leave with information, advice, and possible new leads for other information interviews, to help you decide what your next steps are.

• Search LinkedIn by keywords to find people in your field, and look where they work or previously worked to add those companies to your list.

• Search for companies you're interested in, and contact their employees to get more information about the company and recruitment process. Check out the company LinkedIn page to find their website and if they have other job available. See if you can find the manager's name (for the department you're interested in) if you'd like to use the pain letter strategy.

• Search the "Jobs" section for possible positions you'd be interested in. Also, follow LinkedIn suggestions based on your keywords or profile.

• Learn from more successful professionals in your field by following their profile and updates, connecting with them, participating in groups, etc.

• Get feedback for your profile and resume from others in the same field.

• Increase your visibility and build a good reputation by posting interesting status updates, starting conversations and commenting in groups, writing articles for your LinkedIn profile and sharing them in your status updates and groups. Start a conversation asking for advice about your job search in several groups (not only in those specific to your field). Recruiters and HR specialists are in many groups looking for candidates.

• Get recommendations via LinkedIn from people you worked with, and post them on your profile.

• Use specialty-specific keywords in your profile so people can find you. Set your profile as "open to opportunities" if you want it to show in recruiters' searches matching your career interests.

• Add your website (if you have one) to your LinkedIn profile so the visitors of your profile can get more information if they want. Create a nicer URL for your LinkedIn profile, to add on your resume, website, business cards, email signature, etc.

Twitter (Twitter.com)

When I started to use Twitter I was very confused: "What can you do with a message of 140 characters (called a tweet)?" It turns out that you can actually do a lot! :-)

If you're not familiar with Twitter, it's a social media platform for messaging. I won't cover here in detail how to use Twitter in general. You can check out Joel Comm's book *Twitter Power* to get more details. It's an eye opener for understanding social media in general, and the difference between having a profile and using different strategies to make it more effective. There are many other articles on this topic as well.

If you have a Twitter account or plan to open one, here are my suggestions for using Twitter in the context of your job hunting:

• Use your full name either as your ID or in your description. This will help people find you more easily.

• Add a nice, professional photo and header to your profile. You can even mention in the profile description that you're looking for new opportunities as _____ (fill in the blank).

• Add the URL of your LinkedIn profile if you don't have a website, so people can learn more about you if they want.

• Tweet things related to your expertise and share interesting articles and your opinion, from time to time — so your followers get a better idea of your wisdom, personality, style, and preferences. People can read between the lines, even though a tweet is only 140 characters. Once they land on your profile, they can see your previous tweets.

• If you're new to Twitter, have at least a few tweets on your profile before reaching out to other people. Chances are they will check your profile if you follow theirs.

• Hashtags:

   - If you don't know, a hashtag is a keyword that has a # followed by one or more words without a blank in between (#jobsearch for example). Hashtags are used by Twitter, Instagram, and other social media platforms to facilitate the search for a specific topic. You can even include hashtags in your LinkedIn articles if you want them to be found.

   - If you Google "hashtags for job search" you will find several articles listing the most commonly used hashtags for job search. You will find the most used hashtags for job seekers and for companies/recruiters. They could be very valuable in your job hunt, to help you find companies who have job openings, recruiters, job postings, and even interesting articles to help you through the job search. That's how I found that tip about the sticky notes I mentioned when I talked about organizing your resumes for job fairs.

   - For Twitter, enter in the search bar the hashtags you want. It could be one or more hashtags. For example, enter both #jobsearch and #Toronto if you want to find who tweets about something related to job search in Toronto. This way you'll find people you otherwise might not find, who might post a job opening in Toronto or an interesting article about job search in this city.

- If you want to make people aware that you're available for new opportunities, you can use a hashtag along with what you want to say. For example: "Any suggestions where I can look for a bookkeeping position in Toronto? #hireme "If there are recruiters or companies looking for a bookkeeper in Toronto and are using #hireme to find candidates, your tweet will show up in their search results.

- Use hashtags to find recruiters and recruitment agencies specializing in your field, and follow them on Twitter. Chances are they will post positions regularly, because they want candidates!

- Use hashtags specific to your field and location to find people in your field and ask for information interviews.

• Want feedback about your resume or LinkedIn profile and how to increase your visibility? Why not tweet something like, "Looking for feedback to improve my LinkedIn profile, any suggestion welcome. :-)" and add your profile URL to your tweet so people can actually go check it out. If you have followers, they might be able to see your tweet if they're looking at their news feed.

• If you want to make someone aware of what you're tweeting about, you can include their ID in your tweet with @ as a prefix. For example, if you want me to see what you post on Twitter or you want to include me in a Twitter conversation, add @thoughtdesigner (my Twitter ID) to your tweet before sending it. Like: "Hey, @thoughtdesigner, I'm reading your book and loving it!" By doing this, Twitter will let me know you tagged me, and I can see and reply to your tweet if I want, or retweet your tweet (so my followers can see it too).

• What I like about Twitter is that it makes it so easy to follow someone. After you click on Follow on the person's profile, you can add the profile to a list so you can easily follow all the tweets specific to a category. Possible titles/categories for your lists you can create for job search are as follows: Recruiters, Companies, Job Search Articles, Peers, and so on. When you find a twitter account you're interested in following, add it to a corresponding list.

• By following people on Twitter, their tweets will show up in your news feed, and it can be overwhelming to see all those tweets showing up (sometimes quite fast). But if you populated your list, you can visit a specific list to see what the people from that list shared.

• Imagine a certain recruiter grabbed your attention. You follow him and check his tweets from time to time. One day you see a job posting that suits another job seeker you've just met. You send the information to that person and answer to the recruiter's tweet to thank him. Chances are both people will remember you, because you did each of them a favor. If the recruiter checks your profile after reading your thank you note, he'll notice that you're looking for new opportunities too and will reach out if he has something suitable.

• Here's another way to approach that recruiter: "I told my friends about the position you shared. I'm looking for _____. Do you hire for this type of position too?" If the recruiter answers no, reply back asking if he knows who does or can give you any advice.

• You can reply to someone who shared an interesting article as well, or comment to that tweet, sharing your opinion. It's an easy way to speak up, and you can do it whenever you feel like it, not pressured by a certain event you're participating in or having someone in front of you.

• Find out which recruitment agencies specialize in your field, and follow them on Twitter. Chances are they will post positions regularly, because they want candidates.

• Follow companies you're interested in; they sometimes post job opportunities. Bigger companies might even have a Twitter account specific to their HR department, making it easier to see their job postings than on a general account that shares all kinds of information.

• How Do You Get Followers?

    - You'll need to tweet from time to time: post articles and useful information, comment on others' tweets so they reply back (which will show on your profile), retweet others' tweets you found interesting, and even share about yourself (how your job search is unfolding, or whatever you're comfortable sharing).

    - While writing this book, I often shared something about how the writing process was unfolding (what I found challenging or I discovered) and used hashtags to get followers. You too can use hashtags in your tweets to grab people's attention.

    - When you follow others, some might follow you back.

    - Why is it important to have followers, even if you're not interested in having people read your tweets? Because Twitter has certain thresholds. If you want to follow more than a certain number of profiles, Twitter will not allow you unless you already have a certain number of followers. You can learn more about this by Googling "Twitter following rules and best practices."

What to Keep in Mind about Twitter and Other Social Media Platforms

• As a general rule, before sharing something on social media, read it again and ask yourself if you really think it has value and should be sent out. Many employers and recruiters Google the candidates' names and check their social media profiles, and you might not want them to see something that is not appropriate (and will ruin your application).

• Twitter is a fast-paced environment, meaning many people using it are quite active. If you want to use Twitter for your job search, take your time and stay focused on your goals! Don't get frenzied about all the information coming your way. Just set a certain amount of time per day to use social media, and then move on to your other job-search-related tasks. Otherwise you can spend the whole day and week just using social media, without advancing too much. Believe me, it can be addictive! Been there, done that, learned from it, now monitoring how much time I spend on social media! :-)

• If you're new to social media, start with LinkedIn for your job search. There's so much to do with it, and it is the most professional social media platform. You can add Twitter in time, if you want. Facebook is good for asking for help and advice too (from your Facebook friends), and some companies and recruitment agencies also have Facebook pages when they list job opportunities.

• Reaching out to people on social media platforms like LinkedIn, Twitter, and Facebook, engaging in conversations, and sharing your opinion and useful information is what makes these platforms more effective for the job search (and not only).

• The tone of the conversations you can have on social media is similar to real-life conversations, yet they are shorter and more on topic. And as an introvert, you'll probably like this! :-)

• If you can play the win-win game, you'll be surprised how easy it is to connect with people on these platforms. Because those who are using them are generally open minded.

• Once I went to a film screening in Toronto, which was preceded by a brief introduction of a movie critic. I didn't remember his name, but I liked his presentation. When the film was over, I searched Twitter with the movie name and Toronto as keywords, and found his Twitter account. Then I tweeted about how much I enjoyed his presentation and added his Twitter ID, so he could see it. And he answered me briefly after. You can do the same when you go to a presentation, workshop, or conference, if you want to connect with the speaker without delivering your message in person. This could be your ice-breaker if you want to contact someone. Remember, the win-win game is good, but giving first is even better!

• There are ways of connecting different social media platforms, if you want to post the same message on several platforms. For example, link your Twitter account with LinkedIn so posting a message on LinkedIn will be shared on your Twitter profile too. Hootsuite is a platform that allows you to post the same message at the same time on several platforms. Even if you do that, I still recommend checking and using them independently to engage in conversations and do your targeted research.

• Social media is . . . social! Being too serious will not bring you as much as having a positive attitude.

• And when you have a hard time (it happens), you can also turn toward social media to share what you're going through, instead of blaming others or the system in general. People will relate to your struggles, and some might offer to help, even unknown people who stumble upon your social media profile or message.

I remember one day I was alone and feeling down, and I shared how I felt on an local online chat. Someone answered me briefly after: He was the manager of an Internet cafe not far away, and he invited me to go there. He didn't know my real name, nor how I looked, so I felt okay. I was still down when I arrived there. I booked a computer for fifteen minutes and left before the time ended, without saying a word. I contacted him when I got back home, to thank him for sending me the message that got me out of my house and take some fresh air. It really shifted my mood, and I was already okay by the time I got back home. That's my introverted way of socializing when I feel down or alone: I turn toward social media. :-)

• Studies show that introverts are more open to sharing their opinions and collaborating online. Open source software (developed and updated through the online collaboration of IT programmers, many of them being introverts) is an example of how collaborative and open to idea sharing introverts can be online, without the pressure of urgency and real human connection. You'll also find introverts on social media platforms, so why not tap into these resources to help your job search?

Let's go back to what I said earlier.

What do you think: can social media help you access opportunities, create a more successful mindset, increase your visibility, gain people's trust, make new connections, cultivate professional relationships, get feedback and recommendations, build a good reputation, get new ideas, and stay up to date?

I have given you a few examples along the way to explain how you can combine social media with the strategies presented in chapter 9. Using these strategies in a proactive way could really facilitate and speed up your job hunting process .

If you're like me (putting my thoughts in writing is easier than speaking) you'll find social media a useful tool in your job search toolbox!

Social media is so popular these days and doesn't seem to slow down. It's making things happen faster by making it easier to connect and communicate with others and meet new people. It also facilitates access to information already filtered by those who have a similar focus as us. Just make sure to infuse some discipline (how much you use social media), to not let it steal your time.

As a side note:

I'd like to share that social media helped me, an introvert, step out of my comfort zone and drop down many inner barriers and limiting beliefs. The more I used it, the more I became comfortable sharing what I'm going through and my ideas and insights, and people responded positively to this. It was quite an eye opener for an introvert like me, who didn't open up so easily in the real world. And the beauty of this all is this: by using social media I became more confident and open not only online, but also in the real world. I'm now choosing how I want to behave in each situation, instead of being driven by my default behavior (which didn't serve me in some circumstances).

I personally consider social media the best way for an introvert to build and practice social skills, a real and free self-growth environment where you are present and participate when you want, as little or as much you wish.

Even with social media we can get triggered sometimes, but we have the choice to step back, reflect, and respond (or not) without the pressure of having someone in front of us — a luxury that the real environment doesn't often offer. Plus, practicing your social skills with social media will make you more at ease to meet people in real life as well — which is very beneficial for an effective job search.

Chapter Thirteen

INTERVIEW TIPS TO PRESENT YOURSELF WITHOUT FEELING "SALESY"

It's not about having the right opportunities. It's about handling the opportunities right.
~ Mark Hunter

I have met many introverts who are stressed by job interviews before even getting to them.

Below are a few reasons that could explain why, based on the results of scientific studies. If you'd like more details, check out these two books: Susan Cain's book *Quiet: The Power of Introverts in a World That Can't Stop Talking* and Marti Olsen Laney's book *The Introvert Advantage: How Quiet People Can Thrive in an Extrovert World.*

• A job interview is usually perceived as a competitive environment, while introverts love collaboration (and extroverts love competition).

• Extroverts are more social because their brain is naturally suited for multitasking, while introverts can focus with more intensity on a single task. The job interview requires multitasking, so the introvert needs to focus simultaneously on the question being asked, formulating an answer, monitoring his own behavior, and grabbing any signs of how his performance is perceived — which becomes stressful and overwhelming. That's why, sometimes, their mind goes blank as a natural reaction to multitasking — not because they are not knowledgeable or capable of performing the job tasks well.

• Being more sensitive than extroverts to external stimuli, introverts are not keen on being exposed to new situations. And isn't a job interview a new environment? A friendlier environment would make introverts more at ease and open, leading to a better interview performance.

• When it comes to speaking, introverts' brain pathways are longer than those of extroverts. This makes introverts less spontaneous speakers: their brain needs to access their long-term memory first before formulating an answer (which delays the response). Having shorter brain pathways, extroverts can come up with answers much faster — although they might not be as thorough as introverts.

• Since extroverts are motivated by rewards, a job interview could be a great motivator for them. (Getting the job could be their reward). On the other side, introverts find an inner motivation for working on projects meaningful to them, such projects keeping them focused. Being asked to go through an interview (to prove themselves instead of letting them work directly on the real, meaningful project) could be intimidating and frustrating.

This being said, it doesn't mean that introverts can't handle job interviews well. Having a successful interview as an introvert just requires some preparation and understanding of how to rely more on their strengths and minimize the risks.

I'll divide this chapter in three parts, before, during, and after the interview, because there are things you can do in each of these phases to help you stand out without feeling that you need to sell yourself.

BEFORE THE JOB INTERVIEW

Let's talk about a few factors you can address before going to a job interview:

Stress

When you're invited to a job interview, do you put a lot of pressure on yourself?

Many of my clients approached the job interview thinking: "I need this job, I have to pass the interview!"

If you do this too, you stress yourself so much that you actually sabotage yourself! Because it's not easy to formulate good answers and present yourself well in such conditions.

The employers will notice that you're stressed, and since they don't know from where it comes, they might assume that you're stressed because you don't have the expertise for the position. Would you like to take the risk?

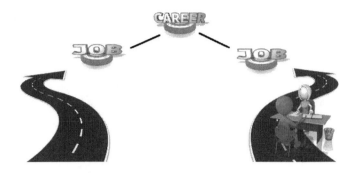

To remove, or at least decrease, the stress caused by that thought, let's put things in perspective a little:

The long-term objective (CAREER) you have in mind can be achieved by taking different paths. There are more options for your next job that could lead to your long-term objective, right?

For example, if you plan to become a manager in five years you can gradually shift from one position to another, taking more responsibility each time so you can build your manager "muscles" until you get promoted as manager or find a manager position. Another option could be, after landing your next job, you start taking management courses, build your network, and manage different projects (at work, on your own, while volunteering), and get a manager position by applying with your updated resume.

If you look from this perspective (more paths can lead to your objective), are you as stressed as before about getting "this" job interview? If it's not this one, there will be another one that will help you move forward toward your long-term objective.

I suggest you instead consider each job interview a stepping stone for sharpening your interview skills to get ready for the right interview! If you pass it, great! If not, learn your lessons (what you did well, what you didn't, what you can do differently for the next job interview, etc.).

Would this perspective be less stressful?

Preparation

While there are similarities between the job interviews, keep in mind that organizations from different sectors (private, public, and non-profit) have different cultures, and so they focus on different aspects specific to what's important to them. The companies from the public sector, for example, focus on financial gains, while the non-profit organizations focus on serving their clients (while the financial aspect is handled through funding). Even in the same sector there are differences between companies.

The size of a company or organization counts also. For example, a small company might be interested in employees who can perform various tasks, because they don't have enough staff. While in corporations, you can find more specialized positions.

Why am I talking about these differences?

If you remember, in chapter 4 ("What I Want") I asked you to define in more detail what you want: what type of company you would like to join (sector, size, industry, work environment, etc.). Through information interviews and your own research, you can find out more about the culture of the specific type of company you'd like to work for. This information could be very useful in preparing your job application. And if you're invited to a job interview, the information you gather about the company (its culture, values, achievements, product, and services, what type of work environment is there, etc.) can help you better prepare and adjust your answers in a way that matches the specifics of this company, thus increasing your chances of getting accepted.

Interview Types and Formats

Types of interviews:

- Screening interview: to preselect candidates (based on salary expectations, for example)
- Telephone interview: to reduce the number of candidates invited to the job interview
- Video conferencing, Skype, etc.: use of technology to interview at a distance
- General group interview/Information session (see John's example below)
- One-on-one interview: between candidate and interviewer
- Panel interview: candidate is interviewed by a group of company representatives
- Group interview: more candidates are interviewed at the same time
- Sequential/serial interview: there is more than one interview before the decision is made (For example, the first interview is with someone from HR, the second with the department manager.)

To exemplify some of the points I'll share in this chapter, I'll walk you through the before and during phases of John's interview process so you can understand what helped him outperform more than 240 candidates and get hired by the company he liked.

After applying for that position, John attended an Information session with a similar company. Knowing what he wanted, John was relaxed and participated during the session. By the end, the session leader asked to speak with him: "I'd like to invite you to a job interview, but I have a sense that you're not quite interested." John admitted he had applied for a similar position with another institution and would really like to get hired by them.

As you can see, the person who conducted this session was actually selecting the candidates based on their personality and other criteria not listed in the job posting. Such sessions allow companies to also asses the candidates' behavior in group settings (which cannot be assessed in a job interview with only one candidate). If you stay in observer mode, you might lose the chance to demarcate yourself from other candidates. One way of getting out of this mode, if you want, is by getting curious: By asking questions that require clarifications or new information, you can make yourself more visible and leave a better impression.

Interview Formats

- *Behavioral interview:* the questions are asked in a way that allows the employer to understand the candidate's behavior in similar situations to those required by the position (so they can predict the candidate's future behavior). For example, "Give us an example of how you handle conflict in the workplace."
- *Situational interview:* the candidates are asked to explain what they would do in a hypothetical situation (and the employers will compare candidates' responses with their own perspective about how the situation should be handled). For example: "How will you handle a client who has an issue but he's not aware of it?" Pay attention: This is a hypothetical question, so you'll have to answer using the same verb tense. If you give an example of what you did in the past in a similar situation, your answer will show that you're not a good listener.
- *Structured interview:* all candidates received the same questions, so the employer can take notes and evaluate the candidates by comparison.
- *Unstructured interview:* a free-flow interview with questions customized for each applicant.
- *Semi-structured Interview:* a combination of the two above formats.
- *Case interview:* the candidates are presented a case with a specific problem and asked how they would solve it (to assess problem-solving skills, creativity, technical knowledge, etc.). When I was invited to an interview for a quality assurance position, I was presented a case study and asked to identify the quality issues and what measures I would put in place to prevent those issues from occurring in the future and ensure better quality services.
- *Testing/assessment:* to evaluate certain competencies required by the position.

For more about interview types and formats see:

http://www.success.uwo.ca/careers/interviews/types_of_interviews.html .

Some of my clients were not aware of the importance of preparing for a job interview. Relying on what you already know about yourself and your background is not enough. Each job interview is different, even if you apply for the same type of position. The company is different; its size, culture, and work environment are different; the opportunities of growth inside the company might be different; what you have in common with that company (motivation, common interests, etc.) might be different as well, including your experience with job interviews for this type of position (based on your previous interview with another company, or no experience with interviewing at all if you're just starting out). All these factors could help you present better at the interview if you prepare yourself.

From an introvert perspective, since every job interview is a new experience, by preparing upfront you will be able to reduce the stress during the interview and feel more confident. There is a stress related to the interview itself, while you're there talking with the employer. By preparing in advance, based on your research about the company and the specifics of this position, you will already have examples and elements to include in your answers during the interview, without having to think about them on the spot (reducing the overwhelm). This research will also help you find commonalities with the company so you'll get a hook to hang on to motivate you during the interview.

When you prepare for the job interview, you will already know what type of interview it will be — the recruiter or employer already told you. Familiarize yourself with what usually goes on in this type of interview by consulting book and Internet articles and talking with people working in the same company.

As for the interview format, you will have to guess which formats the employer will include in your interview based on the type of the position you're applying for. If you did information interviews with people working in a similar position, you'll know from them what the common interviews questions for a such position are (if you asked).

If you're applying for a customer service position, for example, expect questions related to behavior and how you handle certain situations like managing a difficult client.

Having a better idea upfront of what to expect from an interview for a position with a certain company will give you more information you can rely on during the interview.

As introverts, we need time to think and formulate our answers, so preparing some of them in advance could help us when we're under fire.

John did the same thing. He already knew the position he was interviewing for, but he didn't go without preparation. He talked with people who worked for that company, to understand the company's culture better and what they expect from a candidate. He also searched the Internet for common questions specific to that position, reflected on how he could respond in a way that was not only appropriate for the position, but also reflected his great background and his motivation to work for that specific company. Then he prepared five to six examples about his achievements and in what situations he excelled, and identified his strengths related to the position and how he could better present them. He although thought about what weakness he could talk about and how to present it in case he was asked. All this preparation made him more confident, because he knew he could rely on his strengths and his preparation to make a good impression — and he did!

You too can do this type of research and preparation if you want to feel more at ease in a job interview, and better prepared.

Interview Preparation

Here are the steps I suggest when preparing yourself for a job interview:

1. Research

Research information about the company: culture, values, work environment, products/ services, challenges, type of organization, company awards, whether this is a new position or not, etc. Check out their website, articles about the company, and their social media profiles (including LinkedIn page) and talk with their employees, etc.

2. Common Interview Questions

Find out what the common interview questions are for the type of position you applied. Google "interview questions for _____ (position name)". For example, "fraud and security specialist" if that's the position you are interviewing for. Go to the library and check the books on interviewing or on specific careers — the library usually has a lot of resources for job hunting and career advice.

3. Accomplishments or Examples

Write down five or six accomplishments or examples that you're proud of regarding your previous experience in such a position, or when you used transferable skills relevant to this job. Then rewrite each of those experiences in the SAR format (Situation, Actions, Results). You will include these examples in your answers during the interview, to show (not tell) your value. Wouldn't you be more impressed if someone told you he received a certificate of excellence for the work done, instead of saying he is excellent in what he does? The same for the employer: let the examples do the talk about your value instead of you talking about how good you are (which is uncomfortable for an introvert, right?).

So what is this **SAR** format about?

Situation: Briefly describe the situation, so the employer can understand the circumstances. For example, "One day I received a call from a client who was frustrated because . . ."

Here are some suggestions based on the simulation interviews I've done with my clients:

- Do not give too many details about the situation. Otherwise you lose employers' attention. They are more interested in how you handled the situation and if there were any positive results due to your actions.
- The time and company name (where the situation occurred) are often irrelevant. This is especially important when you change the industry: you don't want to remind the employer that your experience is in a different industry, but you want him to understand that you have the right skills to do a great job. Focus more on the tasks, requirements, and behaviors than other details — unless they are important for explaining how your actions led to those results.
- Being concise is a great quality that keeps the employer's attention on what's important.

Actions: What actions did you take to handle that situation?

- I had a client who was so modest he used only "we" instead of "I" when he described the actions taken. Hey, this is your job interview, so the employer wants to know what you did! :-) By using "we" it is not clear if you took those actions or it was a team effort. In the latter case, you still need to talk about your contribution to the team that drove those results.
- Another client was giving so many details that I got lost and a little nervous because it was taking too much time. Again, add to your phrases only what's important to make your point. If you feel that it is important to mention those details: state the main idea first, then provide the details. Otherwise you lose employer's attention by the time you present the main idea. Keep in mind that the employer has a certain amount of time and questions allotted to this interview, and going into too many details might require you to leave out something more important.

Results: What were the positive results based on your action? Were the clients happy? Increased productivity? Solved a problem? In what way did your actions lead to those results?

- I had a client who talked very well about the situation and the actions taken, but forgot to mention the results. And that's the main purpose of using examples in your answers: to let the results speak about the quality of your work!
- Don't forget to choose examples that lead to positive results, because that's what the employers like. Wouldn't you too? :-)

4. Preparing Answers

Now it's time to prepare answers to the commonly asked questions for the position you're applying for:

• Take into consideration what you learned during the research phase (step 1 and 2), and write your answers keeping the employer's perspective in mind: What is he looking for when asking that question? If you don't know, put yourself in the employer's shoes: What would you look for when asking the question? You can also ask other people if you want to better understand the employer's reason, or read articles and books about interviews. Many of them give you ideas of what the employer is looking for (the reason behind the question), and even provide suggestions on how to answer. You can contact the people you did information interviews with again and ask their opinion.

• In your answers, give examples in the SAR format whenever you can to let them talk about your skills and expertise.

• Review your answers and adjust them to be concise and relevant to the questions and the position you're applying for. I can't tell you how many of my clients gave answers that were less relevant for the position, even if they had examples that were more appropriate for the position!

• Asking about your strengths is quite common in a job interview. During the simulation interviews I had with my clients, some of them gave me list of what they considered their strengths. Remember, in the context of a job interview, your answers should be targeted to what the employer needs to know (if your skills, expertise, and personality fit well with the position). If what you consider your biggest strengths are not the most relevant for the job, you might miss the point! While preparing your answer to this question, I suggest you start backward: Think first about the most important qualities someone should have for performing well in that position; then identify which of those qualities are your strengths as well. You need to prepare your answer with two to three of your strengths that are relevant for the position, and give examples that present the positive results of using those skills. You might not need to talk about them all (depending on how the employers react and the time allowed), but examples are more revealing (since they portray a bigger picture) than a list of skills.

• The employers might also ask about your greatest weakness. Give it a thought before going to the interview. Usually, they are interested in seeing if you are aware of your weaknesses and willing to improve them. So I suggest my clients think about a weakness they had related to this position, then to talk about it in the SAR format: Situation (why that characteristic was a weakness for that position), Action (what they did to improve it), Results (how their performance improved after working on their weakness). Any characteristic has two faces: in some circumstances it could be seen as a weakness, in others as a strength. For example, having a keen eye for detail is very useful when you're an editor or work in quality assurance, but it could also make you miss a deadline if you wait until you can fix all the errors. And deadlines have cascading effects, affecting others' work and even the entire project. For your job interview, pick a characteristic that affected your job performance in the past; then tell how you improved it, and the positive effect it had for your work afterward. For example, "When I noticed that my perfectionism was getting in the way of meeting deadlines, I focused on organizing and prioritizing my work better, so I could still provide quality reports in time. I never missed a deadline since, and my reports were well received by my manager." Here's another example from a bilingual client who feared that his level of English was not enough for the position: When I asked what his biggest weakness was, he quickly responded "My English." "Let you employer evaluate if your level of English is enough for the position you apply," I suggested. "And don't draw more attention to what you consider your biggest weakness. There are positions that do not require an advanced level, and the employer has a better knowledge of what's needed." He agreed and found something else to present as his weakness for that specific position. I am not asking you to lie. All I'm saying is to think about your answers in advance and include only what's the most relevant for the position, so you don't shoot yourself in the foot by wasting employers' time with something irrelevant or — even worse — with something that disqualifies you.

• Usually the interview starts with an ice-breaker like: "Tell us about yourself." This might be a trap if you don't think about it upfront. Laureen recently moved into the city when she asked me for a simulation interview, to see if she was well prepared for the upcoming job interview for a social worker position. Looking at her resume, she seemed to have a great background in the field. Getting into the employer's role, I started by asking her to tell me about herself. "Well, I recently moved here with my fiancé because we love this city. We also considered it a great opportunity to . . ." Since she continued to say things unrelated to the position, I stopped her and asked her to put herself in the employer's role: The employer needed to hire someone for a social worker position, and at the first question asked, the candidate talked about unrelated things for a few good minutes. What would she think about the candidate, and how would she feel knowing that a few minutes had already passed while there were a lot more questions to be covered to assess the candidate's suitability for the position during this interview? I suggested that Laureen prepares a one to two minute introduction about herself, but present something related to the position (education, years of experience, etc.). The employer saw your resume before, but if he's interviewing several candidates the same day, he might not remember the background of each of them. Do not get into too many details during the introduction, since you'll have the chance to add them while answering the other questions.

• Also keep in mind that employers are looking for consistency: If you're a project manager but you get lost in the details, you indirectly show that you don't keep an eye on the bigger picture (as every project manager should do!). In a simulation interview, I asked a marketing manager to talk about his background. He told me about all his experience in chronological order, yet he was applying for a position that required experience in a certain area of marketing only. As an employer, I would expect him to tell me about that experience first, then add the rest of it with less detail. This way, not only would I find out what I need from the beginning of his answer, but also he would prove his marketing skills (telling the customer what he or she wants to hear first if you want to grab his or her attention).

• Another question that is quite common is this: "Why should we hire you?" or "Why do you want to work for us?" Don't wait until you're at the interview to think about the answer. Prepare it in advance by thinking about what makes you stand out, based on the combination of your experience, skills, personality, interests, etc. An answer like, "I have the skills and expertise required" will not be enough, because other candidates might have them too. John applied and was hired for a fraud and security specialist position, while there were over 240 other candidates. What helped him stand out, besides his experience in the field? Preparing himself well for the interview: finding interview questions specific for the position he applied, researching information about the company (including how it stands out from other similar companies), and giving a good thought to the answers he'd like to give. When asked, "Why should we hire you?" he started by saying: "Because working for you would be like working for myself." He gave them a few seconds and then he continued: "I have all my bank accounts with your bank, and if I work in the fraud and security department of your company, is like I'm protecting my own money!" And yes, he got hired! What can *you* say to the employer to stand out from the competitors?

• Preparing your answers: When you think about what you can say if asked a common interview question, write down your answers. Read them to see if you have too many or not enough details, and pay attention to whether they are relevant to the position from the employer's point of view. Did you miss something? Does the answer have a good information flow? If needed, adjust or rewrite your answer, then read it out loud a few times to familiarize yourself with that answer. Then I suggest you create a bulleted list with the main points you'd like to cover if you're asked that question. Memorizing the whole answer could be more stressful, because if you forget a word you might not remember how to continue. Memorizing just a few points will be enough, because you can develop them on the spot while keeping the main idea in focus (without getting lost or losing the employer's attention with the details).

• How to prepare for the questions you didn't expect in the interview? Keep in mind that the employer wouldn't ask that question without a reason. Time is money for them, and any question has a purpose, to help them understand something about the candidate to make the hiring decision easier.

Here's what happened at my first job interview in Canada: Although I had IT programming experience, I didn't have the courage to apply directly for such a position, so I applied and got invited to a job interview for a data entry position in an IT company. I passed the technical test, and the interview was going quite well until I was asked, "Do you like routine?" "No," I answered quickly, and that's so true! I don't like routine at all, but I didn't get the job either. :-) I would have handled the question better if I was prepared, because I was willing to start with just a data entry position. So here's what I suggest when you're asked a question you didn't expect or you didn't prepare the answer for before: take a moment to ask yourself why the interviewer is asking the question in the context of that specific position. Maybe he is concerned about something, or wants to understand if you have certain qualities or experience? After you take a guess about what could be the reason for that question, formulate and organize the answer that addresses the employer's concern or what he wants to know. It's okay to take the time to formulate the answer in your mind first; it's much better than jumping into saying something and stopping in the middle to see how you can continue the phrase.

5. Preparing Your Questions

Toward the end of the interview, you will be given the chance to ask your own questions. So you'll also need to prepare in advance two to three questions you'd like to ask the employer. What would you be interested in knowing about the company and the position, to help you understand if this could be a good company for you? Remember, a job interview is also your opportunity to assess the company. Once I asked what other requirements they had besides what was captured in the job description. Another time, when I was interviewed for a quality assurance position, I was interested if it was a new position or someone had left. They answered that it was a whole new department that had been created because they didn't have anyone to monitor and ensure the quality of their services — which gave a totally different meaning to the role I had applied for.

6. Dealing with Your Inner Critic

Pay attention to your inner critic, that voice inside your head saying all kind of things, like, "I don't know why they invited me to the job interview; I don't have enough experience for this position", or "I don't know how to sell myself", or …

Your *inner critic* or *inner saboteur* (as we call it in coaching) is like inertia: When you want to make a change, he'll show up with these kinds of thoughts to help you reflect a little bit more if that's the move you want or not. Actually, his role is not to stop you! If you decide to go ahead, his role is to pop up thoughts in your head about the challenges you have ahead, so you can look into finding ways to overcome them and move forward in the direction you want.

I suggest that you honor and even thank your inner critic, and consider him your ally! After all, that's exactly what he is: an ally who has an unskillful way of communicating with you. But he cares about you and wants to protect you from making the wrong decisions. If, after reflection, you consider that's not the right move for you, thank him for helping you to reconsider your move before you headed toward something you don't really want.

And if you realize that is still something you want to pursue, thank him for pointing out those aspects you need prepare for so you can overcome the upcoming challenges, which otherwise might lead you to failure!

For example, "I don't have enough experience" could be turned around into: "How can I present myself in a way that shows my real value, even if I don't have all the required experience? After all, if they invited me to the interview, they might be interested in giving me a chance." How does this feel? You now start brainstorming with yourself (and others, if you want) how to formulate your answers in a way that shows you in a more positive light.

Can you see the difference it'll make in your attitude just by changing that initial thought with a more positive one? And that attitude will increase the chances of passing the interview (while "I don't have enough experience" won't), right?

That's why I asked you to work on your inner barriers in chapter 5, about mindset. Changing your limiting beliefs and negative thoughts has a positive effect on your attitude, making you more prone to prepare and present yourself well during the interview.

If you are an employer, would you hire someone who doesn't trust his abilities? Or you would hire someone who does, and has the right attitude even if he doesn't have all the experience listed in the job description?

Two Ways to Deal with Your Inner Critic

• Understand the reason behind that thought, and turn the thought around into an inquiry that will help you figure out how to leverage your strengths in the given situation, like in the example I gave you above.

• When you hear your inner critic's thoughts in your mind, switch your thinking toward your long-term objective. Imagine that you've already achieved that, notice how that feels, and take some of the energy from that place with you while preparing for the job interview. That extra energy you get by reconnecting with your long-term objective will give you the boost you need to ignore your inner critic and focus on preparing for your job interview. Without that extra boost of energy, you might get swept into the downward spiral of the negative thoughts, draining your energy, which won't help you do better at the interview. On the contrary, it will decrease your self-esteem even more, which is an important key to a successful interview.

7. Utilizing the Power Game

I'm curious, who do you think has more power in a job interview?

If you answer, "The employer," I suggest you reconsider your thought. Yes, the employer has the final decision, but you have a huge role in what the decision will be.

Putting the employer on a pedestal, thinking that he has all the power, will make you feel less important, less confident that you can actually contribute to his decision, and . . . guess what? That's how you will present in the job interview, unconsciously creating the conditions for someone else to be hired instead of you. It's like a self-fulfilling prophecy, although not the one you want, right?

Remember Aesop's fable "The Lion and the Mouse"? Even if the mouse was much smaller than the lion, he was able to help the lion when he needed it the most.

Don't underestimate your power!

I suggest you consider the employer and you having equal power during the job interview. How does that feel? After all, he's looking to hire the best person that suits his needs, while you have the skills and expertise that will help his company achieve its goals! It will be a win-win if you are a good fit.

So your role during interviews is to answer the interviewers' questions, evaluate their interest in your application, and understand better their company culture (through the way the interview is set up, the questions asked, their attitude, etc.). Your role is to assess the company too. Coming from this perspective, you'll step more into your power, which has a positive effect on the way you'll be perceived.

So before going to the interview, review your short-term goal and long-term objective and the details you wrote in your notebook that correspond to what you really want, and go to the interview determined to find out how much the company and the position fit what you want. That determination will be picked up by the employer, thus showing your assertiveness (a trait very much appreciated by employers).

As an introvert, you'll get a bonus by implementing this approach: it'll will help you stay away from the self-defeating thoughts you might get during the interview, and thus you will be able to use your powerful mind to come up with the best answers you can!

8. Getting a Better Perspective with the Two-Way Simulation Interview

This is my favorite topic! :-) Earlier I talked about some of the simulation interviews I'd done with one-on-one clients. But in the workshop about the job interview, I invited the participants to do two-way simulation interviews. He-he, I just coined this term! :-)

If you're not familiar with a simulation interview in the context of job search:

Whether you received an invitation to a real job interview or you just want to see if you're well prepared for one, you can ask someone to simulate an interview with you for the position you've applied. The person who plays the role of interviewer will ask you similar questions as in a job interview, noticing how well you present yourself. After each answer, or at the end, the interviewer will give you feedback on what you did well and what you can still improve (and how). You will be surprised how much you can learn even from a simulation interview with a person who is not the real employer!

In my workshop, the two-way simulation interviews are done in pairs. Each participant finds a partner, and in the first round they do a simulation interview (one-way) as described above. The second round they switch the roles: the candidate becomes the employer, and the employer becomes the candidate, and they do another simulation interview. This way, each participant has the chance to be both candidate and employer. While being in the candidate role, they notice how well their answers flow, how well they are targeted to the question, and what they need to improve based on their own observations and the interviewer's. From the second round, the same participant will better understand the thought process of an employer: Did the candidates meet my expectations? Were his answers concise and to the point? Does the candidate have the qualities I need for this position? etc.

I highly encourage you to ask someone (friend, relative, colleague, employment counselor) to do a two-way simulation interview with you before you go to a job interview. It will become more obvious to you if you're prepared well enough, if your attitude during the interview project the right image, if you know how to formulate your answers in a way that corresponds to the employer's expectations, etc. You can read as many books and articles as you want, but without putting yourself in the candidate's and employer's roles you will not be so aware on how you actually do in a job interview. I agree with you, a simulation is not a real job interview. But all the participants in my workshops were surprised to see that the interview stress showed up even when they were part of a scenario like this! Your partner in a two-way simulation interview might not be a professional with experience in job interviews, but he can still provide feedback based on his own judgement — and you'll see how valuable that is! He might not be able to catch everything, but if you address even a small part of your mistakes, it's much better than making them during a real job interview, right? And from the experience you'll have by playing the employer's role, you'll get valuable insights about what else you can improve.

Here's what I noticed about some of the introverted job seekers I did one-on-one simulations interview with, from witnessing two-way simulation interviews in my workshops:

• They don't prepare a brief, targeted answer to the question, "Tell us about yourself". And this is your chance to start the job interview off on the right foot!

• They don't take enough time to prepare for the job interview. They rely on their spontaneous talking, which is not the best thing for an introvert to do.

• They don't do enough research about the company, so their answers are not targeted enough to the position in that specific company. Employers love when you include information about their company in your answers. It shows your interest in working for them.

• They don't include (enough) examples in their answers, because they didn't spend time upfront thinking about those examples and achievements. Or they don't present them in the SAR format, to facilitate the employer's understanding. If you want to make a better impression, those examples could do a better job of presenting you than you can do yourself. Plus, these examples will allow the employer to draw his own conclusions instead of relying on your words (which might be tested against the other behavior you show during the job interview).

• They focus only on the verbal communications, forgetting that non-verbal communication (body language) is even more important. The employers are well-equipped to read non-verbal clues. If they get double signals (the verbal and non-verbal clues don't match), they will believe the non-verbal is true. Some studies show that verbal communication accounts for only 7 percent of the message you deliver; the rest is non-verbal (the tone of voice, body language, etc.). That's why I have talked so much about attitudes and soft skills in this book. They do make a difference!

• They don't walk the talk, showing qualities specific to the position they applied (not only talking about them). A marketing manager who doesn't structure and customize his answers well (to what the interviewer needs to know) is not projecting his marketing and management knowledge well. A project manager (PM) who gets lost in the details is indirectly projecting a lack of focus on what is most important for a PM position: the big picture. Someone who applies for a customer service position but doesn't pay attention to all the details in the questions shows a lack of active listening (which is so important for that position).

• They don't do anything to decrease their stress before and during the job interview, thus allowing the stress to hinder their ability to present themselves well in the job interview. I'll give you more tips for decreasing stress in the "During the Interview" section.

• They don't realize what an important role the fear of authority can play in a job interview (and not to their advantage). That's why I asked you to put things in perspective and understand that you and the employer are equal partners during the job interview. If you want another tip: the employer is stressed as well, because quite often the candidates hired don't perform as expected and they need to support the costs and profit loss due to a new recruitment process. Imagine your interview stress could be picked up by the employer, adding to his own, and you'll pick up on the employer's increased stress, increasing yours . . . getting into a stress spiral that doesn't benefit any of you.

• They have a great fear of the formality of a job interview. Often the employer will try to create a more pleasant interview environment, knowing that your normal behavior will show up more in such conditions. And that's what they want to see — how you behave normally — so they can understand if you're a good fit for that specific position.

• They stress too much when an employer asks an uncommon question! First, take a break to ponder the reason behind the question. Think about what you can say that will address that reason, and then speak. Employers are okay if you take the time to prepare your answer!

• "That's how I am!" I've heard some of my clients saying. Some people are not aware they can change if they don't like one or more of their behaviors. While a change in behavior can take time to implement, there are things you can do if you'd like to have a certain behavior in a specific situation (during the job interview, for example). I helped a client decrease his stutter, which was getting worse during job interviews. If he were to continue to apply what he learned, he would decrease the stutter over time and be able to speak without doing it. You can read this blog post to understand how I was able to help him:

http://www.gabrielacasineanu.com/tendency-to-stutter-while-speaking/.

If you like the benefits of a two-way simulation interview, start thinking about who you can ask to be your interview partner and dare to ask. If you receive a no, you can ask someone else.

9. Preparing Mentally

Researching and preparing the answers to the commonly asked questions are not enough if you want to present yourself well at the interview. Mental preparation is as important as the other steps mentioned here.

I mentioned several times that attitude counts, so let's see how you can prepare yourself mentally:

• If you're not comfortable speaking with strangers, especially authorities, ask yourself what exactly makes you uncomfortable. Then address that aspect. For example, if you're intimidated by the power you associate with authorities and interviewers, reframe the way you think about them. They are people too, and in the case of the job interview, you actually have equal power because you both want a win-win situation. What would remind you, when you step into the interview room, to bring this perspective to mind to make yourself more at ease?

• If you're afraid your background and skills are not enough, remember that you got an invitation. The employer saw some value in your application and is willing to find out more. You don't know what the status of the recruitment process, and what the employer has in mind. Trust there is a good reason why you were invited, and go to the interview with more confidence. Remember Ana, the QA specialist who was hired for a school bus driver position? Here's another example: an economist saw a job posting that would be a good fit for her, except of one requirement that seemed the most important for the employer. She found the courage to send her application, and she got the position. Why? Because the employer didn't find anyone who met that requirement, and didn't receive other applications either (probably because the candidates eliminated themselves upfront by not meeting that requirement).

• Talking about confidence, you might be aware of how important it is to have self-confidence, especially during the job interview, so here are a few related aspects:

- The interviewer can pick up quickly how confident you are (or if you lack it). So what should you do if you have too many self-defeating thoughts? Use one of both methods I talked about in the "Inner Critic" section.

- Make a list with all the reasons you are a great candidate for this position, and read it at least three times every day prior to the interview day, plus the evening before and when you're ready to leave your home to go to the interview. Reading those reasons over and over will boost your confidence, and this will make a huge difference in the interview.

- Here's the T-exercise you can use when you create that list: grab a piece of paper and write at the top: "I am a great candidate for this position because ___". Now draw a horizontal line under that phrase, and a vertical line that splits the rest of the paper into two columns (like creating a huge T on your paper). In the left column draw a huge X (like nothing can get in there anymore). Then read your title again. When you come up with a reason why you should get the position, write it down on the right column. And continue to think about the reasons they should give you the job. If you get a positive reason, write it in the right column. If you get a reason why not, say "Cancel. Next!" and let your mind come up with another reason. Don't put the negative ones on paper — you don't have space for that (the left column is closed). Continue to think, and write down all the reasons there are that make you a great candidate. And say "Cancel. Next!" to all the reasons why you are not. Keep pushing yourself to find good reasons; it'll stretch your mind a little, but it's worth it! Think of everything you can bring to that position that will benefit the company: soft skills, hard skills, transferable skills, personality traits, expertise you have in the field, motivation, how having you in that position will benefit them, etc. Then fold the paper to see only the items on the right column (or write them on another sheet of paper), so you can read them over and over to boost your self-confidence and self-esteem.

- Are you aware there is a posture of confidence? Remember a moment from your life when you felt confident, and now allow your body to get the posture you had in that moment. Do you notice you now have a straight back, shoulders back, head high, and you're looking straight ahead? How do you feel now, while holding this posture? This is a posture that exudes confidence (called the power pose), and makes you feel more confident — right? What if you put on this posture for two minutes before getting into the interview room so you feel more confident? The employer will notice it too. I talked in chapter

5 (on mindset) about how our thoughts affect our feelings, which have an immediate effect on the body posture. The other way around is also true: if we consciously choose a different body posture, it will affect how we feel. You might think I'm asking you to fake a power posture, but this is actually backed up by science: When you consciously put yourself in a power posture, you'll feel the same as if you were normally having it. The opposite is also true: If you're looking down and folding up, you're making yourself small (low-power pose). Are you usually doing this while waiting for the interview? Guess what's the effect on yourself: You'll feel disempowered, and presenting yourself this way won't help you behave as you normally do (showing who you really are).

- If you'd like some scientific proof about how our body posture affects our confidence, watch the YouTube video "Your Body Language May Shape Who You Are" by Amy Cuddy: https://youtu.be/Ks-_Mh1QhMc. She's a Harvard scientist, and talks about the research conducted on this topic and what she recommends doing for a job interview. She also shares a very compelling personal story to make this point stand out. If you wonder why I'm talking about the power posture in this "Before" section, it's because it's good to practice your power pose well in advance, so you don't feel like you're faking something when you go to the actual job interview. Introverts are not good at faking, and someone else (the employer, for example) will notice if you try to fake your confidence. Instead, as Amy suggests, try it over and over: "Fake it till you become it" not "Fake it till you make it"! I suggest you practice this confidence posture for two minutes daily: straight back, shoulders back, head high, and look straight ahead. Do it from curiosity at the beginning, to see what you get out of it: do it in the morning (and notice the effect on your day), do it before meeting someone, do it before or during a discussion (even on the phone), etc. The more you do it, the more your body will get accustomed to this posture — so you'll embody it more easily before and during the job interview.

• Think about how you will handle the most difficult moments of the interview. By thinking of this upfront and getting mentally prepared for such situations, you will be less affected by them during the interview. For example, how would you like to react when you realize you didn't answer a question well? If you don't like how you normally react to such a situation, what would you like to do differently? My suggestion in this case is this: let it go! Whatever was said is part of the past; focus on the next questions and answers so you get the most of what is left. If you start thinking about what you didn't answer well while you're still in the interview, part of your cognitive attention will be monopolized by those thoughts instead of giving full attention to the present moment (the next question asked, the next answer to formulate). Not to mention the negative emotions that will show up if you start dwelling on what you didn't do well, which will negatively affect how you will perform the rest of the interview. I know, it's easier to say than do. That's why you need a physical thing to remind you to stay positive, no matter what's happening. What could you use as a good reminder to not take yourself too serious if you miss a point or made a mistake here and there? After all, it's not the end of the world! The way you handle the whole interview is even more important than how you handle those moments that are less than perfect! Employers know job interviews are quite stressful! What color or little sign can you have with you during the interview to remind you that it's okay to move on (instead of beating yourself up for a less-than-perfect answer).

• Looking from a different perspective is something that comes naturally to me, and I encourage you to use this attitude as well. Every time you notice a negative thought in your mind, acknowledge it, then see if you can find a more positive one. I have had many clients who, frustrated by their lack of results, start blaming the system or making all kinds of assumptions. I always tell them, "Blaming the system doesn't help your job search, and such thoughts drain your energy. Find a door to enter the system first; then change it from within when you have time and resources, if you still want to change it."

Here's an example of how to shift your perspective, to not let the initial thought tie you down: If a thought like, "Employers prefer extroverts", crosses your mind, look from a different perspective. "I know many introverts (or I'm sure there are introverts) successful in this kind of position. What can I do differently to get there? How can I present myself in a better way?" This will shift your attitude from feeling like a victim to finding ways to make yourself a more interesting candidate. It's similar with the exercises from chapter 5 (mindset), because all these negative thoughts or assumptions you have could in fact act as barriers in presenting yourself in the best way you can. Practice this attitude of shifting perspective anytime you notice a negative thought in your mind, and challenge all the thoughts you believe as real. You have no way to verify that all employers prefer extroverts for the type of position you're looking for — which means, that's only your own assumption. Replace it with something more empowering!

10. Interviewing in Manageable Doses

Whether you believe it or not, going to a job interview is like performing. Due to the interview structure, this is an interactive performance where you're playing the role of . . . yourself! Take a more objective look at what worked and didn't in your past interviews or when you're speaking with others. This self-reflection could give you some insights on what you need to work more on. I always start a simulation interview asking the client, "Based on your previous experience during job interviews, what do you think you need to improve?" At first some clients say they don't know, but when they really think about it, they remember specific interview moments when they didn't know how to answer a certain question or why the employer reacted in a certain way. If we pay attention, any interview gives us clues which are signs we can look into if we want to do better next time. The clues are quite evident if you pay attention to how an interview unfolded, besides the words being said: when an employer looks annoyed by an answer or loses his attention, or when you feel awkward because you don't know what to say (what question was asked?), etc. Trust your intuition, it'll remember these moments that you need to pay more attention to now while you're preparing for a new interview. Because now you can prepare yourself better. Prepare answers to common interview questions and repeat them out loud (even in front of a mirror) to see how you sound. Ask someone to do a simulation interview, get the feedback, prepare more, and ask for a second simulation interview to see if you've improved. To maximize your chances and reduce the number of interviews you have to go through to get a job, improving from one interview to another is a must. You didn't see a sports champion going from no preparation to a gold medal in one shot, did you? The same goes for you: you'll need to improve your interview performance in manageable doses to get the results you want. I'm not pushing you to become a successful public speaker or improv star, unless you want to. But making progress from one interview to another is a must. If you want something that will also help your whole career, join a Toastmasters club in your area. You can find one on their website: https://www.toastmasters.org. Their supportive and friendly environment creates a structured way to help increase your self-confidence and think on your feet by taking manageable "doses" to improve. It takes commitment, it won't happen in one or two meetings. But if you continue, the results will speak for themselves and you'll no longer feel intimidated when you speak with strangers (like in a job interview). This progress in manageable doses will desensitize you so your fear of rejection is less strong during the job interview (making you feel more at ease and helping you formulate better answers).

11. Being Salesy (Or Not)

I'll start with you: Why do you apply for a position and accept taking a job interview? Because you want the position and to work for that company, right? You have your own deeper reasons why, and that's totally okay. What's not helping you though is refraining from talking about yourself (or in terms that don't show your real value) because you think it's important enough or you're not comfortable talking about you. Yet if you don't talk about yourself, who will?

Introverts are deep thinkers, and some have ideas so big they feel quite small in comparison and not worthy to talk about themselves. Examples of introverts like Mandela and Gandhi show how powerful introverts are if they trust themselves and find their way into implementing those ideas. So should you!

Thinking that your expertise is not good enough or you're not comfortable to mention it will only make you feel small. So will not having the right attitude to enter an interview, even if you know deep inside that you can do a great job if given the chance. I'm not asking you to go to the other extreme either, to brag about yourself if you don't feel like it. It won't come naturally, and it won't serve you either.

So switch it around. Instead of focusing on yourself ("I don't like to talk about myself," "I don't like to be salesy"), focus your answers on the other side! How can your skills, expertise, and motivation can help them, the company?

Think about how you can be of service, and let your answers show that. Not how good you are, but how you can help them achieve their goals!

Including examples in your answers is one way of doing this, because the interviewers can easily translate how your behavior in those situations is relevant to their position. Another way is to do your research well, to understand their specific needs and challenges, and formulate your answers in a way that shows that you understand their needs and you can help them overcome their challenges. This way they'll understand your value pertaining to that specific position better. Remember how John answered the question, "Why do we need to hire you?" for the fraud and security position at the bank? He spotted their biggest need (to keep the information secure) and biggest challenge (prevent fraud) in advance, and his answer showed how motivated he was to make that happen!

You can influence the outcome of the job interview by preparing answers well in advance, so they don't look salesy (and you feel good about them). John was quite excited about his answer and how he played it for a bigger impact (with that brief pause between the first phrase and the explanation).

12. References

Since we are talking about preparation before the job interview, make sure you contact the people you'd like to be referred by, and create a list with their names, coordinates (phone, email, company), and in what role they were when you worked together (for example: manager, colleagues, client, etc.).

If the employer asks for your references at the end of the interview, you can either give the list or offer to send it via email.

13. Take Your Business Card

If you don't have a business card yet, it might be the time. It doesn't have to be something fancy. In chapter 8, I gave you some DIY ideas for creating a business card.

It's useful to have your business card with you when you go to a job interview. You can give it away to the interviewer: "May I give you my business card?" I've found that often when you give a business card, you get the interviewer's in return. If you don't, ask for it so you can follow up with a thank you note after the interview. We'll talk about this note later in the "After the Job Interview" section.

14. Manage Your Interview Expectations

Remember what I said at the beginning? Each job interview helps you hone your interview skills, so you become more comfortable in an interview setting and manage better your answers. There are several paths that could lead to your long-term objective, so there is no need to increase your stress by thinking that you HAVE to pass THIS interview.

Before going the job interview, your focus should be on preparing the best you can. Companies expect you to already have answered prepared for the commonly asked questions. By not doing that you're projecting a less professional image.

During the interview, though, your role is to do your best in the given conditions, because it's the only thing under your control! The rest is the employers' part, based on what they consider important for them. Go to the interview knowing that you can maximize your chances by focusing on your role (to do your best), instead of trying to impress the employer. You don't know what impresses the employer anyway, and if you want to impress you put so much pressure on yourself that it will have a negative effect on the way you present yourself.

DURING THE JOB INTERVIEW

Okay, you've prepared for the job interview the best you could. The night before:

• Go to bed around 10:00 p.m., no matter if you feel prepared enough or not. The stress during the interview will drain your energy, so you need to fully recharge your batteries with a good night sleep and even with a walk in nature, if you can, before going to bed. Otherwise, your mind will be foggy and all the preparation you've done will not serve you well because you simply won't remember much!

• Prepare what you need to take with you the next day: the clothes you'll wear, a notebook and pen (to take notes during the interview), several resumes (to give to interviewers if they ask), references list, business cards, a bottle of water, some snacks in case the commute is too long (stress triggers hormones that can cause hunger; if you feel hungry during the interview you won't have enough energy and mental focus on the interview itself), etc. Some employers might not allow you to use your own notebook, but they provide paper and pen (which remain with them after you leave). If they don't you can ask.

The Day Has Come!

• On your way to the interview, notice the thoughts that come to mind and how you feel. If they're negatives thoughts, let them go by putting things in perspective: if it's not this interview, there will be another one that will take you closer toward your long-term objective. Focus on something more positive, something that helps you relax: your ideal vacation place or your favorite relaxing music, or simply take deep breaths to keep you calm and relaxed. It's important to keep your stress at bay. If not, it'll mess up your interview performance!

• Make sure you leave home early enough to get there in time. I usually go and find the interview place a day before, to figure out where it is and how much time I need to get there. The interview day, I add some extra travel time to have little or no surprises to find the place and be there in time.

• What do I mean by arriving on time? If you get there earlier, present yourself at the reception only ten minutes before the interview. Arriving too close to the interview time will only increase your stress, and you'll not have time to familiarize yourself with the environment and catch your breath before the interview starts. Arriving more than ten minutes in advance is even better, because you can use the washroom, arrange your clothes, and put on the power pose for two minutes — to boost your confidence before meeting any of the company employees.

• Remember, the interview begins the moment you enter the company's door! You don't know who is in the reception area, and the interviewers might ask the receptionist's opinion about the candidates (they'll be waiting in the reception area for about ten minutes, more than enough time for someone to form an opinion). Be polite and professional.

• While you're waiting to be called, instead of feeding your own fears and insecurities about the upcoming interview, get curious! Look around, notice the work environment and the employees passing by: Do they look happy? Do they feel at ease in that company? Does it seem to be a stressful environment? Could you see yourself working in this environment? Etc. Remember, you're there to assess the company as well, not just to be interviewed.

• Take a few deep breaths while you're in the reception area, and put on the confidence pose: straight back, shoulders back, head lined up with your backbone, and look straight ahead. This way you'll enter the interview feeling more calm and confident, and make a good impression from the beginning.

• Keep in mind, you have nothing to lose in this situation. You will gain something no matter the results! Enter the interview with a win-win attitude, and this attitude will help you talk about your experience the best you can!

The Interview Starts

• When you enter the interview room, notice who is there and the environment.

• If the interviewer initiates, have a firm hand shake. In my workshop about the interview, I shake hands with each participant when I talk about this topic. For those who have a very weak hand shake, I ask them to do it again. This time they have to initiate it, and I respond with a weak hand shake and ask what they think about me based on shaking hands this way. They get my point! :-) They understand that the weak handshake comes from someone weak, not interested, or not confident enough. Would you hire someone like this? This is probably your first contact with the interviewer; make it count on your behalf by having a firm handshake.

• Your role is to start building rapport with the interviewer(s) as soon as possible. What that means is this: creating a bond that facilitates communication. Even if you don't like small talk, a simple smile, a positive remark about something positive you've noticed (about the work environment, interview room, an object in the room, etc.) could help you connect with them and break the ice before the interview starts. Finding common ground will put both you and the interviewers more at ease, creating a more pleasant atmosphere. Once I was interviewed by someone who had several photos of horses on his desk and the office walls. I simply mentioned, "It seems you like horses", and he took it away, telling me about how much he likes horses. That simple remark made him feel good (because I noticed something he cares about), and we started the interview in a less rigid way — which made me feel more at ease.

• "Tell us about yourself" will probably be the first interview question. If you've already prepared the answer, it should flow with confidence and ease. This will give you a good start and make a good impression from the beginning. I've heard from different sources that it takes only a few seconds for interviewers to realize if they are in your favor or not. So why not maximize your chances with a well-presented first answer? It shouldn't be too long, because you risk losing the employer's attention. In one-two minutes you have enough time to briefly present your background in a way that's relevant to the position you applied. Pay attention to not give away too much information, too many details, because you want to keep them for the following questions. This question was only to start the interview, not to say everything about yourself.

• Studies show that in a normal conversation, extroverts seem to focus 100 percent on the actual conversation, making them less prone to perceive helpful clues from the environment. For introverts, 75 percent of their cognitive attention is on the conversation itself, the rest being focused on monitoring what's going on (inside and outside). This means, you'll be able to notice the interviewer's reaction to your answers. Use this advantage to adjust your answers on the spot if you notice signs that employers might be getting bored (you're talking too much, for example). If they're interested to hear more, you can add an example.

• The above characteristic also useful in regulating your stress and how you feel in the moment: if you're too nervous or stressed about a specific aspect (how your answer turned out, for example), use self-talk to calm down. Under stress, the introverts' amygdala (which is responsible for the fight or flight effect) is much more active than extroverts'. In her book *The Introverts Advantage*, Marti Olsen Laney PsyD talks about how this powerful tool (self-talk) calm us down if there is no real danger. You can just reassure yourself that it's okay to continue, even in those conditions. It's not the end of the world if one or some of your answers don't turn out the best way, is it? Calm yourself down and be gentle with yourself, instead of beating yourself up for whatever happened. This way you'll be able to get the most from the rest of the interview. An interview is stressful for anyone, especially for the sensitive introvert, so you need to learn some techniques to manage your thoughts and emotions while going through it.

• Another technique is to pay attention to things you're interested in, besides your rich inner world. For example, notice the interviewer's behavior — introverts are good at studying behaviors. Or how you can put your expertise in their service, to help them achieve their goals. Or portray your passion for something related to that position and company. Your role in the interview is not to push to sell yourself, so take that pressure off. Your role is only to give enough relevant examples and answers to make them think: "This candidate would be such a great addition to our team."

• When they ask questions you've already prepared for, remember the points and formulate your answer. Rely on the examples and achievements you prepared in an SAR format, and let them speak about your value. I even used this technique for some questions I didn't expect. Since I already had some examples, I chose the most pertinent for the question and included it in my answer.

• Remember to take your time to formulate an answer to a question you didn't expect. Use your notebook if you need, to write a few points you want to talk about, and develop them in your answer.

• Include in your answers information you gathered while researching the company. Besides the fact interviewers like to see you know something about their company, it also shows that you're interested in that position (not just getting a job in general).

• Active listening is an important aspect of effective communication, especially in an interview. Pay attention not only to the question, but also to key words the employer uses in a question — you can even jot them down on. In your answer, try to use the same key words — it not only shows that you paid attention, but also that you speak the same language, which helps in building good rapport as well.

• Another technique to build rapport is to mirror the mannerisms and the employers' speech pace. This is a technique used in sales, and I was not aware of it until a sales coach pointed it out. Do you happen to speed up your speech when someone speaks fast? And slow down when someone speaks at a slower pace? It might come naturally when you really want to connect with your interlocutor. It seems the same happens when we mirror the interlocutor's body posture, for example. Try it out, with your friends at the beginning. If your friend has a confident posture while talking with you, mirror that posture and see what happens. Don't stress yourself too much with doing this in an interview, because if you force yourself it might have the opposite effect: the interviewer might notice, or you'll pay more attention to using the technique than focusing on formulating good answers. I just wanted to mention this here because I've seen too many introverted clients so caught up in their own world (being insecure about the interview), that it showed up in their body language too. When I asked them to mirror my confidence posture, they noticed a positive change in the way they answered too (speaking with a more confident voice, formulating the answers in a much better way).

• Since the words used are only 7 percent of the message that comes across (the rest being transmitted through non-verbal clues), I encourage my clients to focus on the message they want to deliver and let the words come from that place. What I mean by that is this: If you want a company to understand how useful your expertise is for achieving their goals, believe it yourself first — so your body can also project that attitude while your words talk about your expertise. Your body is a reflection of your thoughts, and if you believe something else than what you're saying, your body language will betray you.

• Believing that the employer has all the power in an interview makes you feel small; your body posture reflects that automatically, and this is what the employer captures when your words say something else. This is called a double signal, and in this case people tend to believe the signal given by your body posture instead of your words. Even if you've applied for a position that's not ideal for you, find something that's really compelling for you regarding that position (or working for that company), and project that attitude when you speak. Be assertive in achieving your goals, and your assertiveness will be much better received than what you project by feeling you're at the employer's mercy.

• Finding something compelling about that position and company will also help you get over your own inhibitions during the interview. Because when you put your attention on and talk about something you really like, your mind won't have enough time to focus on your inhibitions ("I'm not good at this", "I don't know how to sell myself", etc.). When I was invited to the interview for the customer service representative position, I knew that was a job I wanted. I didn't think that I didn't have the right expertise for that position, nor in the financial field. I didn't think that it'd take me two hours to commute one way and that would be tiring. All I thought about was how to present myself in the best way to get that position that would allow me to get into the Canadian job market. I trusted that employer had his own reason for inviting someone like me to the interview, and went there putting on my assertive attitude. I did the same later, when I wanted a job that matched my new career direction. I found something compelling about that position (it'd allow me to use my newly acquired coaching skills), and I put my inhibitions aside (that I don't have experience or enough knowledge for that position). During the interview, being laser-focused on what you want will help you more than focusing on what you don't have or don't do well.

• If you feel that some of your answers don't land well with the employer, please don't take it personally. You're still a wonderful person! They might not agree with what you said, because it doesn't meet their requirements for candidate selection, not because you're not a good person. The way you see things might be different from someone else's point of view. Continue to trust yourself (use self-talk if you need to); otherwise you might screw up the rest of the interview if you allow yourself to feel down. Remember, you can learn from any experience! And we learn even more from those experiences that didn't go as well as we wanted! There's always room for improvement, but leave that for after the interview.

• Maintaining eye contact with the interviewer is perceived, by the Western culture, as having confidence in what you're saying. As an introvert, I feel the need to look away when I formulate an answer in my mind (so I don't get distracted). And that's okay, as long as I still maintain eye contact most of the time I speak. But if you look away all the time, it might be perceived as having something to hide — which won't be to your advantage.

• One of the things to look for during the interview is the employer's concerns. This will show up in the way the employer asks questions, and what questions they ask. It's your role to provide answers that reassure the employer that you're a good candidate for the position, and the way you can do it best is to provide a relevant example or explanation that highlights your point. If, for example, you get a question about not having enough experience related to the position, or any at all. This means the employer is concerned about your experience, so this is your chance to answer in a way that reassures. I didn't have Canadian experience when I was interviewed for my first job here. This is like a chicken and egg situation: How can I have experience if I just got here? But from the employer perspective, this meant that I wasn't familiar with the Canadian work environment and might be risky to take onboard. The way I answered that question was to bring to their attention my ability to quickly adapt. So, after mentioning this soft skill, I gave an example of a four-month internship I did: I was in Romania back then, when I got the chance to do this internship in France in a totally different field (chamber of commerce). Besides considering it a good experience of adaptability (new country, different language and culture), I also mentioned the results of my internship (was considered that best intern they'd ever had, and my evaluation scored 100 percent for adaptability). I concluded my answer with confidence that I can also adapt easily to the new position, if hired. This way, instead of taking the employer's question *ad litteram* (and freak out), I turned it around to show one of my skills that addressed the employer's real concern (the reason behind his question). I'm sure you can do the same, by tapping into the power of your mind! Especially if you're thinking in advance about what you lack (related to the employer's requirements) and what else you can bring to their attention to address their concerns.

• I talked about using your intuition in the chapter 9, about job search strategies. You didn't expect me to ask you to leave it at the door during the job interview, did you? :-) Intuition can help you even in the most difficult moments. In one job interview, the HR representative was talking very fast. That was her communication style. I answered questions one by one, until we got to one that I couldn't understand. I asked her to rephrase the question, and she repeated it the same way. I didn't understand it the second time either. I quickly evaluated my options. Asking her to repeat it again wouldn't serve, and would make me feel stupid. :-) I quickly rewound the question in my mind, and although I didn't understand it, I noticed that it sounded like a closed question. So I gambled my answer, saying "Yes" with conviction (trusting my intuition)! Bingo! It was the answer she wanted to hear! Imagine my relief, and my smile even now, when I describe this situation. :-) The morale of the story is this: When you don't know what to say, trust your intuition to give you an answer, then move on with the rest of the interview!

• If you're asked, "Where do you see yourself five years from now?" put your answer in the context of the position you applied for and the company type. In a simulation interview, a client told me "In five years I want to be a manager" while his job interview the next day was with a small company! If his interviewer is the company manager, this might sound like "I want your job"! :-) Yet this answer could work in a bigger company. Or if you say: "I want to have my own company in five years", the employer might not appreciate your answer because he wants employees who focus on the company they work for (not something else). In this case, you can simply say: I would like to take on more responsibilities." You can also mention if you're thinking about getting a certification in your field, because companies like employees who are assertively pursuing their career.

• Although you might be curious about the salary, during the job interview you might not get a question about this topic. If you do, instead of answering their question directly you can ask if they'd like to disclose their salary range. Based on your research and your salary expectations, you can then answer their initial question to show if you're still interested in getting the position within their salary range. When I was asked this question during the interview for the quality assurance position, I answered: "You now have a better idea of my expertise, and I trust you will make me an offer accordingly." "But this is a beginner position, and you already have experience in this field", the manager said. "There is opportunity to grow, and your salary will be renegotiated after a six-month probation". Since I was interested in having that company on my resume, I continued: "I don't mind starting at this level, because I'm sure I can learn a lot about your company and products before getting to the next level." This way, I also indirectly answered one of their concerns about my experience. I wouldn't recommend you asking about salary, if they don't bring up this topic. It might be too early, because they want to screen the candidates they're interested in first, and bring this topic up when they send the offer to the chosen candidate. Then it's your time, if you want to negotiate. The more expertise you have, the more negotiation power of you have. If their salary range is not what you expect but you still want that position, you can try to negotiate others perks: number of vacation days, health benefits, work from home days, office with a window, etc. :-)

• Usually the last interview question is, "Do you have any question for us?"

This is a polite way to give you the chance to ask something, if you want, but also a way for them to check if you're really interested in working for them. Because if you answer no, they'll think you're not interested (or not enough). If you have time for only one question, ask about the next steps in the interviewing process. This not only shows your interest in the position, but also gives you an idea about how long you can wait to get an answer. If you have some more time and have prepared these questions in advance, this is the time to ask. Start with the most important one for you, because there might not be enough time to get them to respond to all. If you already got your questions answered during the interview, find another one: Now, after all those questions they asked you, what are you still curious to know about the company or position? For example: "How do you describe someone who does an excellent job in this position?" This will give you ideas of what you can do if hired, to meet their standard for excellence. "How would you describe your company culture?" to see how an introvert like you would fit in, or if you can incorporate restorative niches at work. "What is the company's biggest competitor and why? Etc. The questions you ask should be open-ended questions, not those with only two options (yes/no). A simple Google search with "questions to ask interviewers" will give you more ideas.

• Remember the attitudes of effective communication? Use them during your job interview as well:

Lightness: Put things in perspective. Don't take yourself too seriously if you miss something or don't answer well. It's not the end of the world!

Commitment: Rely on your commitment to building the career you want, so you can speak more assertively and put aside the self-defeating thoughts that show up during the interview.

Gratefulness: Appreciate the fact you have the chance of this interview. It will either bring you the job or get you closer to the job you want (by teaching you lessons and allowing you to do better next time).

Collaboration: The job interview is a two-way street. You collaborate with the employer by presenting how you can help and addressing his concerns, so you both get what you want. You have the chance to present your skills, expertise, and motivation. The employer gets the opportunity to see if you're the candidate they want. If it's a good match, you both get a bonus: you're hired and they benefit from your performance!

Curiosity/Awareness: By staying curious to understand the employer's perspective behind each question, you become more aware of what elements to include in your answers for a bigger impact.

Caring: Being fully present in the moment helps you realize what's going on with you and take action before your stress becomes too big to keep under control. Active listening is a form of caring, showing interest. Avoid interrupting while they talk or jumping ahead in your mind thinking you know what they are going to ask (because you might miss something).

Respect: I have no doubt you are respectful of the employer's opinion, but what about yours? Keep in mind, you are a person, and a job doesn't define who you really are. You can talk about the qualities you bring to a job, but you deserve self-respect no matter what job you apply for. If you want your opinion to be heard and taken into consideration, you'll need to speak up during the job interview. It's your chance to say how you see yourself fitting in and helping their company grow! If you hope they'll get it without you giving enough elements, they might not, because they are not mind readers! :-)

Deep Democracy: You have to believe that a job interview is for hearing both voices: yours and the employer's. They might be expressed in different ways (yours in the form of answers, the employer's in the form of questions), but they both count to help each other understand the situation better.

• And at the end, give your business card (if you have one) and get the interviewer's. You'll need the email address to send a thank you note.

That's it! So your role was to handle right the opportunity of having that job interview. I trust you did, the best you could!

AFTER THE JOB INTERVIEW

Okay, the interview is over. Take the time to pat yourself on the back, you made it! I know it was not easy. It's not easy for any of us, so take the time to recognize your efforts.

Then, take the time to think about which of the answers you didn't handle so well and what else was important and you forgot to say. It's time to craft your thank you email. It's better to send it within twenty-four hours, while the impression is still fresh, both for you and the employer. Write a brief email to the interviewer, and give yourself a little time to reread it before sending it (you might have mistakes or want to formulate it differently):

- Thank the interviewer for giving you the time to interview for this position, and how much you appreciate it.
- Mention briefly what was important and you forgot to say or what you didn't say correctly.
- Reiterate your interest in the position and how confident you are that you could be a good fit.

The same day or the next one, take the time to evaluate how your interview was. This is only for learning purposes, not to beat yourself up for what didn't go well. Think about it, and take some notes:

- What did you do right, and what can you learn from that?

- What questions did you find the most challenging? What made them challenging? How would you handle them differently next time?
- What questions did you not expect? What were the reasons for them being asked? Keep them in mind for the next interview, if you have more.
- What did you notice about your behavior: What did you handle well and what didn't you?
- Is there something you'd like to add, remove, adjust in your resume, in case you don't get this position?
- What else can you learn from this experience?

It's important to reflect on your interview now, so you can learn your lessons. Even if you get the position, the lessons learned could have a positive impact for the rest of your career.

Based on the answer received when you asked about the next steps in the interview process, add to your calendar when you'd like to follow-up, in case you don't hear from them.

In the meantime, take a short break from your job search to recharge your battery and rebuild your self-esteem (if it dropped), then continue the job search. Don't wait for the answer from this employer; it might take one to two weeks, or even more, until they make a decision. Waiting is not fun, plus it makes you lose some precious time that otherwise could be used to continue your job search.

If you get the position, congratulations! Take the time to celebrate!

If you don't, I suggest you take a deep breath, and even a short break from your job search. One to two days is okay. You deserve it; you worked hard to prepare for this interview, and you just finished an important step in your job search (any job interview is!). You need energy for the next steps, and some self-care will help you get it!

Also take the time to contact the HR department and ask if they can give you any feedback. Sometimes they answer, and the feedback received will help you learn what went well and the employer's perspective on what you didn't do well — so you can improve.

There is a lot of wisdom in proverbs like this: "Fall down seven times and stand up eight."

Chapter Fourteen

PUT IT ALL TOGETHER

Every project has challenges, and every project has its rewards.
~ Stephen Schwartz

In the previous chapters, I covered different aspects of the job hunting process. In this chapter, we'll put all this information together, to help you create a *job search strategy mix* that suits you best. This is a customized strategy, because you'll be more effective if you focus on what's appropriate for your short-term goal, your personality style, and your specific situation.

Let's start by looking again at some of the examples I gave you along the way, that show how those job seekers customized their strategy mix according to their specific situation.

I met Zara on a hiking trip organized by a local club. When we started talking during a break, she told me how unsuccessful she had been in her job search. She had a great financial background and moved to this city six months ago, and her network was very limited. Her job search relied mainly on job postings found on the Internet, and she was targeting big companies in her field. She was frustrated, not knowing what else to do, yet quite confident that her job search approach was the right one. After all, she applied what she had learned from the employment center she visited when she moved here. Since she needed a job as soon as possible, I suggested she first target smaller and medium companies in her field, close to her home, because they have a shorter recruitment process. I also suggested this strategy because these types of companies might receive fewer applications than the bigger companies (who are usually bombarded with more applications, many of them from candidates with local experience who have already built their visibility, have a broader network who can recommend them, and know to target their applications to get the employer's attention and gain their trust). "Shift from reactive to proactive mode, approach the companies instead of waiting to find listed job postings", I said. "And how can I find such companies?" she asked, without much conviction. I gave her the same ideas you found in the "Research" section of Chapter 9: "Go to the local library (they have printed and online directories of companies, and a librarian can tell you what other resources they have). The Industry Canada website has an on online directory where you can search by industry and geographical area, read the local newspapers, etc." Two months passed by, and I received a message from her via LinkedIn. She found her first position soon after we talked, by following my advice to contact smaller companies. One of the people who received her application sent it to another company, because in his company they didn't have any openings, but the other company was looking for someone with her background. She received a two-month contract. While being there, she continued her job search and got a full-time permanent position in a bigger company.

In summary:

- Understanding the importance of networking, Zina tried to expand her network based on her interests and through one-on-one discussions (which put her more at ease).
- By focusing on what was most important in her situation (finding a position as soon as possible), she adjusted her strategy mix to be more effective in her job search by directly approaching smaller companies.
- She built her path step by step, by accepting a temporary contract until she was able to find a full-time contract with the type of company she was looking for.
- She reached out to thank the people who helped her, to continue to build rapport in those relationships (so they would stay in touch).

Nancy is the senior marketing specialist (Google Analytics certified) who was not interested in learning more about LinkedIn. A nice person, but a very private person, she didn't like the idea of networking — not even online. Without much success in her job hunt, she came to my series of workshops about job search. She became more aware of the employer's perspective and the need to increase the visibility of her own profile. I attracted her to the workshop by saying that she needs to walk her talk: How can an online marketing specialist build credibility if she's not using social media at all? When she realized how resourceful LinkedIn could be for her job search, she changed her mind. "I tried all the strategies you taught us at the beginning, to see which would work for me," she said a month later when she found her dream job. She first contacted other professionals in her field via LinkedIn, and asked for information interviews. They gave her feedback on the resume, plus tips and strategies that are more useful in her field. Then she started to apply them, targeting her resume to each position she applied to. Noticing that her applications were quite well received, leading to invitations to job interviews, she started to be more selective. She knew she wanted to work for an eco-friendly company, so she looked for such companies to approach. She was invited to five job interviews, and she even refused the offers of some companies because she didn't like their culture. Within a month since she started to use these strategies, she was hired by an eco-friendly company she liked a lot, and they were even willing to invest in her professional training. Doing good research about the company, she was well prepared during the interview — which had a nice flow because the company's values and her own were quite similar.

In summary:

- Nancy tried several strategies to see which worked best in her case.
- Information interviews helped her refine and target her resume specific to the industry.
- Applying what she learned from information interviews, she focused only on the strategies that brought her job interviews, narrowing down even more by looking for the type of company she was really interested in.
- The research about the company paid off, because she was more relaxed in the interview and was able to make a deeper connection with the interviewers by sharing the same values.

Lili was a recent graduate when she moved to a new city. With no connections, and no ideas where to start her job search, she attended two of my workshops: Attitudes for Effective Communication and LinkedIn for Job Search." She quietly walked the Wheel of Attitudes, and discovered the lack of assertiveness as her biggest weakness, and how much it affected her job hunting. Motivated by her discovery, she attended the workshop about LinkedIn that opened up her eyes to the opportunities facilitated by this online platform. She started by contacting professionals in her field, via LinkedIn, who were also at the beginning of their career but were already employed. One person referred her to another, and she had a chain of several information interviews in two weeks and a half. One even with a VP, which she wouldn't have had the courage to approach without being referred. Many professionals she talked to mentioned they also found their jobs by using information interviews. The last time Lili called for an information interview, she was asked if she wanted to come to a real job interview instead. Five hours after, she received the job offer for a position they'd created because they needed someone with her skills. She accepted the offer, and it was only two and a half weeks since she started to use LinkedIn and job interviews. Her newfound assertiveness paid off!

In summary:

- Lili's curiosity and willingness to improve led her to the workshops that provided information to facilitate her job search.
- Her willingness to apply the learning helped her become more assertive and reach out to people she otherwise wouldn't meet.
- The information interviews helped her progress, step by step, toward the final interview which led to being hired.
- By stepping out of her comfort zone, not only did she learn new things about herself and the job market, but she also opened a job opportunity. She couldn't find that opportunity otherwise, because the position was created when she increased her visibility enough so the company became aware of how much they need her skills and expertise.

If you paid attention, there is a common thread between these examples: they all succeeded by tapping into the "human factor"! Zara met me while hiking (a common interest), which made us both willing to open up. Nancy and Lili reached out to workshops, where they met new people, got new information, and found the courage and motivation to use the information interview strategy. None of them found the job they wanted relying only on online job postings or books on job search.

Hello captain! :-)

Let me remind you that you're at the helm of your own job search project. As an introvert, you're probably good at complex, focused problem solving, so let's put your strengths to good use by giving you a complex problem to solve: finding the job you want!

We'll start by putting together the information gathered from the previous chapters and exercises, and throw in some more, to see how to create a strategy mix that makes your job search more effective, by taking into consideration your specific situation and the introverts strengths. And we'll do that by looking at the job hunting process as a project with you as the project manager.

One of the challenges of your job search project is not knowing how long it will take to complete it. This project will end when you get the job you want, but how much time it will take to get there . . . who knows? So your role is not only to define the different phases of the project and implement it, but also to make sure you maximize the resources and shorten the process when possible. Even if you're not in a hurry to get a job, you'd like to get the most out of your time and the effort you put into this project, right?

To do that, we'll use some principles from project management and quality assurance. As a project manager you'll divide your project into different phases:

My Job Search Project

Initiate	Plan	Execute	Control	Close
• Self-evaluation	• Strategy mix	• Implementation action plan	• Evaluation	• Got hired!
• SMARRT Goals	• Mind map	• Resources management	• Learn from experience	• Lessons learned from this project
• Project mindset	• Action plan	• Risk management	• Adjust strategy mix	
	• SMARRT goals		• Implement learning	
	• Timeline			
	• Reminders			
	• Checkpoints			
	• Risk plans			

Some of the elements of these phases are not new to you (I mentioned them in previous chapters), but now it's time to actually put them into practice based on your situation and job search project's objective.

Phase 1: Initiate The Project

You probably think you started your job search when you started searching for job openings, but to give a good start to your job search project and make it more effective overall, you need to get together the information from the self-evaluation tools and exercises provided in the previous chapters, set SMARRT goals, evaluate, and set a successful mindset for the whole project. Here's what I mean by that:

Self-Evaluation

• Review your ***current situation***, and I'm not only talking about job search, because other factors could affect your job search as well. Evaluate what's important to deal with, what's urgent, and what to let go. What's important and urgent informs what you need to address first. Being unemployed, for example, leads to a different strategy mix than being currently employed and looking for your next opportunity to advance your career. Sometimes we hang on things and situations without them being necessary — identify them and let go. It will free your mind, time, and energy to put more toward your job search. Watching TV, for example, will eat up your time, distracting you from your job search with all the information it dumps on you. You better use that time in a more beneficial way, so you can recharge your batteries to have a successful job search.

• Evaluate your **strengths** and **weaknesses** using the Wheel of Life, Wheel of Job Search (chapter 2) and Wheel of Attitudes (chapter 11). What's missing? What's important to address? What do you need to adjust?

• Identify your **long-term objective** and **short-term goal** for your job search (chapter 4).

• Review your **skills and expertise** (chapter 6), and decide what you'll take from the past to achieve your short-term goal, and what you'll need more to achieve your long-term objective. Also think about how you can transfer examples from your background toward what you want, even if they don't seem to have a direct connection.

• Check out your **mindset** (chapter 5). Remove the inner barriers you've identified, and replace them with more empowering thoughts that give you more energy and motivation.

• Prepare your **job search tools** (chapter 8), or at least the templates you'll use when you actually start implementing your job search strategy mix.

• Notice what bothers you about the **environment** you're in: Do you have clutter around you? A noisy environment? Stressful? Distractions? Negative people? These will make you feel less at ease and drain your energy. A proper environment will sustain your job search efforts. Introverts flourish in an empathetic environment, with minimal noise; work better individually and uninterrupted; and need peace and quiet time to concentrate or regenerate.

SMARRT *Goals for Your Job Search Project*

The objective of your project is to find the position you want short term, which is aligned with your long-term objective: "I want (this type of position) in (this type of company) with (this type of culture and work environment) by (this date)."

To get there, you'll also need to define some SMARRT goals (like we also talked about in chapter 4). By accomplishing these goals, consistently, your project will progress until you achieve its objective: finding the position you want!

We'll explore what SMARRT goals mean in this context, since it's a bit different than other projects: you might want the new job by a certain date, but there are so many variables that can affect your project completion. You'll define your SMARRT goals in the next phase (plan), so you'll need to know first how to define them:

Specific: Your goals should be specific. The more details, the better. Don't make them too broad, like "I want a position that corresponds to my skills and expertise, and I will send some resumes this week." Because this won't motivate you enough and won't give you specific ideas how to go about it. Something like this is more specific: "Every week I will to add 10 companies to my list, find 30 positions I'm interested in, send 20 targeted applications and reach out to 10 new people." In the Plan phase, after you create your mind map with all the strategies you'd like to use in your job search, you'll be able to set your SMARRT goals by being more specific.

Measurable: You need to be able to measure your progress. If you adopt a goal like the above example, those numbers (10, 30, 20 10) will be your benchmarks that allow you to track your progress each week.

Achievable: Your goals should take you out of your comfort zone, enough to be a stretch but not too much that your inner critic becomes so loud that you don't even try. Goals that are not stretching will make you feel so comfortable that you won't tap into your full potential, thus making the job search process longer. Don't worry if you don't know yet what's a stretch for you, just set some SMARRT goals and you'll adjust them along the way if they are too stretching or too comfortable. Stress is not always a bad thing; it depends on the level of stress you put on yourself. Too much will cause you to become overwhelmed, tired, or frustrated (that you can't do it all). Not enough will make you say, "Oh, I can do it," and you'll relax so much that you lose momentum. Find your so-called "sweet spot," because that'll give you enough motivation to be effective in your job search.

Realistic: You can set whatever goals you want, but if they are not realistic, you're sabotaging yourself by heading into something that has very slight chances of happening. For example, if you just got your MBA, without prior management experience, and you'd like to find a manager position within two weeks — you might not be able to reach employers in such short amount of time, and you might even be disappointed by their reaction (because most prefer prior management experience for such a position). Also, credibility and trust are important factors when it comes to a management position — affecting the hiring decision. So you'll have to work on these factors too, to increase your chances (I gave you a few suggestions throughout the book).

Resonating: Maybe you've heard before about setting SMART goals, but in coaching we add this extra R. It means that the goals you set for yourself should resonate with you! If others pressure you to go several times a week to events, to meet new people, and you don't resonate with that idea, don't put that as one of your goals. Find something that resonates more with you, because in this situation you will come across more authentically. And that's how you want people to see you — not intimidated by the circumstances you force yourself into.

Time-bound: Your goals have to have a time component. By when do you want to achieve each? Or how often do you want to focus on that goal (daily, weekly)? This way you have a structure to help you track the progress of your SMARRT goals, and adjust your actions if required.

For your overall job search project: it's hard to put a time frame, because you don't know when you'll find the company that will hire you. Yet, you can still set a time frame for this project (what you wish as due date), and postpone when you notice the due date is coming without having any signs that the results are close. In which case you can say, "Oops, wrong date. Let's move the completion date to . . . !" Avoid beating yourself up for not getting there yet; there are some elements that are not under your control. But for those that are, like the intermediate SMARRT goals, adjust them and your actions accordingly so you can progress faster this time.

Project Mindset

I developed this topic in more detail in chapter 5 "How My Mindset Affects the Job Search Results" and when I talked about your inner critic in chapter 13. I'd like to bring this to your attention again, because your mindset is a very important key to success! Please use what you learned in chapter 5 throughout your entire job search project. It's something that will help you when you're frustrated, stuck, or have lost the motivation to continue.

Your mind is the best ally you have, and you know how to tap into it! As an introvert, I know you have that power — use it! It can pick you up when you feel down, it can cherish your small successes along the way (when you achieve your daily and weekly SMARRT goals), it can help you make the most of your inner critic's messages or help you get over it when you want more focus on what you can actually do (not who you're not).

Talking about **introverts**, studies show the following:

• They have an inner strength. Tap into it and don't let yourself be swept away by what others say (including me). Take whatever you want from this book and other sources, and create a mental structure that will support you. Decide what you'll do when you're unsure, frustrated, stuck, or have lost the motivation to continue. Giving it a thought upfront will help you along the way, when it becomes harder. Such situations will occur, so decide how you'll handle them beforehand.

• They are patient. Rely on your patience to implement a project plan that bring in results. Hurrying into something, without enough preparation might not be to your advantage, because you're much better off when you think things through in advance.

• They're good at one-on-one interactions. Use this to your favor by encouraging yourself to reach out and tap into the "human factor". It builds bridges otherwise overlooked. And don't forget that "self-talk" can also be used consciously — in a positive way — to get the most out of that conversation. :-)

• They don't like new situations and meeting new people, because it could be overwhelming. Yet, if you set yourself some limits you too can do this because it can be to your advantage. By limits I mean, decide for how long you will be at an event or speak with someone — notice when you have reached your time limit, and be okay with stepping out. By getting there you show some love to your job search goals, while by leaving you'll show yourself some love for being committed to your goals and for honoring your introverted nature. Congratulate yourself when you do that! You made it, and your comfort zone increased just by showing up.

• They are more anxious in the evening of a stressful day. And since the days you'll work on your job search project are quite stressful, be aware of how you feel, and don't force yourself. A good break to recharge your batteries is more beneficial than continuing under stress.

• They like to make other people happy. While that's a good thing, you also need to add you into the picture. You want to be happy too, and to focus on your goals! If you haven't learned yet to say no (when you really want to), now is a good time! Make others understand your priorities so you feel okay saying no to someone (or something) and yes to yourself. Favor quality over quantity, whether it's about people or the actions you take.

• They are successful at things that matter to them, and good at self-gratification. Find what matters to you about this job search, or whatever you are doing at the moment, to help you move forward. And connect often with what matters to you, to keep you motivated. Do not expect others to motivate you; let that come as a bonus — if it happens! :-)

• They're good at solving problems. When one arises during your job search project, get some distance, put things in perspective, and see what you come up with. You can ask others too. There are many people who feel valuable then you ask for their advice. Yet you'll need to pass everything through your own filter before making decisions, because you're the only one who knows your situation, preferences, and priorities, and where your job search is headed.

I have three more concepts to talk about in this section about "Project Mindset":

- High dream/low dream
- Accountability buddy
- The three levels of reality

The first and third concepts are used in Organization and Relationship Systems Coaching (ORSC), and you can read more about them in *Creating*

Intelligent Teams: Leading with Relationship Systems Intelligence by Anne Rød and Marita Fridjhon.

High Dream, Low Dream

To which one are you more attached?

Let me explain the concepts of *high dream and low dream* in the context of the relationship you have with your job search: When you think about finding that position you want, you automatically create a high dream and a low dream.

The *high dream* is when you explore in your mind how great it would be to have the position, and let yourself imagine that situation in more detail. — How does it feel to think about it?

The *low dream* is when you entertain in your mind a thought like, "I can't have this job because . . . (the market is saturated, I'm not good enough for this position, I'm not good at talking about myself, etc." — How does this feel?

You know what? It's okay to have both high and low dreams, because each of them could bring different elements to your attention.

The question is, to which of them are you more attached: the high dream or the low dream?

Because the more you spend time thinking about one of them, the more you facilitate that dream to enter your reality. How? By being too attached to the low dream, for example, you'll miss the energy and inspiration that comes from connecting with the high dream — which will hinder your ability to realize it! By being too attached to the high dream will make you ignore the pitfalls that low dream signals, allowing them to become huge roadblocks on your path of reaching the high dream (get that position).

Now, in the initial phase of your job search project, to which of these dreams are you more attached?

What action will help you get closer to your high dream? Or if you're already attached to it, what action will release your attachment to your low dream?

What ally can you think of which could help you take that action consistently, so you stay on the path of achieving your job search objective? An ally could be a friend, relative, colleague, another job seeker or one of your social media friends. Pick someone who'd be supportive of your action, and you'll do the same for whatever action the other person wants to take. All you need to do is just ask!

Here's a story to give you an example about how the high and low dream exercise works:

I was recently a lead assistant during one of the ORSC courses where this concept is introduced to new students. I joined one of the participants to do this exercise together, and the situation I chose for myself was to get the most of this specific course. As an introvert, the previous two days I was more of an observer, to preserve my energy (so it didn't get drained by being with so many people in the room). During that exercise I realized that I was more attached to my low dream than to the high dream, by playing only the observer role. It didn't allow me to get the most of my time and participation there. It was such a revelation! I chose as my action to be fully present in the moment and participate more! I asked my exercise partner to be my ally. We decided to check in during the breaks to see how we were doing with implementing our chosen actions. To my surprise, I had much more energy at the end of that day than in the previous two days (when I was an observer)!

Accountability Buddy

I highly recommend you get yourself an ally or accountability buddy for your job search project. Even if you have different objectives and goals, the fact that you in check in from time to time (once a week) to report your progress and discuss your challenges will make you more prone to stick with your commitments for the week and will give you some fresh perspectives on what you're doing.

Even if you're like me — you can focus on and progress with your project without having to report to someone else — I can assure you that having an ally or accountability buddy is very useful! It doesn't have to be someone you meet with in person. As introverts, we are more comfortable using the Internet than meeting someone in person weekly — right? A half hour is usually enough to go both ways.

As I'm writing this book I joined a Facebook group of writers, and I got an accountability buddy through this group. We check in every Monday via Skype, and it was very beneficial so far: it helps me notice what I did or didn't do the last week (compared to my goals for that week); what blockages I have encountered, so I can address them; and set my SMARRT goals for the next week. Plus, writing being a lonely activity, getting in touch with someone weekly for a half an hour does a good job of feeding my need for socializing, without putting pressure on myself. Plus, we discuss some important topics, there's no small talk. :-)

Although you meet people during your job search, those are short encounters, while your overall project is still a lonely endeavor (you're the one planning, executing, and controlling your project). Bring in an ally or accountability buddy to touch base from time to time to discuss your job search project's progress and frustrations and celebrate your small successes along the way.

Anyone supportive and working toward a personal goal could make a good accountability buddy. Another job seeker, for example, because you're going through similar challenges. Or one of your social media friends. All you need to do is just ask, and mention the benefits of having such a "partner" for each of you!

Three Levels of Reality

I usually introduce this concept via an example:

Think about something that you wanted and were able to achieve. It could be a personal project you initiated and carried out through completion, the project size doesn't matter.

For example: I wanted to learn Excel. I put time and effort into it, and I was able to pass the Excel test for a position I was interested in. The test result was real proof that I had achieved my goal.

Do you have your example in mind, something you were able to achieve? Now go backward to the first moment you had the idea of that project.

To continue with the above example, I still remember that moment when I got the idea to learn Excel. I wanted to apply for another position, and the requirement to know Excel triggered my interest in learning it! I borrowed a book from the library, spent hours reading and practicing, and I was able to pass the test! Bingo! I achieved my goal, project completed! Isn't this a universal process (idea — action — desired results)? Does it work all the time?

The three levels of reality concept was first introduced by Dr. Arny Mindell, known for his "Process Work" (process oriented psychology). He mentioned that there are three different levels of our experience and perception, equally important, through which we can gain wisdom and knowledge. Here's how this concept applies to your job search project:

1. Essence Level: From this "space" we get any idea for the first time. Call it inspiration, Universal Consciousness or whatever you want. This was the level that inspired you as to what could be a great outcome for your current job search project, or at least the kind of idea you should focus on for this project: something that makes you excited to achieve it.

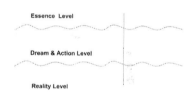

2. Dreaming & Action Level: You enter this "space" right after you get the idea of what you want. You get excited about it and start envisioning in your mind how great it will be. Fed by that excitement, you start taking action: you look for information about what you need to get there, and put yourself in motion. At this point people around you can't see your goal or objective; it's only in your mind (not visible to others).

3. Reality Level (Consensus Reality)**:** After taking the right actions, you achieve your job search project's objective. Anyone can see you're working in that position. This means that your idea made it to "Reality Level" — where anyone can say that's true!

I've seen so many job seekers getting lost in the "Dreaming & Action Level."

That's the reason I wanted to introduce you to the Three Levels of Reality concept, and the 3LR process associated with it: 1) Inspired idea (your job search project's objective); 2) Envisioning it and taking action toward implementing it; 3) Consensus reality validates your achievement (you got the desired position).

That middle level (Dreaming & Action) is the one where a lot of things could happen to block your objective to get into the "Reality Level", and many of those things are actually caused by you:

• **Trust:** If you don't trust there is that type of job out there for you, the one you're excited about, you will not put in the time and effort to find it, right? This way you get yourself kicked out of the 3LR process, and you caused this!

• **Time:** If you decide to drop that objective and choose something else because you didn't get the outcome you wanted for a good amount of time, you're also stopping the 3LR process for the objective! And who knows, maybe you were a few actions away from achieving it! Dropping an idea too early won't lead to its completion. How do you know if it's too early? If you get signs that your job search is progressing well (you get job interviews, for example), you're on the right track. Keep on going, unless your situation suddenly changes (like your financial status becomes an important issue) and you need to change your objective and the strategy mix. Otherwise, you don't want to head on a path and suddenly shift directions, to lose all the momentum you've gained until you reached that point. Talking about time: there is something you can do to decrease the time between the start and completion of your job search project, and that is . . .

• **Feelings:** It's about how you feel while navigating the Dream & Action phase of the 3LR process for your project's objective. Remember the T-F-A-R chain from the chapter 5? If you're thinking negatively during this phase, it will affect how you feel, and that will affect how you take action. Feeling afraid or insecure about what's out there, not having enough self-esteem and confidence, not trusting your background and your capability will make your actions less effective, leading to poorer results. Entertaining thoughts like "there's no such position available", "there's too much competition", "I can't sell myself", will only drain your energy, and you won't have enough to take the right actions that will bring the desired outcome. Not being patient during this process will also affect you, by rushing into taking actions that are not the best for you. It's your responsibility to stay positive and motivated during your job search project, until its completed. If you lose it temporarily, take a break to recharge your batteries, and pick yourself up by putting things in perspective and reconnecting with the objective of your job search project. If it's what you really want, spending some time envisioning how it is to actually have this position will make you regain your motivation so you can continue. By paying attention to your feelings and shifting to more positive ones when you drift away, you actually keep yourself on track while navigating the Dream & Action Level.

When I first learned about the 3LR process, I drew the image with the three levels on a piece of paper and posted it on a door inside my house, as a reminder to stay positive and motivated until I reached my objective I was focused on at that time. Every time I walked through that door, the reminder acted as a helpful ally. I left that drawing on the door long enough for the 3LR process to create the new habit: to believe in my dreams and stay positive until I achieve them. Sometimes life forced me in a new direction, but I don't consider that a failure of the 3LR process. Because every new direction it forced me into was in fact a blessing (with much better outcomes than I had initially envisioned). Like the project of writing this book.

So trust that the 3LR process works to your favor too, if you don't block it.

Let's look now at the next phase of your job search project.

Phase 2: Project Planning

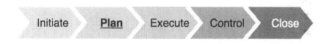

Okay, you've accumulated all this information from self-evaluation, about the SMARRT goals, how to set your mindset to be more successful, and what job search strategies are more effective for introverts. That's quite a lot, right?

You might ask, "Now what?"

In the planning phase of your job search project you'll put all these together and create an *action plan*!

You can make a list of all the things you want to work on, but it will make a long list if you want to capture everything you'd like to include in your plan! The problem with such list? It is long and intimidating, and you might want to rearrange things around (to make it easier to manage your tasks) — so a list is not the right format for that.

Here's what I suggest: create a plan based on your actual situation and project objective, thinking of what job search strategies you'd like to use. I call this your *strategy mix*.

Strategy Mix

It's up to you how many of the strategies listed in chapter 9 you want to use. You can choose to try them all (like Nancy did before narrowing down her choice based on the responses she got), or to try only some of them.

Don't worry if it's the right choice for you at this moment. You'll figure that out in the execution phase of your job search project. But to get there, you have to start with something.

Write down what strategies you'd like to include in your *job search strategy mix*.

Now let's move on to include everything you identified in the initial phase of your job search project.

Mind Map

I suggest you use the mind map concept presented in chapter 9 (about strategies), to brainstorm ideas and organize the information about your job search. This way, you can create your action plan more easily.

Let's create your job search mind map now.

Grab a large piece of paper or use an app like SimpleMind — the one I used to create the mind maps for this book. (The one on this page is for the chapter you're reading right now).

The beauty of using an app like this is that you can just add ideas without thinking of how to organize them; when you're done adding everything you'd like to include in your job search process, you can move the ideas around and organize them by categories, just like I did.

Start with a circle in the middle and name it "My Job Search" (or put your job search project's objective). Then add all the ideas that come to your mind: the job search strategies from your Strategy Mix, what you need to do for each strategy, what job search tools you need to prepare, what actions you need to take to keep you positive and motivated, to improve your communication attitudes, what you need to organize your process, what you'll let go (doesn't serve you during the job search), what you need to change have more time and energy to put into this project, etc.

After listing all the ideas you have, group them into some major categories, subcategories, sub-subcategories, etc. For example: "Strategies" could be a category with subcategories like "Information Interview,", "LinkedIn", "Job Boards", etc. For each subcategory you'll add more. For example, for "Information Interview" you can add as sub-subcategories "Find People to Approach", "Send Messages", "Schedule Interview", "Thank You Note", "Review Info Received", "Adjust Strategy If Needed", "Next Steps".

If you've gotten up to here in this book, I'm sure you have lots of ideas to include in your mind map. Get them all out there, in your mind map. Look at the previous chapters, if you want to refresh your memory. Then get those ideas organized by categories, and you're ready for the next step.

(If you're prefer pen and paper, grab some sticky notes and write each idea on one sticky note. Define your main categories, then stick the notes around those categories. You can add new categories anytime.)

BTW, you can leave this mind map open. When you start implementing your action plan, you might get new ideas to add here and even eliminate some.

Now it's time to get these ideas into an *action plan*.

Action Plan

Take a close look at your mind map. You will recognize that many ideas listed there are actually actions that will help you implement your strategy mix and make your job search process more effective. Check which of your ideas you didn't insert into your action plan yet, and do this now.

I will give you a few more suggestions later on, but for now let's see what you can do with the actions you already have. Examine them from the perspective of which actions can be done in parallel and which in a sequential order.

For example, searching people to ask for information interviews can be done in the same day as looking at job boards. You don't have to wait until you complete one action before working on the other one (because they are not related). But you cannot send a thank you note before actually meeting the person for the information interview — these are actions that have to be done in a sequential order (one after another).

After you look at what actions you can do in parallel and what needs to be done in a certain order, you're ready to organize these actions into an action plan.

Now you can make your action plan as a list that will help you better understand what actions you need to take.

SMARRT *Goals*

Before adding a timeframe to your action plan, define your SMARRT goals: the goals you want to achieve daily, weekly, etc.

Use the SMARRT formula, to help you create more effective goals.

An example of such a goal could be: "I send three targeted applications per day in response to job postings". Another one could be: "I approach fifteen new people per week to ask for job interviews". Or: "I pay attention daily to put aside any negative thoughts that cross my mind, and find new perspectives to look from".

Make your goals a little stretching; that's when you'll mobilize yourself more, leading to a positive effect on your project.

Hint: you can adjust your goals during the execution phase if you want to, but start with something for now.

Based on your action plan, define your SMARRT goals now because you'll need them to create your job search project *timeline*.

Timeline

Based on the actions listed in your action plan, and your SMARRT goals, it's time to create your job search project timeline.

Your SMARRT goals will help you define when each action (from the action plan) needs to take place (when to start, when it ends) so you can progress with your project. You can create an Excel spreadsheet or use your agenda to create your project timeline. It should be something like the chart below.

For those activities that have nothing in common, you can place them on the same day, while those in sequential order need to follow it. Please also schedule some blank boxes of time for new situations that could show up when you execute your plan — so they don't throw out the rest of your timeline when they occur. This is also a way to provide some flexibility to your schedule, because when you start implementing your plan, chances are that not everything will go as planned. Here's an example of a timeline; you can add hours and black spots for unpredictable situations and breaks:

Day 1	Day 2	Day 3	Day 4
do 3 hours of online research	add 1-2 companies to my list	do 3 hours of online research	update my LinkedIn profile
prepare resume, cover letter	find people and send 4 requests for information interviews	send applications	do research at the library
send 2 job applications	do 3 hours of online research	search companies I'm interested in	prepare and send applications
start a discussion in a LinkedIn group, ask for advice on how to get this type of job	prepare 2 applications	send follow-up emails	send 4 more requests for information interviews
send follow-up emails	ask friends for advice	participate in LinkedIn group	prepare for the job interview

Reminders

Just because you create a timeline, it doesn't mean that you'll remember to do everything you said. Life gets in the way, and without reminders put in place you might miss some actions. And guess what happens if you miss them? Your job search project won't progress as quickly as it could and won't be as effective as you want!

One more thing about your action plan and timeline: When you start implementing this plan, you can easily overlook something that's going on but out of your immediate focus (not on your agenda either). For example, not getting interviews because your resume is not appropriate or has some flaws. Or continuing to use a job search strategy that's not working for your situation, as Zara did for six months.

To avoid such situations as much as possible, you need to introduce some *check-points* into your action plan and timeline.

Checkpoints

Checkpoints are appointments with yourself of fifteen to twenty minutes, once a week. Add them to your project timeline so you don't miss them. It's easy to stay focused only on your planned actions and forget to check in and see how your project is doing, but by doing so you increase the risks related to your project. I'll talk more about what to pay attention to during the checkpoints in the control phase of your project. For now just add the weekly checkpoints to your timeline.

Risk Plans

Talking about risks, any project will be faced with some risks during its timespan. By thinking of upfront about risks, and planning ahead how you will handle them, you give your project a better chance of running smoothly and having fewer delays.

Of course, not all risks can be envisioned from the beginning, but some of them can. And by doing this, you'll feel more mentally prepared to handle them, because you'll have backup plans to handle these risks to minimize their negative effects on your project.

Here are some risks I would associate with the job search process:

• *Your Situation Suddenly Changes*

In such circumstances, we can usually get carried away by the momentary aspects, and forget about the bigger picture (your project). Have a plan you can rely on for handling such situations. It can include reassessing your priorities according to the new situation and adjusting your strategy mix and action plan if needed.

An example could be when you get sick and take a few days to recover. Reassessing your priorities for that period of time is better than beating yourself up because you can't follow your schedule (which will only drain your energy and weaken your body even more, slowing down the recovery). Another example could be when you have a family emergency, something you need to deal with before it gets worse.

• *Your Situation Gradually Changes*

For example, you're unemployed and your financial situation deteriorates slowly. Even if you're aware of this, you need to decide what is the bottom line for you when you can still function well. Before reaching it you can continue with your current plan. But if you don't get results by the time you reach that limit, you need to reassess your priorities and your short-term goal, create a more aggressive strategy mix, and adjust your action plan accordingly. Please don't to wait for the situation to get too bad, before making changes. Because if you do, you'll be so stressed by your financial situation that moving ahead with your initial plan will lead you nowhere! That stress will affect your interview performance. Plus, no employer wants to hire a stressed candidate when they have other candidates to choose from!

This situation happened to me: several years ago I was let go from a position while I was paying a monthly rate to get rid of my debt. When I noticed that I had reached my bottom line, instead of panicking, I totally changed my strategy mix: I picked up the phone and called people out of the blue, something that I very rarely do even in a normal situation. I totally went out of my introvert comfort zone, but it worked! I got a job soon after, and while working there I got back to my initial plan of looking for what I really want.

• *You Run Out of "Gas" (Energy)*

Job searching is like a full-time job, and if you don't pay attention, you're swept in so much that you can get tired of . . . the job search. If you don't take measures to change this, it will affect your job search project outcome.

If you're determined, like me, when you work on something you really want, you can get so tired that you can't keep your negative thoughts at bay anymore, and you have no more energy to take the actions you want to get you there. Have a backup plan for this too. This was mine during my first job search in Canada: I first noticed and accepted that I had hit that state. Then I reevaluated my priorities and urgencies, adjusted my schedule and gave myself a three-day "vacation" to recharge my batteries! I didn't do anything job search related during those three days. I focused only on myself and what I like (for example: sleeping well, spending time in a park, and taking pictures of nature — my favourite way to get recharge my batteries).

Think of what you like and what usually works for you, and have your plan ready for when you need it.

• *You Get . . . Rejected!*

It happens, to everyone. The question is, how do you normally handle rejections?

If you let them affect your self-esteem, it'll drain your energy (so you won't have enough to carry on your planned actions). It will also affect your performance during the next job interview(s). If you had high expectations about a job interview and it didn't go well, you'll be disappointed — not a good feeling to continue your job search, right?

So how you handle rejections can put your job search project at risk. I suggest including this in your plan for handling rejections: Put things in perspective (short term vs. long term) so you don't get disappointed by having expectations that are too high. Learn from your rejections. (What didn't work well? What can you do differently next time?). Support your self-esteem with your accomplishment list (read it over and over, to boost your self-esteem and confidence).

Also, don't take rejections personally. Remember that it's not about you, it's about what the employers consider the best candidate for that position and their company.

• Can you think about other situations that could put your job search project at risk? Add them to your risks list and the plan you create of managing each of them.

• When you start executing your project, you might find other situations that put it at risk. Add them to your risk list, and create a plan to handle each (in case they show up again in the future).

By having plans for handling the risks associated with your job search project, you avoid being knocked out or temporarily derailed from its normal course, thus managing it more effectively!

Environment

I talked about the environment in the initial phase of your project, to help you get familiarized with how the environment you're in can affect your job search project productivity.

In the planning phase, you need to add to your action plan and timeline the actions you'd like to take to create a more auspicious environment for your job search.

Your environment affects your life more than you think. It could be empowering (making you feel good, giving you energy, supporting you in achieving your goals), or it could weaken you. We always have options. What kind of environment would you choose for your job search?

Identify what you'd like to change for these three types of environments:

• *Physical*

This is about your surroundings, the space where you conduct your job search: furniture, light, sounds, ergonomic desk, neatness, etc. A noisy environment is stressful for introverts. The clutter could influence you more than you think. Often distractions could affect your productivity, since it takes time for you to refocus on what you were doing. I personally work better in well-lighted environment with minimal noise. When I'm not working from my home office, I choose to work in places with large windows that let the sunlight in (coffee shops, libraries), and have my headphones handy. What works best for you?

• *Relationships*

The relationships we have (friends, family, colleagues, pets, mentors) influence us. For introverts it is even more crucial to pay attention to what type of relationships we have, because our energy gets drained even in normal interactions with people we already know. And if we have some negative or unsupportive people around us, it will affect us even more.

Take an inventory of your relationships and see how you can handle them in way that doesn't affect your job search. Use the attitudes of effective communication from chapter 11, to respectfully communicate what you need. Set boundaries that work for you and let them know. You also need time to regenerate; add breaks to your timeline and let those around you know that you need that time for yourself.

• *Personal*

This is about the relationship you have with yourself: your mindset, your physical body (strength, eating, sleep), clothing, etc. It is important to have a good relationship with yourself in general, even during the job search, because it can help you!

As discussed in chapter 5, your negative thoughts affect your job search results. Allowing yourself to get too tired will decrease your productivity. Physical exercise will make you feel better, and project more energy. It doesn't have to be in a gym; even a little movement during your break could help. I love to dance to music that makes me happy during some of my breaks, and I can see the difference in my productivity. I also do some stretches from time to time when I work at the computer. What works best for you?

Think about these types of environment as faucets of energy that could replenish your energy or drain it. What can you let go, adjust, or add in regarding each of the above aspects to make your environment less stressful?

Add those actions to your action plan and timeline!

By removing the stress caused by certain elements of your environment and replacing them with something that brings more joy (or, at minimum, don't affect you), your energy will be less drained so you can focus it on your project more.

Phase 3: Project Execution

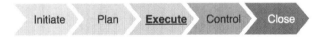

Okay, by now you have an action plan (associated with your job search project timeline).

It's time to start . . .

Action Plan Implementation

From your timeline you'll create, either in the evening (for the next day) or in the morning, a list of the activities you'll focus on that day. Pick either evening or morning to make this daily plan, whatever works best for you.

Check with yourself to see if there are any other priorities and urgencies to consider, and adjust your list if needed.

Then go implement those actions throughout your day, one by one, and strike them through on the list when they're done. That's such a great feeling, right? This way you'll also see that you are making some progress.

By having a mix of actions for each day, your job search will progress through various strategies in parallel, without spending most of your time on only a few actions or getting completely lost in one action (like searching the Internet all day).

Resource Management

Here are a few ideas to help you manage better your resources (time, energy, technology):

• *Single Action*

Introverts are not good at multitasking, and doing so could become overwhelming. Focus on one action at a time.

• *Use a Gmail Address and Google Calendar*

An email address like firstname.lastname@gmail.com is considered more professional. Plus, with all the Google features, you can get some more benefits:

> - Create folders in your inbox, and save all the job search communication in one or more folders for easy access when you need it (for follow-ups for example).

> - Synchronize all your activities in one place (including your interviews) with Google Calendar, and access your calendar from anywhere (via a computer or phone).

> - Set reminders in your Google Calendar, to not forget something (do a follow-up, for example, or go to an interview).

> - Use Google Drive for documents you'd like to have access from anywhere. I have a folder in my Google Drive called "Job". If someone asks me for my resume, I can login on any computer/laptop with Internet access, adjust my resume, and send it without waiting to get home. Even with smart phone you can do this, although the screen is much smaller. I suggest this method to all my clients, since it's an easy way to apply for a position if you're in a rush.

• *Avoid Eye Strain*

If you stare too much at the computer daily, you can get eye strain. Believe me, it's not pleasant: besides your eyes getting red, they hurt too! And you don't want to go to an interview with red eyes, do you? :-)

Since someone told me about EyeCare (a Chrome browser extension), I don't have eye strain anymore, although I wrote for more than seven hours a day for this book and learned (about self-publishing from the Internet) another two to three hours daily. EyeCare lets me know every twenty minutes to stop working and do some eye exercises. It really helps! No more red eyes, and no hurting either. You can adjust the time if you want, but I wouldn't recommend it. There is a similar extension for Firefox: 20-20-20.

And if you like to use the computer late in the evening, get software or an app like f.lux (to make the color of your computer's display adapt to the time of day, warm at night and like sunlight during the day) so it doesn't affect your sleep.

• *Job Search Spreadsheet*

I talked about the job search spreadsheet in chapter 9 (strategy IS 20). You can create this document in MS Excel or Google Spreadsheet (in Google Drive). It'll help you keep track of your applications, so you won't miss a follow-up and you'll quickly remember what resume you sent when an employer calls.

• *Get Organized*

Find ways to organize the amount of information you want to save for later use in your job search.

You can save URLs for articles or interesting websites in the Favorites folder of your browser. Being more visual, I created a Pinterest board "Book" for all the interesting information I found on Internet that relates to my book topic, so I can find it easily by browsing the images. You can create a "Job Search" board on Pinterest too. Or even several boards of each topic you're interested (for example: companies, job board, etc.). If you don't have a Pinterest account, you can create one and get the Pinterest Save button (extension) for your browser. This way, you can save your preferred websites and articles in your Pinterest boards.

• *Small Breaks Throughout the Day/Pomodoro Method*

Your mind can get tired when you focus on an activity for a longer period of time. And a tired mind leads to a tired body! Introverts think a lot, and the brain "eats" a lot of energy, so they get tired more easily. Not only will you not have much energy to get the most of the following activities, but if you continue that way you'll accumulate fatigue — which will also affect your productivity for the following days! Can you afford that?

So taking small breaks throughout the day will prevent your mind from getting fatigued. Since the job search is a quite lengthy process, you need to take care of yourself to not get too tried to continue.

One way of doing that is to use the Pomodoro Technique. This is a method that increases your productivity by hyper-focusing and getting things done in short bursts, while taking frequent breaks in between to get some fresh air and relax. Search the Internet if you want to know more. You can find an app to help you use this technique, if you want, whether you have Windows, Mac, or smart phones. A few minutes break is okay; it helps you recharge.

Did you know that you can also get some energy by moving your body? I love to put on my preferred song, and dance for a few minutes before I get back to writing (in my case). It lifts my mind too.

• *Take a Longer Break When You Feel Too Tired*

If you don't, it could affect your job search project in a bigger way. Remember when I gave myself a three-day vacation? I came back with a lot of energy and channeled it again into my job search. Do whatever you like during such a break. There are things you can do even when you are on a budget, like a walk in the woods or read a book you enjoy (borrowed from the library).

• *Make Your Weekend (or at Least One Day) "No Job Search" Day!*

You're a human being, not just a job seeker! You deserve to have at least a day off, to do whatever you want. You can make it "no talk" day if that's what you want. I bet you'll get some new insights about how to improve your job search when you actually don't think of your job search at all! I prefer to do some hiking, or at least walk in nature. What helps you recharge your batteries?

• *Reward Yourself*

Introverts do well by providing rewards to themselves. Don't wait until you find the job to give yourself a reward! Every day you have smaller achievements, like those strike-through actions. Give yourself credit for them, even a pat on the back, and eat that chocolate (if you want). These rewards will give you some extra energy and motivation to carry on your job search.

• *Honor How You Are*

No need to envy others for how they are, what they do and achieve. That will leak your energy, instead of keeping it for your job search!

Honor your own style, focus on your strengths, and pay attention to your own progress. Since we are all unique, you can only compare your actual you with who you were and what you knew before. Do you notice any improvement? Do you have more information now about your job search? A yes to both questions will show you're on the right track. For any no, ask yourself what else you can do — or do differently — to make some progress.

Risk Management

In the execution phase of your job search project, you'll need to keep an eye open to identify the risks that might affect your project. You already have plans for how to handle some of the risks that may occur; keep them handy so you can refer to them when needed. For the risks you didn't think about upfront, use your judgement: How can you handle them to best minimize their effect on your project, to still achieve your project's objective and long-term goal?

Don't let yourself be swept into the turmoil created by a sudden situation. Chances are that you'll learn something useful for your job search project too, if you keep your head up and take the necessary actions. Since you put your energy and time into your project, the unpredictable situations that occur may help you develop the skills needed to take your project to completion.

Acknowledge the situation in the early stage — maybe see it coming (if you can) and start taking the appropriate action to handle it.

Use your mind to turn things around in your favor — sometimes that is possible. Ask yourself, "What can learn from this situation that could help me move forward?"

Instead of getting into the victim role (feeling pity for yourself and that you're at the mercy of the situation), asking yourself open-ended questions will get your mind thinking of what could be useful and help you find solutions.

Once I had a client who was not open to feedback. He went on to find another service provider, and another one — continuing to do things his own way — and concluded that there is discrimination everywhere. Then he started to feel victimized by society in general, and his behavior got worse, to the point that he was denied services because he was verbally abusing everyone he got in touch with. He had a legal background, yet not being open to feedback threw him into a series of situations that affected his job search project as well.

Employers don't like negative people, because they could poison the work environment if hired. (The work environment is stressful enough because of the organizations' goals; throw in a negativist and things can get worse quickly.

Phase 4: Keeping Your Project under Control

Just because I put the control phase after the execution phase, it doesn't necessarily mean that you have to wait until you implement all your job search related actions before you start keeping your job search project under control.

Remember those checkpoints I asked you to add to your project timeline?

They are a way to evaluate your project evolution along the way. Weekly, have that appointment with yourself to do the following:

• Verify what actions planned for the last week you were able to do and not do.

• Notice what got in the way and figure out how you can overcome that.

• Understand what went well and what didn't.

• Learn from your last week of job search experience.

• Check if you have any new insights about your job search now, a week more into your project.

• Analyze if anything changed regarding your situation, project goals, and how you perceive the job market now.

• Check your level of motivation and belief in your success (remember the 3LP process?)

• Verify if any changes are needed in the way you manage your job search project.

• Decide if you want to make any adjustments to your action plan and time-line, to incorporate what you've learned from this self-reflection.

Besides having these checkpoints periodically, you can use the above questions anytime a new situation occurs, which has the potential to have a bigger impact on your project.

That's what Nancy did: She started by trying all the job search strategies she learned, and noticed that information interviews gave her more useful infor-mation about how to look for a job in her field (online marketing), and how to craft her application to be more attractive to employers. Then she took that information and applied it to the strategy that gave her more invitations to job interviews (targeting her resume to specific companies and applying online). Then she narrowed down the search to find companies who better suited her choices. She got five job interviews with such companies: She refused two job offers because she didn't like their company culture, and accepted a third one from a big eco-friendly company (exactly what she was looking for).

After learning more about useful job search strategies for introverts, Lili changed her strategy mix from applying everywhere, to information inter-views. And she stuck with them when she noticed how much information she got, and how each interview informed her next step. Encouraged by the fact that people interviewed used the same strategy to get their jobs in the same field, she continued the series of information interviews until she got a job — in two and a half weeks — and the job was created when she approached the company (helping them understand that they needed someone with her skills).

From a quality assurance perspective, the flow of your job search project should actually have feedback loops, to improve the job search process along the way based on the new information and experience acquired during the execution phase.

To reach your objective even if something occurs during the execution phase or your situation drastically changes, you'll need to go back to the planning phase or adjust your project execution.

It might require only a change in your strategy mix, to accommodate the new situation or information, or a modification in the way you implement your plan.

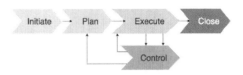

In the above flowchart, the two arrows from "execute" to "control" signify the checkpoints required to capture the new information and analyze the situation in order to make the required changes.

This way, you ensure that your project stays the course without delays due to a lack of monitoring your job search project.

A note of caution though: Don't make adjustments to your strategy mix too early in the execution phase, because it takes some time for a strategy to show its effect. It is better to first try to improve the results of the strategies used in your strategy mix, before changing what strategies you use.

Phase 5: Close Your project

Okay, the time has passed, and you've taken action after action to advance your job search project and adjust it when required until . . . BOOM! You got the job!

Congratulations!

Well, actually, it was not really a BOOM . . . You saw it coming, because you worked on it! Yet for those around you (the Reality Level) it might look like you got that position overnight, you were plain "lucky"!

When Nancy came to share her successful job search story with other job seekers, someone said: "Oh, you were lucky to get that position in such a short amount of time!"

I really liked Nancy's answer: "Behind that *luck* was a lot of work involved. I made it happen through the actions I took!"

It happened to me too: I was working for a few months, when a colleague from another department asked how I got this position. After sharing my story, she said: "You were lucky! It took me much more time to get mine." What she didn't realize was the whole chain of actions that led me to being "lucky."

Congratulations on making yourself a *lucky* person! :-)

Before closing your job search project, there's one more step: Take a moment (or two, or more) to evaluate what you've learned from the whole project:

- What went really well?
- What would you like to avoid if you decide to look for another position in the future?
- What you would do differently next time?
- What did you like most about being the project manager of your job search project?
- What did you like least about being the project manager of this project?
- Which of your introvert strengths helped you the most?
- What can you take away to implement in future projects you have?
- Who did you become in the process of going through this project?
- What did you learn about yourself that you didn't know before (or you didn't trust enough)?
- At what level is your self-esteem and self-confidence now, compared with when you started your job search project? What will you do to keep it at that level, or even get it higher (if possible)?
- How will this job search project influence the way you think and act in the new position, to help you move along toward your long-term objective?

You can write your answers in the notebook, to have them for future reference.

Now go and celebrate your success, and close this job search project! :-)

If you would like a visual overview of the whole job search process, you can download it here: GabrielaCasineanu.com/JSfilesfree

---

Chapter Fifteen

POWERFUL QUESTIONS TO ASK YOURSELF

We get wise by asking questions, and even if these are not answered, we get wise, for a well-packed question carries its answer on its back as a snail carries its shell.
~ James Stephens

I cannot emphasize enough the power of asking yourself questions! They can take you from feeling hopeless to being assertive and proactively looking for what you want.

I'm curious, did you notice the difference in the energy you have while holding one perspective versus the other (hopeless vs. assertive and proactive)? One is weakening to you, the other is empowering. I'll let you decide which one is which. :-)

So why not use this "trick" to get some extra energy to pour into your job search? Introverts need to take more regenerating breaks, because their energy gets drained much faster. Did you know that the brain consumes about 20 percent of what the whole body consumes? And with introverts' brain being super active (paying attention to all the thoughts and inner and external stimuli), no wonder why they feel depleted and tired more often than extroverts.

Employers also prefer assertive, proactive people instead of those feeling hopeless or complaining. One more reason to change from feeling victimized to taking charge of your own job search project.

Below, I've listed a few attitudes (A) that I've noticed in my clients, and how you can turn them around with powerful questions you can ask yourself (refer to the previous chapters for answers). These questions (Q) usually begin with "What" and "How":

A: Feeling a victim of the system. *"Employers favor extroverts,"* etc.

Q: How can I find introverts that work in my field, to get ideas from what worked for them? What articles/books are out there for introverts looking for a job?

This approach will make you curious and give you the energy to look for what you need, instead of feeling hopeless. In this world full of people and information, you surely can find something that could inform your next steps.

A: I don't know how to find ... *"Show me websites with job postings, so I can apply."*

Q: How can I find websites with the type of positions I'm looking for?

By using a question, your mind will start looking for answers, instead of getting stuck in "I don't know."

A: Taking the situation for granted. *"I sent many resumes, but no one contacted me." "There are no jobs in my field."*

Q: What is going on here. Did I miss something?

Shifting to being curious will help you find out what you can do differently to get the employers' attention. There are so many potential employers out there. Don't rely only on what's more visible. Dig deeper!

A: I don't have enough experience *(all the skills required, etc.).*

Q: Let's see, what do I have to offer, and how can I find employers who might be interested in someone with my (lack of) experience/skills?

This question puts you into a more proactive mode, helping you realize your strengths and motivation. From there, you can start looking for employers (who would appreciate your potential) or for people who can help you find them. If you focus on what you don't have, you'll miss what you do have can do for you!

A: I don't like to talk about myself.

Q: It's not about me. What does the employer need to know to understand that my skills and expertise can help them?

By shifting your perspective (from "me" to "them"), you can then play a matching exercise: Think about the employer needs and find examples from your background showing that you can meet those needs. Then craft your job search tools and the answers to common job interview questions to reflect how your expertise and motivation can help them.

A: I have a great background; I don't understand why they don't hire me.

Q: How can I present my background to make it easier for the employer to understand that I'm a good fit for the position?

It's good to be proud of your background, but relying only on that might not bring the results you want. The employers don't know you! It's your role to make it easier for them to understand who you are and what you can offer, by presenting a targeted application. Plus, such a resume shows respect for their time and needs.

A: I don't know why the employer invited me to this job interview.

Q: What if the employer is interested in my application, even if I didn't meet all the requirements?

By asking such question you take on a more confident attitude: You're not questioning your ability and expertise anymore. Instead, you become more curious to find out which qualities and experience you already have could be relevant for the position. Such attitude will not only make you more prone to prepare better answers, but will also boost your confidence (a very important factor for success).

A: I'll take anything; I just need a job.

Q: Even if this is not my ideal job, what would be good about this position to help me short or long term?

By finding something you like about that position, you'll have something to boost your motivation—so you show up more determined at the interview. Plus, you will prepare better (because you see the connection with your goals), which will increase your chances of getting hired.

A: I don't like to talk with strangers. Why bother to do information interviews and meet people at events?

Q: I'm interested in knowing more about _____ (this type of company, the recruitment process in this field, etc.). Where can I find people who know more about this?

Again, shifting to an attitude of curiosity will help you get out of your bubble and gather useful information for your job search. This way you'll also tap into the "human factor," increasing your visibility and credibility in a world where being at the right place at the right time is called seizing the opportunity! Would you like to? Or do you want to leave it for someone else?

I hope by now you understand the importance of asking yourself powerful questions every time you get stuck in a thought or situation that makes you feel weak or hopeless.

I'll leave it to you to practice this "trick" in any other situations I didn't capture here. I know you can!

Chapter Sixteen

COMMON JOB SEARCH PITFALLS

A man must be big enough to admit his mistakes,
smart enough to profit from them, and strong enough to correct them.
~ John C. Maxwell

In this chapter you'll find what I consider common job search pitfalls, and why. I mentioned these throughout the book, but I wanted to create a special section where I could summarize these points, because they affect your job search!

So let's get started:

• Setting Too Broad of an Objective for Your Job Search

When I mentioned this idea in my workshops, my words were usually met with resistance: "I don't believe this! I increase my chances of getting a job by broadening my job search!" the participants often said.

Really? My idea might sound counterintuitive, but by looking in too many directions you actually take small steps in each direction. Plus, you divide your time by creating different resumes and gathering information about different directions.

But by narrowing down your objective you can actually advance much faster! Because you don't divide your time in so many directions, you more quickly gather the information you need specific to that direction, to advance faster in your job search. Plus, narrowing your objective down will help you get the most of the "human factor" (information interviews, for example), thus increasing your visibility in one direction, and building trust, which increases your chances of finding the position you want.

Choosing an objective that is too broad and believing that you increase your chances this way, comes from a scarcity mindset: "I don't think there are enough positions available in this direction, so I better broaden my view." Keep in mind that, what you come across in your job search is only the tip of the iceberg! There are more companies and organizations than what you can find directly, so it's not such a limited offer as you think. Plus, there are companies who are able to create positions, if the right candidate shows up to help them overcome their challenges. When you start taping into the potential of the hidden job market, you'll increase your chances of getting the job you want even with a narrow objective.

Here's an example: After getting his PhD in a very narrow niche of physics, Edward realized that he wanted to work in the private sector. Many other PhD graduates remain in academia, either by preference or because many companies are not investing in someone at that high of a level. But Edward set his mind on finding a company where his expertise in that narrow field would be beneficial. Using his researching skills, he was able to find such a company. Via LinkedIn, he identified and approached several employees who worked at that company, to understand its challenges, culture, and values, before he reached out for employment. And guess what? His approach was successful; he soon started to work for that company!

• Neglecting the Importance of Soft Skills

I've met so many people who rely only on their hard skills and experience in their job search. Please don't be one of them. You know, from chapter 6 (Skill Set Inventory), that in many cases the skills required to carry on a successful job search are different from those required to perform well in the position, if hired.

As an introvert, you have many strengths. Use them to your advantage during the job search! Don't rely only on your application to give the right message to the employer, because they might miss the chance. And for interviews (informational or for jobs), prepare well in advance to put yourself more at ease and give well thought out answers.

Being invited to many job interviews and not getting positive results could be a signal to pay more attention to how you can improve your soft skills and attitude. If the employers invite you to job interviews, it means that your applications captured their attention. Maybe you lack proper preparation for the interviews or your soft skills and attitude aren't good enough. This doesn't mean you are a bad person. It just means that some aspects of your personality can be improved in some way.

I had a client who had an attitude of superiority, believing so much in his managerial experience that he actually failed to adapt his answers to correspond to the required position. With his attitude, he spoiled the interviews to which he was invited.

• Lack of Confidence

While confidence is usually considered part of soft skills, I want to talk about it separately because it is so important! On one side, employers can easily notice the lack of confidence. On the other, you do yourself a huge disservice by not trusting yourself and your ability to handle a situation.

Look, I'm writing this book directly in English, and I'm not a native English speaker. I've been in Canada for thirteen years, and more than a half of those I spoke only French in the professional environment. But as I'm writing this book, I'm quite surprised at how the English words are flowing through me. Sometimes I get words I have never used, which are exactly what I needed for that sentence. How's that possible? My intuition plays a huge role, and I entice it with powerful questions. :-) That's something you can do too! Trust that your intuition will help you find the right words and will bring the right opportunities for you even if you don't everything now. Trust the process! There is a bigger force than us, whatever you call it, that can inspire us if we're open to it.

If you need to boost your confidence more, remind yourself of all the situations you managed well in the past. Talk with people in your field, and you'll sometimes be surprised to see that others perceive your skills and expertise better than you do.

Don't let your inner critic to have too loud of a voice. Befriend it, by learning how to turn his messages around. I talked about this in chapter 13.

• Getting Stuck in Your Own Perspective

There's nothing wrong with having your own opinions about what's going on in the job market and your job search. What's important though is to notice if your opinions are blocking you from moving forward, to advance your job search. If they are, use the exercises from the chapter 5 (about mindset) to help you come up with more positive perspectives that actually help you move forward.

If you can't come up with another perspective, ask! Reach out to someone else, someone who has a positive attitude, someone you admire or already works in your field. I know it takes courage, but it's worth it. Their perspective might not be what you're looking for, but just by speaking with someone else, it might help you shift perspective. It happened to me many times — speak with someone and having a shift in of perspective just by talking.

To help me get unstuck, I have other methods too: going for a walk in nature, writing in a notebook in the form of questions & answers, getting good sleep (if I'm tired). The walk in nature, for example, always clears my mind and helps me come up with new perspectives. The writing in the notebook, I start by saying what bothers me and ask a question; then I write what comes to mind (sometimes I have to write one word to get the next). Then I continue my writing Q&A, until something shifts: I feel better, and I get a new idea or perspective. See what works for you. But don't stay stuck too long, because the more you stay, the harder it is to get out of that state (affecting your job search negatively).

• Ignoring the Checkpoints

Please don't be like Ron, who, six months and three hundred resumes later, decided to try the job search strategies I suggested. I've had many clients who've made this mistake.

Do not neglect to stop and reflect on how your job search is unfolding. Because if you do, you might miss the chance to make the adjustments required to accelerate your job search. Wave in periodical checkpoints in your agenda, so you don't forget.

• Not Understanding the Employers' Perspective

This showed up in many simulation interviews I did with my clients. By not making an effort to understand what the employer was looking for or not paying attention to employers' needs and challenges, you set yourself up for failure. Because otherwise, by preparing well in advance to address the concerns they might have about your application, you increase your chances of being seen as a good candidate, gain their trust, and even pass the interview.

Another example: Adil was new in town, and his employment counselor referred him to me. In the past, he organized big music festivals and really enjoyed it, but he was not versed in job hunting. He couldn't find job postings in his field either, and had a nice, quiet personality. I suggested he put himself in the employer's role. What would he do to find a good festival organizer? He knew how this industry works, so he quickly understood that looking for job postings in this field might not be the right strategy for him. I told him about a few cultural hubs in Toronto where he could start to gather more information about what was going on in his field. And the next time I saw him, he was on the stage presenting (as an organizer) the biggest summer festival in Toronto. He approached me after: "Do you remember me? You're the one who told me how to go find what I want. Thank you!"

Now, in case you need it, you have my blessing to go out and find the employers you're interested in and try to understand their perspective! Then use that information to make your job search more effective.

• Not Taking the Time to Prepare Every Step Well

I can understand that every job seeker wants to get the desired position as soon as possible, but not preparing every step well will actually delay the process. Take the time to create well-targeted applications, the questions for information interviews, answers to commonly asked questions, examples that show your expertise instead of you talking about it, etc., to maximize your chances. I talked more about this in chapter 13, about the job interview.

• Ignoring the Importance of the TFAR Chain During the Job Search

I'm not just talking about when you interact with other people (in job interviews, for example).

I'm asking you to pay attention to your thoughts and feeling daily, while carrying on the job search. I know it's not easy to keep yourself motivated all the time, especially when you don't see results yet. But your success depends on how well you manage your frame of mind during the whole job search project: Do you believe you'll get what you want? Do you believe you'll find a way to get there, even if you don't know how yet? Do you believe that others can help, so you can reach out to ask for help? Do you believe in yourself?

The difference between two people who take the same action, one being successful and the other not, is mainly how they carry on that action. One believes in a successful outcome, which gives him energy and motivation to forge forward. The other, by not believing success is possible, will put less energy into it leading to a different result.

And, as you already know from chapter 5, the TFAR chain plays a huge role in people success. Make it work for you too. Do not block yourself by holding on limiting beliefs and negative thoughts!

• Not Thinking of Turning a Situation Around

I personally love challenges! I invite my mind to help me make lemonade if life throws lemons at me. I love to find new perspectives when I look at a situation. Changing careers and wanting a job in the new field? No problem! "What can I do about this?" I asked myself and others. I really loved my new direction; step by step the opportunity showed up, and I seized it!

Got a sudden idea to write this book, without writing experience while going through a burnout (barely walking and lacking enough focus)? No problem! Hanging on to the enthusiasm generated by this idea, I took baby steps: showing up daily, adjusting my writing process, connecting with a group of authors for support — and I ended up here: almost finished writing this book!

What can you do to turn the situation around when you run into challenges during your job hunting? There's always something to learn, to adjust, and someone who could give you a hand.

You know what? You're more prone to thinking about how to turn things around than an extrovert! You just need to be more aware of this quality you already have, and use it to your advantage!

Susan Cain mentions in her book *Quiet* that in a situation, introverts and extroverts pay attention to different things. Extroverts notice what is here, now. While introverts process the information in their mind, imagining things, making plans, asking "What if . . . ?"

Use this introverted quality to help you get ideas that could help you move forward. Then follow your ideas with appropriate actions! Otherwise . . . (you know what I'm gonna say, right?) :-)

Part Three

WHAT'S NEXT

Chapter Seventeen

GOT THE POSITION, NOW WHAT?

The more you praise and celebrate your life, the more there is in life to celebrate.
~ Oprah Winfrey

Okay, you've signed the offer, and soon you'll get started with the new position. Congrats!

I bet you're excited, at least that your job search project came to an end. Did you notice that ending a project brings joy and comes with a self-esteem boost? You made it!

It's a new achievement you can add to your list. It also boosts your confidence that the 3LR process works.

Are you a little nervous about the new job? Relax. First you deserve to give yourself some consideration for the hard work you did to get here!

Did you celebrate?

Even if it's not the position you initially wanted, it still is a milestone reached on your career path. You deserve to celebrate . . . your way! :-) I don't mean confetti, loud music, and all that jazz . . . unless you want it. Some introverts have a quieter way to celebrate, and that's okay. Whatever works for you!

Then, if you didn't yet, reflect on the lessons learned from your job search experience. What worked well? What didn't? What will you do differently next time? How did your introvert strengths help you? Which ones did you not use enough?

Since you'll soon move to a new "chapter" of your career path, you now need to capture and anchor the lessons learned. Otherwise you might forget these lessons and might repeat the same mistakes next time you look for a new position.

And you know what? The lessons you learned from this experience can help you in other areas of your life as well. Take a moment and to reflect how, and integrate the learning.

Even if you plan to become an entrepreneur, these lessons could still help you: you learned how to use your strengths more and how a successful mindset leads to achieving your objectives. You also learned how good management of your (project) actions could make the process more effective, and that small breaks waved in could actually increase your productivity!

I didn't look at life as a series of projects until I created my first photo exhibition. It was a few months' project, and I really enjoyed taking it through the different phases to completion. Since then, I've continued to give myself projects, and I noticed that this works well for me: each project has a beginning and end, and a lot of focused activities in between (keeping the end objective in mind).

Did you enjoy being the project manager of your job search project?

If you didn't, I'd be curious what would've make your journey as a project manager more enjoyable.

And if you liked the experience, I encourage you to treat this new "chapter" (the new position) as a new project. Take a look at how this position fits into your long-term objective. Go back to the flowchart "What I Want" from chapter 5, to see where you are now (after accepting it) and what else you need to move forward on your career path.

In the next chapter we'll talk about how to use the time spent in this new position to gather the skills and experience you need for your next career step.

Chapter Eighteen

EMBRACING MY CURRENT POSITION AS A STEP FURTHER

Planning is bringing the future into the present so that you can do something about it now.
~ Alan Lakein

Many people have experienced or witnessed someone being laid off. In today's ever-changing economy, with companies going bankrupt, merging, or resizing, a secure job remains only a dream. Yet some of the clients I had were dreamers. When asked to define in more detail what they want, the first thing that came out was: "I want a secure job!"

They believed that a secure job was the ideal, and I can agree that it'll take some pressure off knowing there is a paycheck coming every month. But my question is, do really think you can be happy by staying in the same position all your life? Because with the years passing by, our preferences change, we become more aware of what we want and don't want. I bet you have different preferences and see the world differently than how you saw it ten years before, don't you?

That's why I encourage people to proactively take charge of their careers, instead of allowing themselves to be at the mercy of the employers. When you hold a certain position, and in parallel you work on your Plan B (that helps you take the next step toward what you want), being laid off will not be as critical as suddenly not knowing what to do.

I had a client who told me in a quiet voice: "I'm a nobody." When I became curious why he was saying that, Thomas mentioned his background (neurological doctor in his home country, thirty years of experience), but that he's unemployed because he couldn't find a position in his field since he immigrated to Canada. I know that the Canadian medical system requires certain accreditations that are difficult to obtain if you're a foreign health practitioner, but I cannot agree with the fact that he's "nobody"! No one took his knowledge and experience away, nor who he really is: an intelligent human being!

But if he identifies himself through what he is able to achieve, and suddenly that aspect is no longer in his life, he sees himself as a nobody. When I asked him to consider himself being in between jobs, I noticed a change in his attitude.

Why I'm telling you about Thomas?

Because I want you to be fully aware that who you really are is different than the job you have. When you don't have that job anymore, you will still be yourself, put yourself together, and find something else. And, even better, if you plan your next steps while you're still working in that position you might not experience being laid off, because you can move to the next right position for you when you want!

In other words, you can embrace your current position as a stepping stone while you're preparing your next move, this way designing your career the way you want!

I'm not inviting you to be like a butterfly, to fly from one position to another often. Because each position has something to offer you, to help you build the skills and experience you need for the next step, and just a few months are not enough. Plus, you'll want to build the network and relationships that will help you make a smoother transition to your next job — instead of going through a stressful job search again. And this requires time as well.

Plus, you'll not be trustworthy for employers either, if you change positions too often.

So I wanted to include in this chapter some ideas you can ponder while working in the new position, to help you prepare for your next step, whenever you decide to take it. In other words, to help you have a plan B in mind (or project B, if you enjoy working on projects).

Benefits of Having a Plan B

• Thinking of your next step (which will take you closer to your long-term goal) will give you a bigger purpose to focus on, and mobilize your time and energy in a direction of your choice.

• That energy boost will be infused in the actions you take in your current position, and you'll do an even better job. You'll be happy with that, and good references are always beneficial when you decide to move on!

• If there's something you don't like about your current position, you'll look from a more detached perspective. This will give you a more objective view on what's going on and what can be improved, and you'll feel good about yourself so you can contribute in a bigger way. Introverts like to help. Just make sure you talk with your manager before implementing something that could affect the team's work and objectives. Managers see things from a higher perspective, having access to more information than you have.

• Besides coming with ideas for improvement in the workplace, what you don't like could be opportunities to help you grow. Don't like how a colleague or your manager is treating you? Apply the attitudes of effective communication to improve your relationship with them! Noticed an area that needs more attention, and you'd like to get involved (because it is part of your plan B to get that kind of experience or develop those skills)? Ask if you're allowed to get involved! In other words, constantly look for opportunities that could relate to your plan B.

• If you want your next move to be a position in the same company, find ways to meet the colleagues from that department or someone with a similar position within the company. Information interviews can be done internally as well, and will help you understand what skills are required for that position and what you don't have yet. Mary was very upset when her colleague was promoted as a team leader. She was expecting to get that role, because her performance in her current technical position was very good. What she didn't realize though is that a great performance in a position doesn't necessarily make you a good candidate for the upper position — unless you demonstrate that you have the extra skills required for the new position. In that case, going from a technical position to team leader required management and good people skills, which you have to demonstrate before being considered for the new position (as her colleague did).

I remember when I was enrolled in a management course, a colleague asked me: "Why are you taking this course? I'll be interested in such courses when I have a management position." "I take it to be ready when the opportunity shows up," I answered. To be honest, I was curious to understand a manager's perspective and it really help along the years that followed. I was a curious person, are you?

• Having a Plan B in mind will give you the time and opportunity to build your social media network and presence that will help you achieve your Plan B and beyond. When someone showed me the different features of LinkedIn, I immediately understood its importance from a career building and business perspective. Although I didn't plan to change my job soon at that time, I gradually built my LinkedIn network and relied on it whenever I needed to later. Proactively building a career takes time and perseverance; it doesn't happen overnight or without effort from your part.

How to Manage Your Energy

Now let's talk about the new work environment, since it has a huge impact on your energy, as an introvert. And you need energy to both perform your work-related tasks and prepare and implement your plan B.

• As you integrate into a new team in the workplace, use the attitudes of effective communication to build strong professional relationships with your colleagues and manager. This will make you feel more at ease in the workplace, creating a good atmosphere so you can leave work less stressed. You will also find that you have some energy left to put into your plan B, instead of lying flat on the couch or in front of the TV for hours) when you get home.

• Introverts prefer freedom instead of peer pressure. Working independently suits introverts much better than working in teams. What can you do in your workplace to give you a little more freedom?

• See if you can change your physical work environment to better suit your needs: the location of your office/desk, light, plants, less noise, etc. The physical environment can drain your energy, so do what it takes to protect yourself. When I read Susan's book *Quiet*, I understood why I don't like open space offices (too much going on around), lunch birthday parties, potlucks, and team building activities. They drain the introverts' energy quickly. But avoiding them completely also creates a "space" between you and your colleagues that might affect your work relationships as well (and makes you feel isolated). What I have chosen to do about such events: I show up so people can see I'm not an outsider, and I find a way to leave earlier. :-)

• Introverts are more sensitive than extroverts to various kinds of stimulation: loud voices, coffee, a lot going on in the room, etc. That's why meetings are not welcomed by introverts. Yet, if it's part of your role, make an effort to be there and be fully present. Share your opinion, instead of just being an observer. Your deep thinking will give you real ideas and insights that will help others better understand the situation or problem, and will also help them understand you better! Besides making you feel good when you see that others understand and take into consideration your points, it can also help your plan B. You will need good references when you decide to move on to another position. And you can also ask for recommendations for your LinkedIn profile, to gain the trust of those find you there.

• If you find it hard to speak up, take one step at a time. Share an idea, notice how it lands, adjust the way you deliver your ideas (if needed), and speak up again later on. Being so sensitive, introverts might find harder to take the feedback or criticism than extroverts. But keep in mind to look for the reason underneath the criticism, complaint, or feedback if you don't agree. Try to understand others' perspective by putting yourself in their shoes. And if you still don't understand, ask for more details. This way you build your interpersonal communication "muscle" that is so useful for implementing your plan B and the career you want.

• You can also team up with someone else who is more skilled at verbal communication. This way you rely on each other's strengths to get things done. Just make sure it is someone with good ethics, who doesn't take advantage of your work to look good in front of your managers and colleagues. If you notice that does happen, adjust the way you work. Make others more aware of what you're doing, instead of feeling victimized. I once attended a workshop, and asked, "What do you do when you notice that your manager is not aware of all the great work you're doing?" That's how I was feeling at work, so I was curious what the answer would be. I loved when the leader replied: "It's your responsibility to keep the manager informed about what you're doing. He is busy with his own tasks and might not see or understand everything you do." Learning how to work with someone else is another great skill that will help your career, because we can't live in an isolated bubble (even if we, as introverts, might love to).

• Talking about isolation, a position that doesn't allow you to work independently is stressful. Find out how you can introduce some "me" time so you can recharge your batteries during work hours too — especially if some of your activities require a lot of talking and meeting people. If you can't take such breaks, you'll be too tired when you get home. And you'll need to plan time for more of these types of breaks outside work. It's so important to take the time to replenish your energy, because if you don't it could lead to burnout (which will also postpone the achievement of your long-term objective). Just let your colleagues know why you take breaks by yourself, instead of joining them in the cafeteria, for example. Otherwise they might feel ignored, which extroverts don't like, and they will isolate you as well. Once they know your real reason, you will not only open their eyes to the difference between extroverts and introverts, but they will also be more understanding. This will also help you to learn to ask for what you need and want, such a great tool in your career toolbox! :-)

• Did you know that probably one-third to one-half of the workforce are introverts? But you might not recognize them if they show a more extroverted behavior in the workplace, to get by. By sharing that you're an introvert, you'll help them recognize their introverted strengths as well, and gain some allies in the workplace. This will help you cope with any work-related stress, and even brainstorm with like-minded people. And if you build relationships with other introverts, you can support each other's plans (including your plan B).

• Collaboration is well appreciated in the workplace. If you feel more comfortable collaborating and communicating in writing (email, surveys, reports), offer this as a way to accommodate the other required tasks. Keep in mind that written communication can be understood in a different way than it was intended, since it lacks human interaction. I once sent an email to make a colleague aware of some mistakes in the database she was managing (that were affecting all our work), and she replied, "Everyone makes mistakes." If you notice something like this happening, clear up the misunderstanding by talking with the person if you don't want the situation to escalate. Others might prefer direct communication (phone, meetings). You can mention the way you like to communicate and collaborate, so you can come to a common agreement instead of blaming each other for not being understood. If you both decide that verbal communication is more appropriate for the task, it might stretch you a bit, but it'll also help you expand your comfort zone. Becoming more skilled in different communication styles won't change your preferences. But it might be useful sometimes when implementing your plan B, and advance your career.

Chapter Nineteen

OOPS, MY TURN!

All good thoughts and ideas mean nothing without action.
~ Mahatma Gandhi

Yep, now it's your turn to put into practice what you learned from this book! :-)

When I got the idea of writing this book, I became more aware of the frustration I had felt over the years because I knew a lot more than what I could say in the workshops on job search related topics or when working with individual clients.

Yet I soon realized that I have a bigger purpose for this book: to help introverts shift their perspective about the job search, from a reactive to a more proactive approach empowered by their strengths! Which, actually, fits into my higher purpose: to build a better world by tapping into introvert power.

So I immediately embraced this book idea and launched myself on a writing journey for about seven months, to make it possible for people like you to get this info in your hands.

I did my best to capture all these concepts, techniques, and ideas in this book, so you get the chance to read them. But that's not enough!

You need to apply what you learned from this book, and the insights you got from the exercises, to make your job search more effective and advance your career . . . one step at a time!

Along the way, you might find yourself taken in a direction you didn't envision before.

If you like it, embrace it!

If you don't, adjust your direction toward what you want more.

You are a powerful human being!

Use your introvert strengths, and in a gentle way, you can shake the world — as Gandhi said, and he walked his talk!

Will you?

AFTERWORD

Did You Enjoy
Introverts: Leverage Your Strengths for an Effective Job Search?

First of all, thank you for purchasing *Introverts: Leverage Your Strengths for an Effective Job Search*.

I am extremely grateful! I hope that it adds value and quality to your career, and ultimately to your life.

If you enjoyed this book, I'd like to ask you a big favor. Please let me know if my mission was accomplished:

- Did this book change your perspective about the job search process? In what way?
- What did you find useful about this book?

Please post a review for this book on Amazon.

Your feedback will help others make a more informed decision when considering buying this book. And who knows, maybe your review will also help others discover this book and change their lives!

It will also help me improve my writing craft and understand how this book can be improved.

Your feedback is greatly appreciated.

Let's build a better world together by tapping into introverts' power!

All the best,

Gabriela Casineanu

I am preparing the "Workbook and Quick Reference Guide" for this book. Until is ready, I created for you a visual format of:

- **7 Networking Tips for Introverts** (checklist)
- **LinkedIn for Job Search** (flowchart)
- **Job Search Process** (overview).

All three pages in one PDF file, as a easy reminder. **FREE download** here:

GabrielaCasineanu.com/JSfilesfree

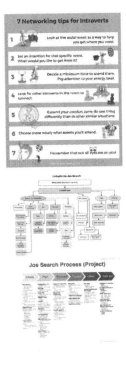

Introverts: Leverage Your Strengths for an Effective Job Search

is the first in a **series of books for introverts** titled:

To **get notified** when my **upcoming books and workbooks** will be published, sign up here:

GabrielaCasineanu.com/series

ABOUT THE AUTHOR

Gabriela Casineanu has always been intuitive and curious. With her mother's help, she learned logical thinking at an early stage, paving the path for the technical profession at the beginning of her career. She ended up making a full circle by turning toward coaching, which puts her intuition to good use.

By applying coaching to herself, and through a daily meditation practice since 2007, Gabriela's intuition has sharpened and her creativity has increased, leading also to artistic expressions.

She is passionate about self-improvement and walking a path of heart.

She finds strength in nature and loves intuitive painting, nature photography, outdoor activities, visiting sacred places, the Holographic Universe concept, and . . . wearing that turquoise ski jacket! :-)

GabrielaCasineanu.com
Building a Better World by Tapping into Introvert Power

For more information:
GabrielaCasineanu.com
gabriela.casineanu@gmail.com

ACKNOWLEDGMENTS

I would like to thank . . .

. . . *my friends, who understood my need for solitude (especially during the last seven months while I was writing this book)*

. . . *my clients, who made me realize that changing careers from engineering to coaching was my best decision, and helped me realize the powerful potential of coaching*

. . . *my editor, Stacey Kopp, for her great suggestions and patience*

. . . *my wonderful book launch team members* for their support and valuable feedback

. . . and the *SPS community of authors,* such a knowledgable group who made me feel welcomed while embarking on this writing journey.

Gabriela

BIBLIOGRAPHY

Susan Cain, *Quiet: The Power of Introverts in a World That Can't Stop Talking*, (Broadway Books, 2013)

Marti Olsen Laney Psy.D, *The Introvert Advantage: How Quiet People Can Thrive in an Extrovert World*, (Workman Publishing Company, 2002)

Paul D. Tieger, Barbara Barron, Kelly Tieger, *Do What You Are*, (Little, Brown and Company, 2014)

Tom Rath, *StrengthsFinder 2.0*, (Gallup Press, 2007)

Richard N. Bolles, *What Color Is Your Parachute?*, (Ten Speed Press, 2016)

Anne Rød, Marita Fridjhon, *Creating Intelligent Teams: Leading with Relationship Systems Intelligence*, (KR Publishing, 2015)

Joel Comm, *Twitter Power*, (Wiley, 2015)

Steve Krug, *Don't Make Me Think: A Common Sense Approach to Web Usability*, (New Riders, 2014)

Erik Myers, *Overcoming Shyness: Break Out of Your Shell and Express Your True Self*, (CreateSpace Independent Publishing Platform, 2017)

Laurie A Helgoe, *Introvert Power: Why Your Inner Life Is Your Hidden Strength*, (Sourcebooks, 2013)

Elaine N. Aron Phd, *The Highly Sensitive Person*, (Citadel, 2013)

Nancy Ancowitz, *Self-Promotion for Introverts: The Quiet Guide to Getting Ahead*, (McGraw-Hill Education, 2009)

Amy Cuddy, "Your Body Language May Shape Who You Are", (YouTube, 2012): https://youtu.be/Ks-_Mh1QhMc

http://www.success.uwo.ca/careers/interviews/types_of_interviews.html

Liz Ryan: http://www.humanworkplace.com/whats-pain-letter

Liz Ryan: https://www.forbes.com/sites/lizryan/2015/03/01/how-to-write-your-first-pain-letter

Liz Ryan: https://www.forbes.com/sites/lizryan/2015/01/24/why-you-need-your-own-business-cards

ALSO BY GABRIELA CASINEANU

How else can Gabriela Casineanu help you?

1-on-1 Coaching   Workshops for Introverts

For more details:

GabrielaCasineanu.com

Want to get notifications about Gabriela's **upcoming books**?

Sign up here:

http://www.gabrielacasineanu.com/series

Made in the USA
San Bernardino, CA
18 July 2017